THE ASIA BOOK

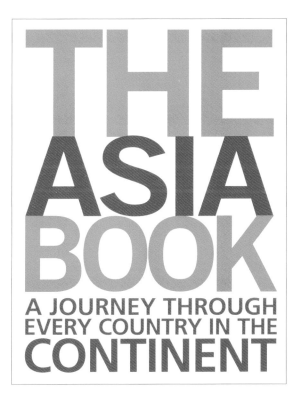

THE ASIA BOOK

A JOURNEY THROUGH EVERY COUNTRY IN THE CONTINENT

CONTENTS

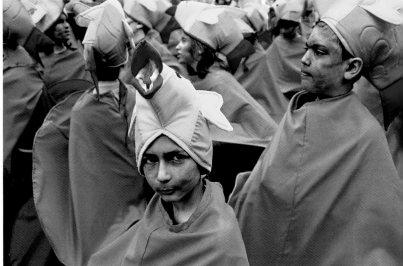

FOREWORD

WHAT IS A CONTINENT? IT'S NOT EASY TO DEFINE: A PHYSICAL LANDMASS, COUNTRIES IN GEOGRAPHICAL PROXIMITY, A UNITING CULTURE – NONE OF THESE QUITE CAPTURES WHAT MAKES ASIA ASIA.

Asia means different things to different people. It's the tranquillity of a watery rice terrace reflecting the clouds; it's the eternal emptiness of the desert; it's the über-modernity of a neon-bathed city. It's all this, and infinitely more.

A continent is certainly more than just a list of countries. In creating a book about every country in Asia, we faced a challenge in deciding exactly what that meant. There's no definitive list to refer to, experts disagree, and to add to the confusion some countries are transcontinental, like Turkey, divided along the Bosphorus, and Russia, whose vast Siberia has its feet in frozen Asian soil.

You won't find these two countries in this book. Turkey's bid for entry into the European Union helped place it in our Europe Book. And while most of Russia's landmass is in Asia, its capital and most of its population, historical and cultural activity is firmly in Europe. Similarly, we've reserved transcontinental Georgia, Armenia and Azerbaijan for Europe, but several other republics of the former USSR are undoubtedly part of Central Asia.

The Middle East is much closer in culture to North Africa than to Thailand or Japan, but it is traditionally understood to be part of Asia and is sometimes known as Western Asia. Two countries in this region are transcontinental, but we've divided them along the geographical line of the Red Sea, keeping Yemen in Asia and including Egypt in our Africa Book.

Australians and New Zealanders consider themselves part of the Asia-Pacific region. But for the most part, there's a clear dividing line between what's Asia and what's Pacific, with the possible exception of Indonesia and the world's newest country, East Timor, which straddle both but which we've included here.

But the diversity of our final list of countries didn't present a problem – rather, a joy. This is a region laden with history and yet bursting noisily into the modern world. From the austere silence of the Mongolian steppe to the sweaty and raucous jungles of Malaysian Borneo, and from the holy pilgrimage site of Mecca to the temples of fashion in Hong Kong, Asia offered an almost impossibly varied palette of experiences for our authors to draw from.

But there are unifying themes to the concept of Asia. We've explored some of these in the essays at the end of this book: the deep spirituality of the region that has spawned all of the world's great religions; the importance of the landscape and its influence on lifestyle and traditions; the pop culture whose endless creativity delights the world on celluloid, on the airwaves and on the streets; and the tradition of adventurous travel this continent has inspired, which began with Marco Polo, had its renaissance with the backpackers' hippy trail, and continues to thrive today.

The traveller's perspective led us to structure this book into five distinct regions, with the countries of each ordered by a logical travel route, meandering from east to west. For the traveller, the experience of each of these countries is unique, with its own sights, sounds, people, trademarks and surprises.

To further inspire readers to become travellers, we've suggested a number of routes, both famous and challenging, by which to see the best of this intriguing continent. Using our Great Journeys section, follow the path of the mighty Mekong, uncover the mysteries of the Silk Road, or trace the footsteps of the great adventurer TE Lawrence.

In addition we've asked our community of travellers to contribute mementoes of their own encounters with the continent. Among the images and text from our regional expert authors you'll find the photographs and words of everyday travellers sharing a moment in time and reflecting on what Asia has meant to them.

Many journeys have gone into the creation of this book, as inimitable and surprising as the continent itself. Yet here, we hope, begins a new journey, wherein both the uninitiated and the most seasoned of Asian travellers will discover something new.

ROZ HOPKINS,
PUBLISHER, TRADE & REFERENCE,
LONELY PLANET PUBLICATIONS

INTRODUCING ASIA

WHEN MARCO POLO FIRST VENTURED INTO THE COLLIDING WORLDS ALONG THE SILK ROAD, HE BROUGHT BACK TO THE ISOLATED WEST SUCH MAMMOTH AND MYSTERIOUS TALES THAT MANY LISTENERS COULD NOT FATHOM SUCH A PLACE.

And when Christopher Columbus sought to carve a new route to the Indies from Europe, it allegedly came as a disappointment that a new continent stood between the two. Whether story collectors, merchants or ordinary travellers in search of adventure, intrigue, solace or spirituality, all have found what they're looking for in Asia. And all return home with the same euphoric disorientation, unable to fully articulate what it is about so incomprehensible a continent that fixates them. For how can a region of such contrast, controversy and contradiction be expressed in a way that captures the experience of it?

DEFINING ASIA

What is meant by the word 'Asia' has been debated for centuries; its borders have been fought over and redrawn, its cultures exoticised and eroticised, its nationalism assumed and imposed and its people feared and misunderstood. To some, 'Asia' is merely a term that became synonymous with the world's largest continent, which begins at the eastern part of the Eurasian landmass and its adjacent islands, distinct from Europe and separated from it by the Ural Mountains, and stretches east until it fronts the Pacific. And for others, Asia can be divided into parts, including Northeast Asia, the subcontinent and the

Middle East: regions which were in turn bestowed with the loaded labels 'Orient', 'British India' and 'Arabia'. These Occidental terms romanticised, colonised and homogenised the landscapes, cultures and people whose identities were ascribed to them. Ultimately, the European empires that once presided over Asia came to refer to it in definitional defeat as the 'Mysterious East'.

HISTORY REPEATS ITSELF

This continent has contributed a cast of villains and heroes to global history. Most of the significant achievements of the modern world had their infancy in Asia. Ancient trading routes sliced across epic terrain as expanding empires competed to trade goods and ideas throughout the continent and beyond. Immense expanses of desert, seemingly impenetrable jungles and inhospitable mountains were all surmounted by the ambitious civilisations that ultimately gave rise to some of the world's most revolutionary ideas. Asia is the birthplace of Buddhism, Hinduism, Judaism, Islam and Christianity. Siddhartha Gautama's enlightenment continues to be shared across generations and continents as his 14th successor Tenzin Gyatso teaches the meaning of peaceful conviction.

Historical figures like Jesus Christ and Mohammed advocated compassion over conflict. But no matter how profound and peaceful Asia's religious revelations, ancient struggles to reconcile differences continue to mar the human story.

ASIA ASCENDING

In an age when one person's terrorist is another person's freedom fighter, and when aggression can be carried out using bigger weapons and louder mouthpieces than ever before, the eyes of the world look to the east in trepidation and hope. Asia, with its prolific economic, cultural, social, political and ideological influences, will continue to shape the direction of the world. You don't have to have been to Asia to have experienced it. Its people, cuisines, philosophies and inventions are themselves the quintessential travellers, having spread so far for so long that their origins become hard to recall. More than 100 million people around the world practise Hinduism in the form of yoga. Chinese acupuncture is increasingly used alongside mainstream Western medicine. The compact disc has circumnavigated the globe since it first appeared in Asia in 1982. Japanese technology has infiltrated European homes, and American cars are fuelled by Arabian oil. Indian, Chinese, Japanese and Middle

Eastern cuisine are all familiar to the Western palate. World-class writers, artists, musicians and filmmakers from this creative continent are fêted by critics around the globe. China and India vie for superpower status, and places like Běijīng, Dubai, Hong Kong, Tokyo and Singapore have stepped forward to take their place among the recognised global cities.

Indian-born British writer Rudyard Kipling said that 'East is East and West is West and never the twain shall meet'. But in resistance to the powers that tried to define it, Asia boldly projects its ever-evolving identities into the global consciousness, reinventing and reclaiming itself from Occidental simplifications. The increasing prosperity, ingenuity, spirituality and unsurpassed hospitality of this continent have made the Occident realise its accident. Since Asia has revealed itself to the rest of the world and travellers have deepened their affinity with it, the once 'Mysterious East' has more affectionately come to be considered 'the same, but different'. Indeed, by looking into the complicated continent of Asia, we see that the struggles of humanity to define and express itself remain the same the world over, and that it is the exchange of difference that makes the attempt worthwhile.

TIMELINE

563–483 BC »
Siddhartha Gautama, born in Lumbini, Nepal, becomes the historical founder of Buddhism.

500–400 BC »
Persian Empire (modern-day Iran) conquers the Middle East.

334 BC »
Alexander the Great of Macedonia claims the Middle East.

c 200–300 BC »
Romans gain control over all of the Middle East (except for Persia).

c 30 BC »
After the Roman conquest of Egypt, trade between Europe, the Middle East, India and China increases along the famed Silk Road.

8–2 BC »
Jesus Christ born in Bethlehem of Judea.

3RD CENTURY AD »
Gupta dynasty oversees India's golden age.

570–632 »
Mohammed founds Islam and leads the beginning of an Arab-Islamic empire.

802–50 »
King Jayavarman consolidates the Angkor Empire based in Cambodia.

11–13TH CENTURIES »
European kingdoms crusade against the Muslim empires of the Middle East, in a bid to reclaim the Holy Land for Christianity.

1206–1360 »
The Mongol empire expands through the Asian continent, helping re-establish the Silk Road. Marco Polo reaches the Mongol capital Khanbaliq (Běijīng) in 1266.

1368–1644 »
Ming dynasty rules China.

15TH CENTURY »
Ottoman Empire expands into almost all of the Middle East, except for Iran.

1511 »
Melaka (in present-day Malaysia) falls to the Portuguese, marking the start of European colonisation of Southeast Asia.

1526–1707 »
Mughal empire rules Hindustan (the Indian subcontinent and parts of Afghanistan and Iran).

1644–1911 »
Qing dynasty rules China.

1912 »
Sun Yat-sen establishes the Republic of China.

1932–1971 »
Colonised countries in the Middle East, Indian subcontinent and Southeast Asia gain independence.

1939–45 »
World War II. Japan occupies much of Southeast Asia. The war ends with the atomic bombing of Hiroshima, Japan.

1947 »
The United Nations partitions Palestine into a Jewish and an Arab state.

1949 »
The Communist Party of China, under Mao Zedong, establishes the People's Republic of China.

1967 »
Six-Day War between Israel and an alliance of Egypt, Syria and Jordan results in Israeli control of the Sinai peninsula, the West Bank and the Golan Heights.

1973 »
Saigon falls to the North Vietnamese, bringing an end to US military action in the region.

1987–1989 »
The Intifada (uprising) of Palestinian refugees living in Israel begins.

1990–1991 »
Iraq invades Kuwait; the first Gulf War, backed by a multinational coalition, ensues.

1995 »
Prime Minister Yitzhak Rabin of Israel is assassinated by a Jew opposed to liberal policies on the peace process between Israel and the PLO.

1997 »
Economic crisis hits Southeast Asian countries.

2001 »
The September 11 terrorist attacks lead US President George Bush to launch an invasion against Afghanistan and to overthrow the Taliban regime.

2003 »
The US and its 'coalition of the willing' invade Iraq on the basis that it is harbouring weapons of mass destruction. No such weapons are found.

2004 »
Tsunami strikes in the Indian Ocean, killing approximately 230,000 people.

2008
Games of the XXIX Olympiad take place in Běijīng, China.

ASIA AT A GLANCE

READING THE QURAN IN THE MOSQUE OF THE PROPHET, SAUDI ARABIA

RIDING A DRAGON DOWN THE YANGZI RIVER, CHINA

INDONESIA'S FORMIDABLE KOMODO DRAGON

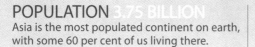

POPULATION 3.75 BILLION
Asia is the most populated continent on earth, with some 60 per cent of us living there.

AREA 30.3 MILLION SQ KM
Asia covers almost nine per cent of the earth's total surface area or 30 per cent of its land area.

COUNTRIES 44
OFFICIAL LANGUAGES 40

HIGHEST MOUNTAIN
At 8848 metres, Mt Everest, which straddles Nepal and Tibet, is the highest mountain on earth.

TALLEST BUILDING
The 509-metre Taipei 101 has been the tallest building in the world since 2004 – though it's likely to be superseded with the completion of Burj Dubai in the United Arab Emirates (UAE).

BEST OFF-THE-BEATEN-TRACK DESTINATION
The only country in the world to have a gross national happiness indicator, Bhutan also has strong policies to limit tourism.

BEST SUNRISE
Pilgrims of different faiths gather at Adam's Peak, Sri Lanka, to watch the mountain form a perfectly triangular shadow as the sun rises. The lotus flower that emerges with the rising sun in Angkor Wat is also a wonder…

MOST CONTROVERSIAL TRAVEL DESTINATION
Is travel in Myanmar a means of reducing the isolation of its people, or does it merely bolster the power of the military regime?

MOST BIZARRE ANIMAL
The Komodo dragon on the Indonesian island of Komodo proves that tales of prehistoric beasts aren't just bedtime stories.

MOST ELUSIVE CHARACTER
Kim Jong-il succeeded his father in 1994 to lead North Korea – is he a great leader or a crazy dictator?

MAJOR INFLUENTIAL LITERARY WORKS
The Bible and the Quran both have their origins in this epic region of the world.

LONGEST RIVER
The Yangzi, Asia's longest river, flows through 6211 kilometres of China, and is spanned by the world's largest hydroelectric dam, the Three Gorges Dam.

NEWEST COUNTRY
After years of struggling against Indonesian oppression, East Timor became independent in 2002, and was the first new country of the 21st century.

LARGEST ETHNIC GROUP
There are some 1.2 billion Han Chinese in Asia.

MOST EPIC RAILWAY JOURNEY
The Trans-Siberian Railway, spanning 9288 kilometres and eight time zones, connects Russia with Mongolia, China and the Sea of Japan.

WETTEST PLACE
Mawsynram, Assam, India, is the wettest place in Asia, with an average rainfall of 11,873 millimetres per year.

LOWEST PLACE
The Dead Sea between Israel and Jordan is almost 420 metres below sea level.

MOST TRANQUIL PLACE TO WATCH THE STARS
The Gobi Desert in northern China and southern Mongolia (Asia's largest desert) lies prostrate for the nightly display of the Milky Way.

GREATEST MAN-MADE CONSTRUCTION
The Great Wall of China, India's Taj Mahal and Petra in Jordan are impossible to compare and rank.

BEST PLACE TO SPECULATE
One day, visit Iraq and ponder whether the Hanging Gardens of Babylon and weapons of mass destruction ever existed.

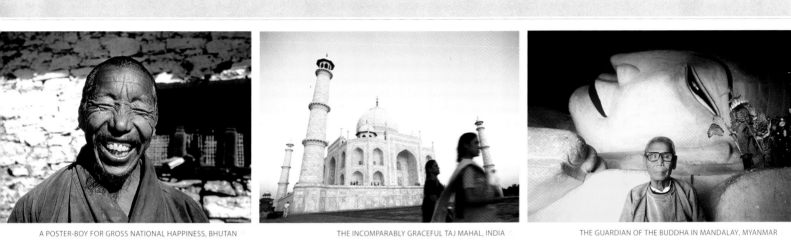

A POSTER-BOY FOR GROSS NATIONAL HAPPINESS, BHUTAN   THE INCOMPARABLY GRACEFUL TAJ MAHAL, INDIA   THE GUARDIAN OF THE BUDDHA IN MANDALAY, MYANMAR

GREAT JOURNEYS

Strap in for the flight to Mumbai and start your journey across the subcontinent. Get your fill of curries in India's largest city, then ride the rails south to Goa for beaches and parties. Detour inland to Hampi, then continue south to tropical Kerala, and around the tip of India to Tamil Nadu. On the east coast, essential stops include Chennai (for the food), Mamallapuram (for the temples), and Puri in Orissa (for the festivals and beaches).

Finish the India leg in Kolkata before boarding a flight to Yangon, the temple-strewn capital of Myanmar. (Visiting this embargoed nation is a controversial decision; alternatively, you can always fly directly from Kolkata to Bangkok.) Follow the Ayeyarwady River north to Mandalay and the ruined temples of Bagan, or head south to the golden boulder temple at Kyaiktiyo and the rain-drenched city of Mawlamyine.

Continue by air to Thailand, taking time to explore Bangkok, Asia's most energetic city. Detour north to Chiang Mai and west to Kanchanaburi near the border with Myanmar. There are two alternatives for the next stage – south to Singapore or east to Vietnam.

The most logical route to Singapore is via the party islands of Ko Samui and Ko Pha-Ngan to Hat Yai, on the Malaysian border. From here, buses run regularly to Georgetown on the island of Penang, known for its tasty street food. Hop across the isthmus to the dive mecca of the Pulau Perhentian, then go south to Kuala Lumpur, Malaysia's fast-paced capital. Finish up by taking the air-conditioned train to Singapore, a melting pot of all the cultures in Asia.

Alternatively, you can cross east from Thailand to Cambodia at Poipet. Visit the temples of Angkor near Siem Reap and take a boat along the Tonlé Sap to Phnom Penh, the Khmer capital. From here, Highway 6 cuts east to Ho Chi Minh City, Vietnam's second city. Scoot up the east coast of Vietnam all the way to Hanoi; you can finish here, or continue north to make your way into the vast expanse of mainland China.

A BREATH OF MIST LIES OVER THE TEMPLE RUINS OF THE BAGAN PLAINS, MYANMAR

At the bottom of the Thai Peninsula, Asia breaks down into a series of islands strung out across the Pacific.

Kick off in Kuala Lumpur, then take the ferry from Melaka to Dumai on the Indonesian island of Sumatra. Get back to nature at Danau Toba lake and the orang-utan sanctuary at Bukit Lawang, then fly from Medan to Jakarta, the noisy capital of Indonesia.

Take time to explore Java. Go east to the old capital, Yogyakarta, and see the Hindu temples at Prambanan and Borobudur, before continuing by boat from Ketapang to Bali. Drop in on Kuta Beach and climb to the peak of Gunung Batur. From here you can island-hop east through Lombok, dragon-inhabited Komodo and Catholic Flores, continuing by boat to Dili in East Timor.

Alternatively, fly north from Denpasar to the colourful port of Makassar on Sulawesi. Sip local coffee in the longhouses of Tana Toraja, then pick up the ferry to Kalimantan, the Indonesian half of Borneo. Roam the dense jungles and fly north from Banjarmasin to Pontianak and on to Kuching, on the Malaysian side of the island. Heading northeast, you can ride a roller coaster in Brunei and visit numerous national parks on the way to Kota Kinabalu.

Next, fly north to Cebu in the Philippines, heading quickly on to mysterious Bohol, with its famous Chocolate Hills. Continue northwest by bus and boat to beautiful Boracay, with the best beaches on the islands. Outrigger ferries go on to Mindoro and the popular dive resort of Puerto Galera, which has regular boats to Batangas on Luzon, the largest island in the group.

From here, you can visit amazing volcanoes near Legazpi and soothing natural springs around Los Baños. Head north through hectic Manila to the rice terraces of the Banaue and the tribal villages of the Cordillera Mountains. Finish off by flying from Manila to Busuang for some of Asia's best wreck diving, then reward yourself with some downtime in wild Palawan, the Philippines' last frontier.

GOOD AS GOLD: A RAINBOW ENDS OVER THE CHOCOLATE HILLS IN THE PHILIPPINES

THE OVERLAND TRAIL

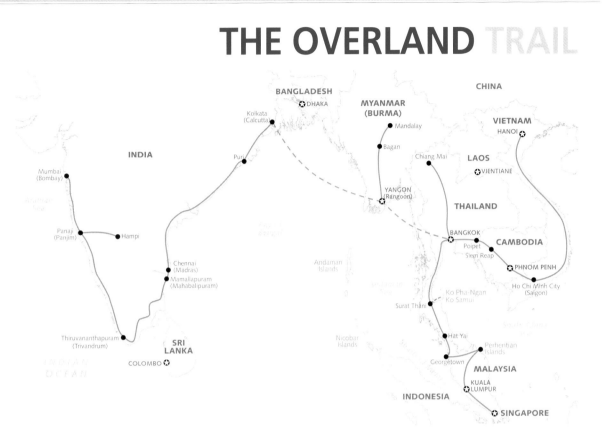

BANGLADESH
🕸 DHAKA

MYANMAR (BURMA)
● Mandalay
● Bagan

CHINA

VIETNAM
HANOI 🕸

Kolkata (Calcutta)

INDIA

Puri ●

Mumbai (Bombay) ●

Panaji (Panjim) ● ● Hampi

Chennai (Madras) ●
Mamallapuram (Mahabalipuram) ●

Chiang Mai ●

LAOS
🕸 VIENTIANE

YANGON (Rangoon) 🕸

THAILAND

BANGKOK 🕸
Poipet
Siem Reap

CAMBODIA

🕸 PHNOM PENH

Ho Chi Minh City (Saigon) ●

Andaman Islands

Ko Pha-Ngan
Ko Samui
Surat Thani ●

Thiruvananthapuram (Trivandrum) ●

SRI LANKA
COLOMBO 🕸

Nicobar Islands

Hat Yai ●
Perhentian Islands

Georgetown ●

MALAYSIA
KUALA LUMPUR 🕸

INDONESIA

🕸 SINGAPORE

ISLAND HOPPING
AROUND ASIA

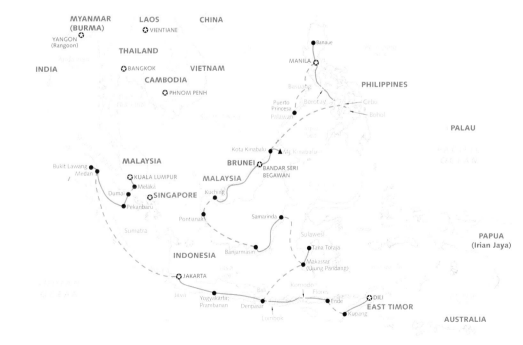

MYANMAR (BURMA)
YANGON 🕸 (Rangoon)

LAOS
🕸 VIENTIANE

CHINA

THAILAND

INDIA

🕸 BANGKOK

VIETNAM

CAMBODIA

🕸 PHNOM PENH

● Banaue

MANILA 🕸

Basuanga

PHILIPPINES

Puerto Princesa
Palawan

Boracay
Cebu
Bohol

PALAU

Kota Kinabalu ● ▲ Mt Kinabalu

MALAYSIA

BRUNEI
BANDAR SERI BEGAWAN

Bukit Lawang ●
Medan

🕸 KUALA LUMPUR
Melaka ●

MALAYSIA

Kuching ●

🕸 SINGAPORE

Dumai ●

Pontianak ●

Pekanbaru ●

Samarinda ●

Sumatra

Banjarmasin ●

Sulawesi

PAPUA (Irian Jaya)

Tana Toraja ●
Makassar (Ujung Pandang) ●

INDONESIA

🕸 JAKARTA

Java
Yogyakarta;
Prambanan

Bali
Denpasar

Komodo
Flores
Ende ●

🕸 DILI

EAST TIMOR

Lombok
Kupang ●

AUSTRALIA

ALONG THE
MEKONG RIVER

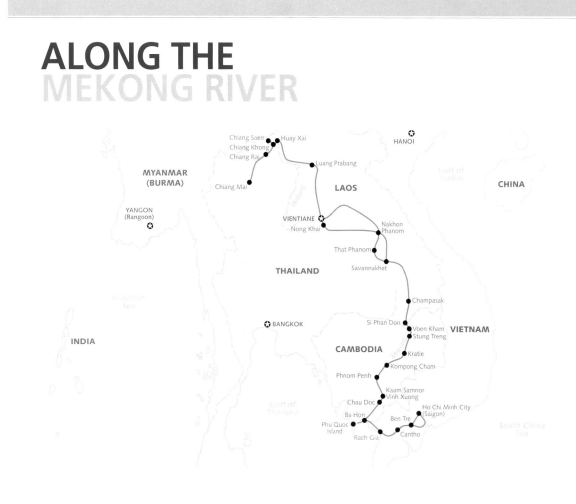

THE GREAT SOUTH
ASIA LOOP

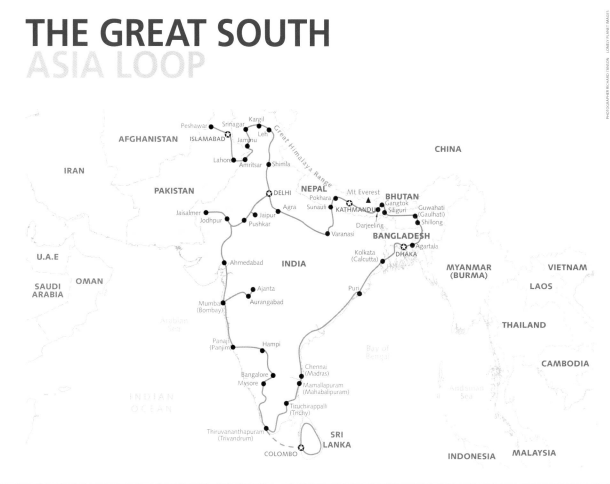

HARD AT WORK AT A FLOATING MARKET ON THE MEKONG DELTA, VIETNAM

Living up to its name – Mother of Waters – the Mekong River is the defining artery of Southeast Asia. Rising high on the Tibetan plateau, the river charges down to the South China Sea, dividing Myanmar from Laos and Laos from Thailand, cutting through the heart of Cambodia and splitting into dozens of tributaries at its mighty delta in Vietnam.

There are no easy border crossings between China, Myanmar and Laos, so start in Thailand, taking the night train to Chiang Mai, then the bus to Chiang Rai. Local buses run north and east to tiny Chiang Saen, facing Laos across the Mekong. Cross the river between Chiang Khong and Huay Xai and take a boat south to Luang Prabang.

Laos' second city is a living museum of French colonial buildings and Buddhist monasteries. From here you can take a ferry trip or an overnight bus ride to the capital, Vientiane. Dragonboat races are common on this stretch of the river and you can continue south on either side of the Thai–Lao border, crossing at Nong Khai, Nakhon Phanom or Savannakhet.

From Savannakhet, take a bus to the riverside hamlet of Champasak and continue to the 4000 river islands of Si Phan Don, close to the border between Laos and Cambodia. Crossing here involves a boat and bus trip to Voen Kham, and an onwards bus ride to Stung Treng, where you can connect with the boat south to Kompong Cham (keep an eye out for freshwater dolphins around Kratie). The next leg is by bus, down to the Cambodian capital, Phnom Penh.

After trawling the markets and bars of Phnom Penh, jump another riverboat south to Kaam Samnor and cross into Vietnam at Vinh Xuong, continuing to Chau Doc at the foot of Sam Mountain. The final stage snakes around the southern tip of the delta, through Ba Hon, Rach Gia and Cantho, with a detour to the paradise island of Phu Quoc to unwind after all this river travel.

Explore Cantho's floating markets and continue to Mytho, the gateway to the Mekong Delta. Charter a boat to explore the tributaries or take the ferry to the backwater village of Ben Tre. The run to Ho Chi Minh City is easiest by bus; die-hards might want to negotiate passage on a freight boat for the slow but scenic trip by river and sea.

EYE-POPPING COLOUR ON DHAKA'S RICKSHAWS, BANGLADESH

With a six-month Indian tourist visa, you can zigzag all the way around south Asia, taking in the sights and sounds of India, Nepal, Bangladesh and even Pakistan.

Start off in Delhi, the dusty but invigorating capital of India, for mosques, temples, forts and fabulous North Indian food. Take a train to Jaipur, home to the famous sandstone 'Palace of the Winds', then continue west to Pushkar, one of the original hippy hang-outs, and on to Jodhpur and the desert fortress of Jaisalmer.

Skip through Gujarat, Gandhi's home state, to Mumbai, India's largest city. Take in a Bollywood blockbuster then turn inland to the cave temples of Ajanta and Ellora. Follow the Konkan Coast south to Goa for raves and beaches, then head east to the sprawling ruins of Hampi. Move on to Bangalore by train for a glimpse of the new India, and on to Mysore with its incense factories and famous palace.

Continue south through the jungles and backwaters of Kerala and fly from Thiruvananthapuram to Colombo for a glimpse of beachfront Buddhism in Sri Lanka. Returning to India, follow the east coast through Tamil Nadu, busy Chennai and temple-tastic Mamallapuram. From Chennai, take the fast train to Kolkata and the bus to Dhaka in Bangladesh.

Take your time exploring this little-visited nation, then cross the border to Agartala in Northeast India and join the bus convoy north to Meghalaya and Assam. From Gawahati, go west to Siliguri for the ride to the Buddhist state of Sikkim, then head to Darjeeling and cross the border into Nepal.

It's a long bus ride across the Terai plains to Kathmandu. Tour the temples then head west for a trek near Pokhara, before crossing back into India at Sunauli. Travel to Varanasi on the River Ganges, then head to Agra for a peek at the Taj Mahal. Connecting through Delhi, go north to mountainous Himachal Pradesh, Kashmir and the remote Buddhist enclave of Ladakh.

Loop back to the plains via Amritsar, with its legendary Golden Temple, and cross into Pakistan at Attari. If it's safe to travel, take your pick – the architectural wonders of Lahore, the string of ancient cities along the Indus or the rugged cities of the northwest. Brave souls can even enter Afghanistan via the Khyber Pass near Peshawar.

Nepal's most famous trek is still the one by which others are measured. From the tiny village of Besisahar, in the hills east of Pokhara, the Annapurna Circuit covers more than 200 kilometres as it winds around the peaks of the mighty Annapurna Range, passing over the grit-testing Thorung La (5614 metres), allegedly the world's highest navigable mountain pass.

The road to the mountains begins in Kathmandu, Nepal's stunning medieval capital. It's worth staying a few days to acclimatise to the Nepali way of life and see the temples and stupas of Hanuman Dhoka, Bodhnath and Swayambhunath. Meals on the Annapurna Circuit are mainly *daal bhaat* (curried lentils and rice), so enjoy the international food available on the streets of Thamel.

When you have all the equipment you need, pay the fee for the Annapurna Conservation Area and take the bus to Dumre to pick up a jeep to the trail head at Besisahar. The trek takes a minimum of 16 days but most people allow several extra days to acclimatise to the increasing altitude.

The first few days follow the rushing Marsyangdi stream, passing through tiny tribal villages to Chame, the regional headquarters of Manang district. From here the trail enters the mountains proper; most people stop and rest for one or two days at the village of Manang to enjoy the mountain scenery and adjust to the altitude before pushing over the Thorung La, the highest point on the trail. Acute mountain sickness is a risk at this elevation, so be prepared to bail out if you detect any symptoms.

Once over this mighty obstacle, the trail descends through rocky country to Muktinath, a Hindu and Buddhist pilgrimage centre with a temple lit by a natural flame. From here it's a steep descent to Kagbeni, on the edge of the forbidden kingdom of Mustang (only accessible with a US$700 permit), and Jomsom, where you can fly back to Kathmandu or Pokhara.

We recommend gritting your teeth and continuing for the final seven days to Pokhara, on the edge of the beautiful Phewa Tal lake. In Pokhara the weather is warm, the streets are flat, restaurants serve every cuisine under the sun and bars rock till the wee hours with trekkers celebrating the end of weeks of toil.

⌃ THE FORMIDABLE PAUNGDA DANDA ROCK FACE LOOMS OVER UPPER PISANG, NEPAL

The old Silk Road from Tashkent to Běijīng is one of the most evocative overland journeys in the world, cutting across the wind-scoured plains of Xinjiang and Inner Mongolia. It takes a special kind of traveller to survive the rigours of travel on these unforgiving roads, but people even mountain bike along the Silk Road, so it can be done.

Start the journey at Tashkent in Uzbekistan, once the fourth-largest city in the USSR. Head south to ancient Samarkand, perhaps the most romantic and atmospheric of all the towns along the Silk Road. The old city is a mass of ruins and Islamic monuments, including the famous *medressas* (Islamic colleges) of the Registan. Nearby is Bukhara, a sprawling city of mosques, minarets and mausoleums.

Return to Tashkent and continue by bus or train to Bishkek, the tree-lined capital of Kyrgyzstan – or fly, saving yourself several bumpy days. Pick up the Silk Road again at Issyk-Kul lake, surrounded by dramatic mountain scenery and thermal spas, then push on to Osh. The journey to China involves joining a jeep tour for the tortuous ride over the 3752-metre Torugart Pass to Kashgar, an ancient Silk Road bazaar town full of markets and mosques.

From Kashgar, the Silk Road branches into two, passing either side of the Taklamakan Desert. The northern route skirts the Tian Shan mountains to Ürümqi, offering interesting detours to ruined cities and Buddhist caves. You can also travel the little-visited southern road through the desert city of Hotan, known as Khotan in Silk Road times.

From Ürümqi, follow the modern road east through Turpan and on to Lánzhōu, before cutting north into Inner Mongolia. Follow the Yellow River across the grasslands to Hohhot then turn south to Dàtóng, home to the stunning Cloud Ridge Caves, filled with 50,000 Buddhist statues. Finish off with a tour of the silk shops in Běijīng, China's buzzing capital city – and be glad you didn't have to follow the whole route by camel!

⌃ A DONKEY'S TOOTHY DISPLAY AT A KASHGAR MARKET, CHINA

THE ANNAPURNA CIRCUIT

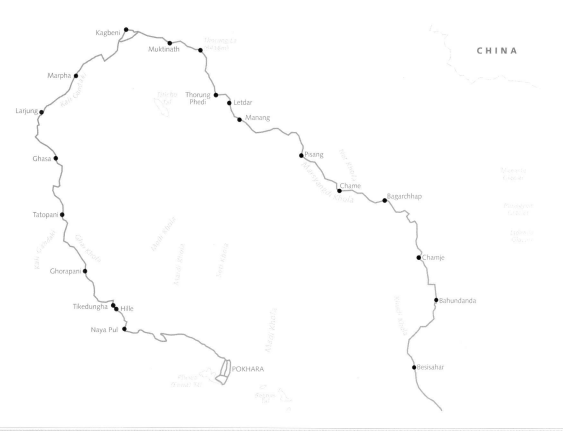

CHINA

Kagbeni
Muktinath
Thorung La
6416m
Marpha
Thorung Phedi
Letdar
Larjung
Manang
Ghasa
Pisang
Chame
Bagarchhap
Tatopani
Chamje
Ghorapani
Bahundanda
Tikedungha
Hille
Naya Pul
Besisahar
POKHARA

THE SILK ROAD

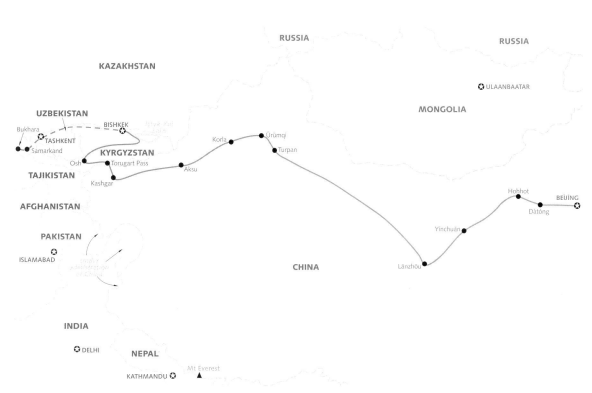

RUSSIA

RUSSIA

KAZAKHSTAN

✪ ULAANBAATAR

MONGOLIA

UZBEKISTAN
BISHKEK
Bukhara
✪ TASHKENT
Samarkand
KYRGYZSTAN
Osh
Torugart Pass
Aksu
Korla
Ürümqi
Turpan

TAJIKISTAN

AFGHANISTAN

Hohhot
BEIJING
Dàtóng

PAKISTAN

Yínchuān

✪ ISLAMABAD

CHINA

Lánzhōu

INDIA

✪ DELHI
NEPAL

Mt Everest

KATHMANDU ✪

EMPIRES OF
THE EAST

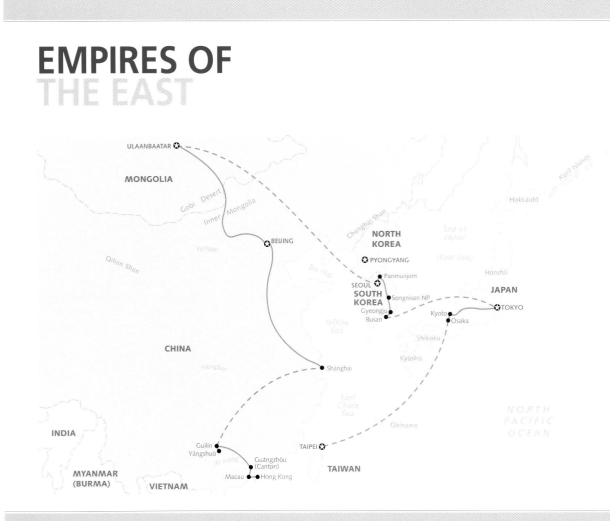

ULAANBAATAR

MONGOLIA

Gobi Desert

Inner Mongolia

Qilian Shan

Yellow

BEIJING

Bo Hai

Changbai Shan

NORTH
KOREA

PYONGYANG

Sea of
Japan
(East Sea)

Hokkaidō

Kuril Islands

Honshū

Panmunjom

SEOUL
SOUTH
KOREA

Songnisan NP

Gyeongju
Busan

JAPAN

TOKYO

Kyoto
Osaka

Shikoku

CHINA

Yangtze

Yellow
Sea

Shànghǎi

Kyūshū

East
China
Sea

Okinawa

NORTH
PACIFIC
OCEAN

INDIA

Guilin
Yángshuò

Lí Hé

Guǎngzhōu
(Canton)

Macau   Hong Kong

TAIPEI

TAIWAN

MYANMAR
(BURMA)

VIETNAM

IN THE FOOTSTEPS OF
LAWRENCE OF ARABIA

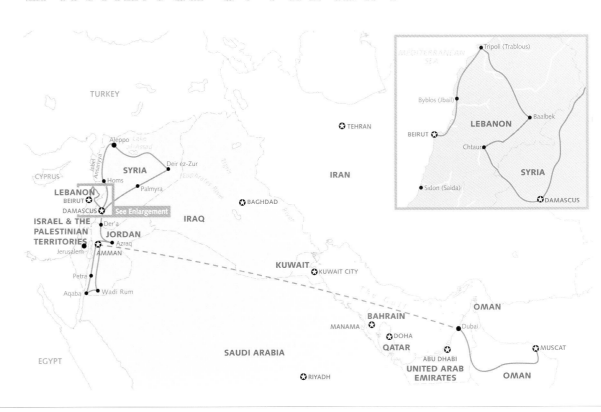

TURKEY

Aleppo   Lake al-Assad

Jebel Ansariyya

SYRIA

Deir ez-Zur

CYPRUS

Homs

Tigris

Euphrates River

IRAN

TEHRAN

LEBANON
BEIRUT
DAMASCUS   See Enlargement

Palmyra

BAGHDAD

ISRAEL & THE
PALESTINIAN
TERRITORIES

Der'a

IRAQ

JORDAN

Azraq

Jerusalem   AMMAN

KUWAIT

KUWAIT CITY

Petra

Aqaba   Wadi Rum

EGYPT

SAUDI ARABIA

BAHRAIN

MANAMA

DOHA

QATAR

RIYADH

OMAN

Dubai

ABU DHABI
UNITED ARAB
EMIRATES

MUSCAT

OMAN

Enlargement

MEDITERRANEAN
SEA

Tripoli (Trablous)

Byblos (Jbail)

Baalbek

LEBANON

BEIRUT

Chtaura

SYRIA

Sidon (Saida)

DAMASCUS

The nations of East Asia share a common history and culture. Hong Kong, China, Mongolia, Taiwan, South Korea and Japan were forged by rival empires, each struggling for domination of the East.

The logical starting point for a jaunt around East Asia is Hong Kong, the last Asian outpost of the British Empire. Take the boat across to Macau to see the Portuguese take on Chinese culture, then hop on the bus or train to Guǎngzhōu on the mainland, a major rail hub for the rest of China. Ride the night train to Guìlín and spend a few days unwinding among lakes and mountains in idyllic Yángshuò. From Guìlín, fly northeast to Shànghǎi, China's most dynamic city.

After taking your fill of the sights on the Bund, ride the overnight sleeper to Běijīng to stroll through the quiet quadrangles of the Forbidden City. Whatever else you do, make time for a day trip to the Great Wall of China. Next, book a seat on the Trans-Siberian Railway to the surreal capital of Mongolia, Ulaanbaatar. From there, take a trip to the wild interior to ride a horse along the steppe and stay in a traditional *ger* (nomadic tent house).

Getting out of Mongolia is easiest by air, so jump on the next flight to Seoul, the futuristic capital of South Korea. Explore Gyeongbokgung Palace and Bongeunsa Temple, then book onto an official tour to Panmunjom for a peek at the heavily fortified border with secretive North Korea.

Head south via mountainous Songnisan National Park and the medieval city of Gyeongju, and finish up with few days at the hot springs and beaches near Busan. Flights leave regularly from Busan to Tokyo, the space-age capital of Japan. Take your pick of sumo wrestling, Zen meditation or sushi, then climb the perfect volcanic cone of Mt Fuji. Rest your legs on the high-speed bullet train south to the temples and gardens of Kyoto, and on to Osaka.

Finish off your East Asia jaunt with a short flight to Taiwan, founded by the exiled president of post-imperial China, Chiang Kaishek. The capital, Taipei, is another bustling Asian metropolis, and around the island are mountains, beaches, aboriginal tribes and stunning natural scenery. Flights go on from Taipei to just about every nation in the world – except, ironically, China.

A DISPLAY OF DISCIPLINE AND UNITY AT THE ARIRANG MASS GYMNASTICS FESTIVAL IN NORTH KOREA

Thomas Edward Lawrence – more commonly called Lawrence of Arabia – is perhaps the best-known traveller of the Middle East. Between 1914 and 1919, Lawrence fomented revolt against the Ottoman Empire in Palestine, Jordan, Syria, Lebanon and Saudi Arabia, redrawing the map of the entire region.

If things are politically stable enough in the region, start your journey in Lebanon. Spend a few nights in Beirut, before heading north to ancient Byblos and Tripoli's distinctive Mamluk mosques and *hammam* (Turkish baths). Go south to fabulous Roman ruins at Baalbek, then head to Chtaura to pick up a bus to Syria.

You'll be dropped off in the Syrian capital, Damascus, which Lawrence seized with his Arab allies in 1918. Roam the streets of the Old City, then head north to the fortresses of the Jebel Ansariyya and the ruined cities around Aleppo. Go east past huge

Lake al-Assad and follow the Euphrates to Deir ez-Zur, before turning south again to the desert city of Palmyra.

There's time for one last peek at Damascus, then it's on to Jordan via the border crossing at Der'a. Detour east to the oases and castles at Azraq, then head on to Amman, the chaotic but lovable capital. Continue south through the desert to famous Petra, following the King's Highway. The rock-hewn city is an incredible spectacle, so allow several days before heading on to the seaside at Aqaba.

Next, loop north to Amman via Wadi Rum, where David Lean shot the film of Lawrence's life. Although Lawrence travelled widely in Saudi Arabia, getting permission to visit is fraught with difficulty. To experience some of the same culture and landscapes, fly from Amman to Dubai in the United Arab Emirates, then travel across the desert to famously friendly Oman.

WHO NEEDS A HEALTH SPA? A MAN APPLIES MUD TO HIMSELF AT THE DEAD SEA

SOUTHEAST ASIA

DOWN HERE IN THE TROPICS, LIFE MOVES A LITTLE SLOWER. THE CLOCKS ARE SET TO AN AGRICULTURAL RHYTHM THAT MEASURES THE PROGRESS OF RICE FROM TENDER BABY SHOOTS IN FLOODED PADDIES TO BOWING FEATHERED STALKS IN DRY, CRACKED MUD.

The temperature is a natural mellowing agent, and the back-breaking labour of the farmer is rewarded with long periods of rest and waiting, during which the natural inclination for conversation is tuned like a beloved instrument. Perhaps no other place on the continent is as affable as Southeast Asia, where friends are made with a mere handshake and where a stroll through town invites smiles, stares and inquiries.

Whether fresh or salt, water is a constant in the identity and landscape of Southeast Asia. The lifeblood of this region is the mighty Mekong River, which swells and contracts with the rains, draining the remote and mountainous reaches of Laos through the rice basket of Thailand, Cambodia and Vietnam, until it blurs the distinction between land and sea into a half-breed delta as it empties into the South China Sea. Just as the ocean begins to stretch freely away from the land, it bumps into the island chains of the Philippines and Indonesia, the continent's last grasp into the deep blue.

It was along these choppy seas that the great sailing ships blew into the region's harbours, including those of the spice-rich islands of Indonesia and the trading cities in Malaysia. Merchants from India and China exchanged goods, religion and some DNA with the locals, resulting in the spread of Hinduism, Buddhism and Islam, as well as the introduction and adaptation of noodles and curries. Later, the sleepy underside of the Asian continent was carved up by Western empires and their corporations, and these colonies struggled for independence well into the 20th century. Pleasant remnants of the colonial age remain in the scenic architecture of Vietnam's cities and the delicious inheritance of crusty baguettes and thick coffee.

Long before Southeast Asia was viewed by larger countries as an unwed maiden, the region was betrothed to its own empire builder: the great Angkor kingdom, based in present-day Cambodia. The Angkor kings built elaborate monuments, carved Hindu myths into stone walls and designed their holy city as a mirror of celestial geometry. Today, the temples have emerged from the undergrowth of the jungle and the insecurity of civil war to claim their rightful place among the world's greatest man-made treasures. Making a trip to this part of the world without visiting Angkor is the definition of 'missing the boat'.

Always a few degrees below boiling, Southeast Asia is also a playground for those from colder climes. Almost every country in the region boasts a voluptuous coastline and underwater coral gardens that rival the visual spectacle of an Asian fruit market. Of the celebrity beach spots, Bali, Phuket, and Boracay remain top contenders but little islands filled with coconut trees and hammocks have their share of sun-loving devotees.

Whether they're temple-hopping or island-hopping, visitors find that Southeast Asia quietly colonises the tender territory of restless souls.

TEXT: CHINA WILLIAMS

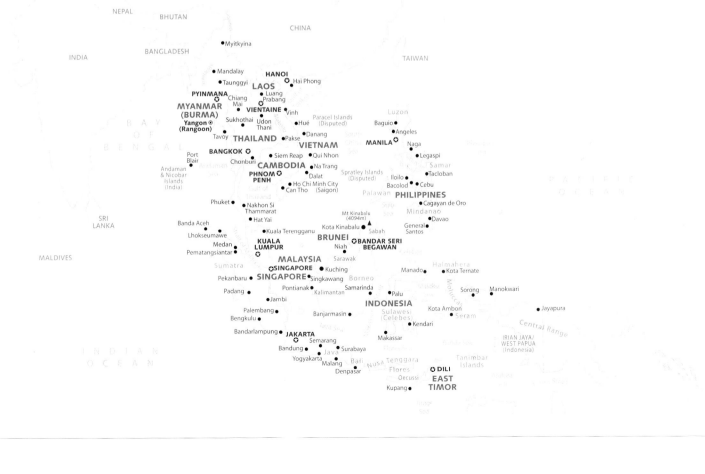

THAILAND

A GOLDEN COUNTRY WITH A GENTLE AND FRIENDLY NATURE, THAILAND IS ONE OF ASIA'S MOST ACCESSIBLE EXOTIC DESTINATIONS.

CAPITAL CITY BANGKOK   POPULATION 65 MILLION   AREA 514,000 SQ KM   OFFICIAL LANGUAGE THAI

LANDSCAPE

Central Thailand has the geographic equivalent of 'child-bearing hips': an arable landscape fed by nutrient-rich rivers. In the northwest, it begins to climb into the mountain range that divides Southeast Asia from China. Tapering south is the narrow Malay Peninsula, lined with sandy beaches and jewel-toned waters. On the western side of the peninsula, the photogenic limestone cliffs carve up the coastline into elegant horseshoe-shaped coves.

HISTORY IN A NUTSHELL

The area now known as Thailand was once made up of independent city-states and farming communities based in the fertile river valleys. During the 14th century it was the western frontier of the Angkor kingdom, until the city-state Sukhothai, considered to be the first Thai kingdom, gained control. Sukhothai was later upstaged by Ayuthaya, which in 1782 was sacked by the Burmese, leading to the foundation of the present-day capital, Bangkok. During European imperialism, Thailand avoided colonisation partly because of its stable monarchy and cohesive national identity, and partly because of its strategic 'buffer' location between French Indochina and British Burma

and Malaysia. The country became a constitutional monarchy in a bloodless coup in 1932. In the late 1990s, Thailand experienced a currency crisis, along with other racing Asian economies, but has since recovered and has ambitions to establish itself as a regional hub for politics, transport and culture.

PEOPLE

On the surface Thailand seems homogeneous, with 95 per cent of its population practising Buddhism and only one official language. But each region (northern, northeastern, central and southern) has a distinct identity and dialect. Central Thais define the national identity, including the dialect widely accepted as proper Thai. Northern Thailand has a distinct and regal history dating back to one of Thailand's earliest city-states. Minority hill tribes in the far northwestern corner maintain their own tribal languages and customs. The northeast forms the true grit of the country: hardscrabble rice farmers and a soulful culture that acts as a ballast to central Thailand's haughty refinement. In southern Thailand, the culture has been greatly influenced by Muslim Malaysia. In the deep south, many southerners speak a Malaysian dialect called Yawi. Four per cent of all Thais are Muslim.

MARKETPLACE

Thailand is an agricultural economy, with 50 per cent of its population working in the sector; major products include rice, cassava, rubber, sugar cane, coconuts and soya beans. Tourism is also important, as are textile production and light manufacturing. The average minimum wage is about US$4.

TRADEMARKS
- Hedonism
- Chillies
- Land of smiles
- Temples
- Beautiful beaches

MYTHS & LEGENDS

Thailand's leading epic is an adaptation of the Indian Ramayana, known locally as the Ramakian. The Ramakian uses Thai artistic forms to depict the struggle between good Prince Rama and the 10-headed demon Ravana. In temple murals Rama bears distinctly Thai facial features and daily village life is often depicted in the corners. Not to ruin the ending, but the Thai version of the story opts for a fairytale finale, a departure from the original.

⌃ A MOKEN CHILD CAPTURED IN AN INSTANT OF WEIGHTLESSNESS, MU KO SURIN ISLAND

PHOTOGRAPHER: CLAVER CARROLL : LONELY PLANET IMAGES

⌃ WATER FEATURE: WORSHIPPERS FLOAT A TRADITONAL *KRATHONG* FOR THE ANNUAL LOY KRATHONG FESTIVAL IN TAK PROVINCE

⌃ A GYMNASTIC MOVE FROM A *TAKRAW* (FOOT VOLLEYBALL) PLAYER

PHOTOGRAPHER DEAN CHAPMAN PANOS

A KAYAN WOMAN HAVING RINGS RUN AROUND HER, KARENNI REFUGEE CAMP, MAE HONG SON

FAMILY BUSINESS IN A RICE FIELD IN NORTH THAILAND

FROM THE TRAVELLER

This photo was taken in Ayuthaya in Thailand. This statue of the Buddha holds a smaller Buddha in his hand. I have a lot of Thai friends who, although they're Buddhist, have different views to their parents. I liked the idea that the older Buddha is supporting and guiding the younger Buddha.

ALEXANDER KYRIACOU   UK

NATURAL BEAUTY

Thailand's most stunning natural attributes are its beaches and the jungle-topped islands poised in the shallow Gulf of Thailand or Andaman Sea. Along the river valley is the country's rice basket, where the landscape is a sea of tender green rice shoots stretching to the horizon.

URBAN SCENE

Bangkok is one of Southeast Asia's most dynamic cities. It's crowded, polluted, superficial and totally amazing. Relatively cooler in climate, Chiang Mai is the more studious and bohemian alternative.

ON FILM

For a long time the only movies about Thailand that reached international movie houses were about the Vietnam War or featured B-grade action heroes. This meant a lot of fight scenes, hooker bars and a golden temple thrown into a musical montage. Recently, though, home-grown filmmakers have lit up the silver screen with engaging only-in-Thailand stories. Pen-Ek Ratanaruang's *Last Life in the Universe* (2003), a tale of two mismatched people in Bangkok who accidentally become friends, is just a darn good flick. Cannes applauded Apichatpong Weerasethakul's *Tropical Malady* (2004), a gay love story wrapped up with Thai mythology and an experimental artistic style.

CUISINE

Thai cuisine dazzles foreign diners with a complex interplay of four major flavours – spicy, sweet, salty and sour – and a combination of zesty ingredients. Some popular favourites include phàt thai, green curry and tom yum. Then there's a cornucopia of amazingly sweet tropical fruits. The key to enjoying a Thai meal is to order complementary dishes: a soup or curry, a meat or fish dish, and a stir-fried vegetable dish. Meals in Thailand are communal and informal. Dishes are served family style and everyone makes sure that their fellow diners are fed and watered beyond capacity.

CULTURE

Thailand's customs have been influenced by China, India and the former Cambodian kingdom of Angkor, and many rules of social etiquette are based on Buddhist precepts. Buddhism mixed with animism dominates much of daily life and formal celebrations. Each morning, shopkeepers set out offerings to the various guardian spirits to ensure a prosperous business. Various shrines, temples and holy places are paid respect by passers-by with a respectful *wâi* (a palms-together gesture of greeting). The monarchy is also highly revered and any image of the king (such as on money or stamps) is treated with respect.

TOP FESTIVAL

Songkran, also known as the water festival, is Thailand's most famous celebration. It used to be a fairly subdued family affair marking the Thai New Year in April. Scented water was gingerly poured over the hands of the family elders to express respect and appreciation. These days, when family and temple visits are concluded an all-out water fight breaks out, featuring long-range supersoaker water guns and truck beds full of armed water guards. Bangkok is especially notorious for this battle of the uninvited bathing, while Chiang Mai's celebration is considered more tame and scenic.

FUTURE DIRECTIONS

Thailand is changing rapidly. What was an agricultural feudal society with a small elite and a large labouring class is beginning to develop an educated middle class based in the cities and towns. As economic success continues, more Thais will move away from the country and lose touch with their agricultural roots. Tourism will continue to dominate the economy, but domestic tourism will grow as Thais take trips of nostalgia into the villages, searching for lost customs.

PHOTOGRAPHER EVERNIGHT IMAGES / ALAMY

◦ CAMPING OUT: PERFORMERS AT A BANGKOK CLUB

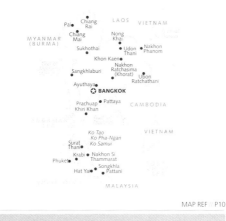

ESSENTIAL EXPERIENCES

◦ **Hanging out in a hammock next to a palm-fringed beach on Ko Pha-Ngan**

◦ **Getting stuck in traffic in the middle of gridlocked Bangkok**

◦ **Wiping back the tears after tucking into Thailand's fiery cuisine**

◦ **Diving among the colourful coral gardens near Phuket**

◦ **Being twisted and poked in the name of relaxation during a Thai massage**

◦ **Surviving temple fatigue in scenic Chiang Mai**

MAP REF P.10

BEST TIME TO VISIT OCTOBER TO MAY

PHI PHI ISLAND RISES OUT OF A TRANQUIL SEA

RICKSHAW DRIVERS KICK BACK WHILE THEY WAIT FOR FARES AT THE CHIANG MAI NIGHT BAZAAR

CAMBODIA

CAMBODIA HAS BEEN TO HELL AND BACK, BUT WITH THE MOST MAGNIFICENT TEMPLES ON EARTH DRAWING BIG TOURIST BUSINESS AND PEACE REIGNING FOR A DECADE, IT SEEMS HEAVENLY DAYS LIE AHEAD.

CAPITAL CITY PHNOM PENH   POPULATION 13.9 MILLION   AREA 181,040 SQ KM   OFFICIAL LANGUAGE KHMER

LANDSCAPE

For most visitors, who only make it to Phnom Penh and the temples of Angkor, Cambodia is pancake flat and covered by a blanket of rice paddies. However, there are important mountains, including the Cardamoms in the southwest and the Dangrek range in the far north, forming a natural border with Thailand. Water is a dominant feature. The Tonlé Sap lake, the largest in Southeast Asia, is the heartbeat of the country and the mighty Mekong River brings life and vitality to the land.

HISTORY IN A NUTSHELL

'The good, the bad and the ugly' is the simple way to sum up Cambodian history. Things were good in the early years, culminating in the vast Angkor empire, which was unrivalled in the region during its four centuries of dominance. Then came the bad, as the empire began to implode and ascendant neighbours started chipping away at its edges. In the 20th century things turned downright ugly, when a brutal civil war erupted as a sideshow to the American war in Vietnam. This culminated in the genocidal rule of the Khmer Rouge (1975–79), Cambodian communists responsible for the deaths of almost two million people. The Vietnamese invaded and overthrew the Khmer Rouge in 1979, but liberation soon turned to occupation – they stayed for a decade. The United Nations oversaw the country's first postwar election in 1993, but the civil war rumbled on until 1998. Unfortunately, the legacy of the war lingers on, with somewhere between four and six million land mines littering the countryside. However, the country has now enjoyed a decade of peace.

PEOPLE

According to official statistics, the population of Cambodia is overwhelmingly ethnic Khmer: they make up about 95 per cent of the population. In reality, there are far larger communities of Chinese and Vietnamese living in the country than this figure suggests. Cambodia also has a large population of Cham Muslims, numbering perhaps 400,000. The mountains of the northeast of the country are home to several minority hill tribes known as Khmer Leu (upper Khmer).

MARKETPLACE

A gecko compared with the Asian dragons of the region, the Cambodian economy is still recovering from the decades of conflict. Tourism is the biggest business in town at present and the temples of Angkor are attracting more than a million visitors every year. Textile and garment manufacturing is another big industry, and Cambodia is attempting to carve out a niche for itself as an ethical producer with good labour conditions.

TRADEMARKS

○ Angkor Wat
○ The Killing Fields
○ King Sihanouk
○ Apsara dancers
○ Prahoc (fermented fish paste)

URBAN SCENE

At times beautiful and bewitching, at times downtrodden and depressing, Phnom Penh is a crossroads of Asia's past and present, a city of extremes that rarely fails to captivate. Blessed with a beautiful riverfront, the royal palace compound is a focus for most Khmers. Hip restaurants and bars point the way to a fashionable future, and with more budget airlines putting Phnom Penh on the map, there's clearly a lot more to Cambodia than Angkor.

PUT 'EM UP – A SMILING CHALLENGER AT ANGKOR WAT

PHOTOGRAPHER MIKAEL OSTERGAARD / PANOS

A FAMILY TRAVELS HOME FROM MARKET ON THEIR ELEPHANT, RATTANAKIRI

SUNRISE OVER SERENE ANGKOR WAT IS NOT TO BE MISSED

FLOWER CHILD: AN *APSARA* DANCER AT ANGKOR WAT

BURNT OFFERINGS: AN ELDERLY CAMBODIAN OFFERS INCENSE AT THE BAYON IN ANGKOR

BANANAS BRISTLE AT A PHNOM PENH MARKET

RANDOM FACTS

WILD THINGS

In contrast to the long-suffering Cambodian people, the wildlife didn't fare so badly during the bad old years. However, rampant deforestation and widespread poaching have since nobbled the numbers. The Cambodian forests conceal wild tigers and elephants, as well as bears and leopards. Large water birds flock to Cambodia's swampy waters in abundance and include rare adjutants, storks, cranes and pelicans. Under the water is the freshwater Irrawaddy dolphin, which can be seen in the Mekong, north of Kratie.

CUISINE

The consensus is that Cambodian food is either a bit like Thai with fewer spices or like a slightly spicier version of Vietnamese. However, this downplays the unique aspects of Cambodian cuisine and reflects the fact that the country is only just re-emerging from the shadows. The closest thing Cambodia has to a national dish is *amoc*, baked fish in banana leaf scented divinely with coconut, lemongrass and a dash of chilli. Angkor is the national beer, but in the countryside rice wine and local moonshine are the brews of choice.

IN ART

Much ink has been spilt on the tragedy of modern Cambodia. François Bizot was the only foreigner to survive kidnap by the Khmer Rouge during the civil war and *The Gate* (2003) is his account of his ordeal. *Sideshow* (1979) by William Shawcross is a brilliant book on Kissinger's meddling in Cambodia and how the country was sucked into the Vietnam conflict. One of the best survivor accounts is *First they Killed My Father* (2001) by Luong Ung. When it comes to the big screen, think *The Killing Fields* (1984), the story of journalist Sydney Schanberg and his photographer colleague Dith Pran. Many a tear has been shed over its final scene.

SURPRISES

○ Snakebites cause almost as many amputations as land mines in Cambodia.

○ Ho Chi Minh City in Vietnam began life as the Cambodian village of Prey Nokor back in 1700.

○ The Khmer people are incredibly friendly, given their horrific history.

TEMPLE TRAILS

When it comes to temples, no other country comes close to Cambodia. The kingdom is littered with the lavish legacy of the god kings and the epicentre of this empire is Angkor, which is fast becoming the hottest cultural stop in Asia. But beyond the awe-inspiring capital of old, hundreds more temples lie dormant in the jungles, testament to the might of the ancient Khmers. Choose from majestic mountain-top temples, forbidding and forgotten jungle fortresses, incredible carved riverbeds and pre-Angkorian brick cities.

IMPORT

↗ Japanese four-wheel drives
↗ Temple-seeking tourists
↗ Land mines
↗ The world's sympathy and compassion
↗ Baguettes

EXPORT

↖ Rubber
↖ Clothing (not rubber clothing!)
↖ De-mining know-how
↖ Exquisite silk
↖ Stolen carvings

FUTURE DIRECTIONS

Politically Cambodia is more stable than it has been for many years, but some would ask at what cost? Democracy exists at the ballot box, but the culture of democracy is hardly ingrained in government actions and attitudes. But stability is better than the chaos of the past and for now most Cambodians are happy for the chance to look to a future they were once denied. Tourism is set to make its mark in Cambodia. Angkor has been discovered and is a must on any trip to the region. Thailand gets more than 10 million tourists a year. Tread carefully, Cambodia.

ESSENTIAL EXPERIENCES

○ **Heading for the mother of all temples, the world's largest religious building, the one and only Angkor Wat**

○ **Checking the pulse of resurgent Phnom Penh, one of Asia's most enigmatic capitals**

○ **Playing Robinson Crusoe on the isolated tropical islands off the south coast beach mecca of Sihanoukville**

○ **Journeying to the wild east of Mondulkiri, a world apart where elephants are still used as a mode of transport by the minority Pnong people**

○ **Riding the bamboo train, Cambodia's home-made commuter express, around Battambang**

MAP REF // Q11

BEST TIME TO VISIT NOVEMBER TO MARCH

PHOTOGRAPHER ANDREW BURKE // LONELY PLANET IMAGES

☆ A MAN FINDS SOLITUDE ON THE ROOF OF A CARRIAGE OF THE BATTAMBANG TO PHNOM PENH TRAIN

A FEARLESS FAMILY TAKES A THRILL-RIDE THROUGH THE STREETS OF PHNOM PENH ⨠

A SLOW DAY ON THE SANGKER RIVER, BATTAMBANG ⨠

VIETNAM

PANORAMAS OF VARIEGATED NATURAL BEAUTY SET THE BACKDROP FOR THE DRAMA OF VIETNAM'S THRUMMING FUTURE, TO BE IMPROVISED BY ITS CAST OF DETERMINED, EMINENTLY RESOURCEFUL OPTIMISTS.

CAPITAL CITY HANOI   POPULATION 84.4 MILLION   AREA 329,560 SQ KM   OFFICIAL LANGUAGE VIETNAMESE

LANDSCAPE
The long, sinuous 'S' of Vietnam creates the curvature of mainland Southeast Asia's coast, while the Truong Son mountain range forms the backbone of the svelte central region. Mist-shrouded mountains in the north stretch as high as 3143-metre Mt Fansipan, dropping down to the fertile Red River Delta near Hanoi. At Vietnam's southern end, the Mekong River terminates in a fertile delta emptying into the South China Sea. Between the extremes, the geography ranges from rainforest to rich volcanic highlands, with limestone karst formations and outlying islands lacing the coast.

HISTORY IN A NUTSHELL
Several distinct cultures settled in what is present-day Vietnam between the 1st and 8th centuries AD. While the Indianised kingdom of Funan flourished in the Mekong Delta, the kingdom of Champa ruled the central coast, and conquering Chinese descended into the Red River Delta. Though a thousand years of Chinese rule greatly influenced Vietnamese culture, the national identity was as strong then as it is today, and in AD 938 the Vietnamese wrested independence from China. Thus began another thousand years of

nearly uninterrupted rule by Vietnamese emperors, during which the nation expanded southward, absorbing the Cham civilisation and repelling the Khmers. The French would ultimately colonise Vietnam, beginning in 1847. After the end of World War II, Ho Chi Minh's Viet Minh league began a full-scale war with the French to regain independence. The 1954 Geneva Accords split Vietnam into north and south, but they were reunified in 1975 at the end of the Vietnam (American) War.

PEOPLE
About 87 per cent of the population are ethnic Vietnamese (known as Kinh), who share a common language. Of the three distinct dialects and accents distinguishing speakers of the north, south and central regions, the northern dialect is recognised as being 'correct' Vietnamese. Most Vietnamese practise the religion known as *Tam Giao*, a blend of Buddhism, Taoism and Confucianism, while about nine per cent identify as Catholic. The largest, most assimilated sector of Vietnam's minorities are the ethnic Chinese, but the remaining population comprises 53 separate ethnic groups, who mostly inhabit the highlands. Collectively, these hill-tribe people are known as

Montagnards, and though most hold animistic beliefs, their languages and cultures are distinctly different.

MARKETPLACE
With the implementation of mid-1990s *doi moi* (economic liberalisation), Vietnam opened the door to foreign investment and revitalisation and experienced a boom that then busted in the Asian financial crisis of 1997. But Vietnam's economy is bouncing back, growing at eight per cent a year. Exports of agricultural products, along with manufacturing and tourism, form the mainstays of the economy. The average per-capita income is US$550.

TRADEMARKS
○ Ho Chi Minh
○ Vietnam (American) War
○ Pho
○ Conical hats
○ Apocalypse Now
○ Women in *ao dai* (traditional Vietnamese tunics worn over trousers)
○ Rice paddies
○ French colonial architecture

ELEGANT RANKS OF SCHOOLGIRLS WEARING THE TRADITIONAL *AO DAI* »

⌃ A FISHING JUNK ON THE CALM WATERS OF HALONG BAY

PHOTOGRAPHER ANTHONY PLUMMER · LONELY PLANET IMAGES

⌃ SCHOOLGIRLS PASS IN A GRACEFUL BLUR, NHA TRANG

⌃ BLACK HMONG WOMEN SHARE A JOKE

MEMBERS OF THE CAODAI SECT, FAMOUS FOR ITS FUSION OF PHILOSOPHIES, AT PRAYER IN TAY NINH

BALANCE AND SYMMETRY ON THE SHORE OF HOAN KIEM LAKE

SPEED DEMONS RACE MOTORBIKES ON A CITY STREET

NATURAL BEAUTY

Most iconic of Vietnam's natural wonders are the unusual karst islands of Halong Bay, gracefully surreal in fair weather or fog. Along the coast lie miles of windswept beaches facing the South China Sea. Bright-green rice shoots undulate in the breeze from the alluvial Mekong Delta paddies to the spectacular terraces cultivated up the slopes of the Hoang Lien Mountains. National parks protect pockets of rainforest dotted along the length of the country.

URBAN SCENE

Hanoi and Ho Chi Minh City hold the most obvious appeal for those seeking urban immersion. Sophisticated restaurants, the buzz of international commerce and high concentrations of expats make these cities the most cosmopolitan in Vietnam. But downshifting into the smaller hubs affords its own pleasures – going consumption-mad for tailored clothes in the charming, bustling alleys of Hoi An, perhaps, or bar hopping in beachside Nha Trang.

MYTHS & LEGENDS

The Vietnamese origin myth begins when Lac Long Quan, a dragon king, falls in love with Au Co, a beautiful fairy. After they marry, Au Co lays 100 eggs, which hatch 100 sons. Sadly, the marriage becomes untenable, as Au Co is a land fairy and Lac Long Quan a water dragon, and they decide to separate. The fairy takes 50 sons to live with her in the mountains, while the dragon king takes the other 50 sons to live on the coast. The descendants of these children are the people of Vietnam.

CUISINE

Vietnamese cuisine uses the country's wealth of seafood, vegetables and herbs to delicious advantage, with rice as the staple of every diet. Fiery chillies, basil, mint, coriander, lime and fish sauce are the essential condiments that spice up the thousand dishes that feature these complex flavours in simple culinary combinations. Diners usually eat communally, unless they are taking a quick bite on the street, and guests will be topped up eternally unless they are savvy enough not to leave their bowl or glass empty.

TOP FESTIVAL

In the weeks leading up to *Tet* (Vietnamese Lunar New Year), the holiday frenzy builds to a palpable pitch as Vietnamese living abroad pour back into the country to spend this auspicious time with their families. As the population swells and people prepare to make cross-country peregrinations, vendors sprout along roadsides, selling potted flowering trees, red envelopes for lucky money and special holiday snacks. Traffic jams clog temple entrances as visitors arrive to burn incense and pray for a prosperous year. The colourful and manic pace suddenly drops off when *Tet* finally arrives, however, and everyone retreats towards home or visits with friends and family.

ESSENTIAL EXPERIENCES

o **Kayaking among the limestone islands of serene Halong Bay**

o **Zigzagging through chaotic Ho Chi Minh City traffic as the front-loaded passenger in a pedal-powered *cyclo* (pedicab)**

o **Going underground at the Cu Chi Tunnels for a claustrophobic taste of wartime subterranean survival**

o **Trekking past stunning rice terraces to diverse hill-tribe villages surrounding Sapa and beyond**

o **Stopping streetside for a steaming breakfast bowl of *pho* (flat rice noodles)**

o **Taking a time-out on the white-sand beaches of Phu Quoc Island**

o **Toasting your travels (and getting toasted) at a *bia hoi* with litres of cheap, fresh draught beer**

DRYING RICE PAPER BEFORE CUTTING IT INTO NOODLES, AN GIANG

PHOTOGRAPHER PATRICK BEN LUKE SYDER · LONELY PLANET IMAGES

FROM THE TRAVELLER

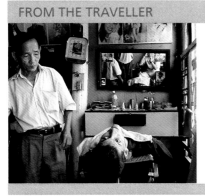

One thing I love about travelling in Asia is that I never have to shave: for a very small outlay you can have the relaxing experience of getting someone else to do it for you and it's usually a great shave. Not always, though – on this occasion in Hoi An, Vietnam, my friend went to the local shack for a shave and when he saw how much the old barber's hands were shaking I could see the fear light up in his eyes. Fortunately I had my camera handy to capture the moment. He did walk away clean-shaven and unscathed, physically anyway.

SEAN LUCAS   UK

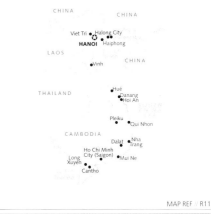

MAP REF // R11

BEST TIME TO VISIT **ANY TIME OF YEAR**

SLANTING LIGHT CATCHES THE SMOKE OF A BLACK HMONG WOMAN'S COOKING FIRE

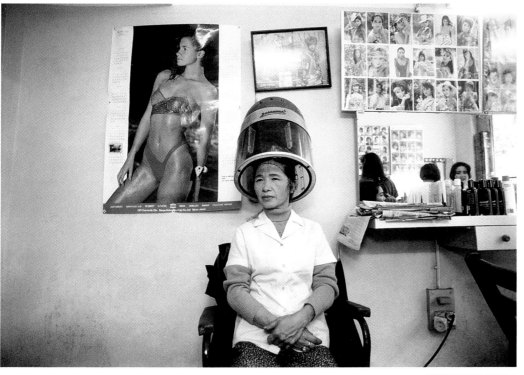

PHOTOGRAPHER MARK ANDREW KIRBY · LONELY PLANET IMAGES

DOING THE DO IN HANOI

A DZAO TODDLER IN SAPA

LAOS

LAOS IS ONE OF THE MOST ECOLOGICALLY INTACT COUNTRIES IN ASIA AND IS QUITE POSSIBLY THE MOST LAID-BACK COUNTRY ON EARTH.

CAPITAL CITY **VIENTIANE**   POPULATION **6.4 MILLION**   AREA **236,800 SQ KM**   OFFICIAL LANGUAGE **LAO**

THE ARCHETYPICAL IMAGE OF ASIA: WOMEN WORKING IN RICE FIELDS, SEKONG

LANDSCAPE

The majestic Mekong River is the lifeblood of Laos, flowing 1835 kilometres from China all the way to Cambodia. More than 10 per cent of Laos is officially protected, and vast swaths of virgin forest blanket the stunningly beautiful mountains that dominate much of the country. Fortunately, the lack of major population pressures mean that the biodiversity in these hills remains impressive.

HISTORY IN A NUTSHELL

Chao Fa Ngum became the first king of what would later be called Laos in 1353; he called his kingdom Lan Xang Hom Khao (Million Elephants, White Parasol). The kingdom slowly fell into decline and by the late 18th century the Thais, Burmese, Vietnamese and even Chinese had all been busy annexing and looting Lan Xang. The French arrived in the late 19th century and made Laos a part of French Indochina. After they departed in 1953, Laos became a Cold War pawn and eventually a secret but very bloody battleground during the Vietnam (American) War. In 1976 the communist Pathet Lao took power, ending royal rule once and for all. Laos remains a one-party socialist state.

PEOPLE

The Lao live in extended-family units and divide themselves into four broad categories, roughly reflecting the altitudes at which they live. The Lao Loum (about 50 per cent of the population) live mostly in the Mekong River valley, while the Lao Thai (10 to 20 per cent) live mainly in upland river valleys. Both are predominantly Buddhist. The mainly animist Lao Thoeng live on mid-altitude mountain slopes, while the Lao Soung (High Lao) live at altitudes above 1000 metres and consist mainly of the marginalised Hmong and Mien. Within these groups are dozens of smaller tribes speaking many dialects.

MARKETPLACE

Until the mid-1990s, Laos' main foreign exchange earner was the fees paid by overflying airlines – the economy remains blissfully unsophisticated. Despite 20 years of rapid growth, agriculture still employs about 80 per cent of the population, many of them at a subsistence level. Mining, construction, logging and tourism are other significant employers. In 2005 Laos spent about US$11 million on its military, compared with US$81 billion in neighbouring China and US$518 billion in the USA.

TRADEMARKS

- Swaying hammocks
- Saffron-robed monks
- Golden Triangle opium
- Beer Lao
- Luang Prabang monasteries
- Homes made from bomb casings

WILD THINGS

Laos is like a repository of all those animals that have been hunted to near extinction elsewhere in the region. They generally keep a pretty low profile, but the jungles hide small but significant numbers of tigers, clouded leopards and spindlehorns, and the highest proportion of elephants to humans in Asia. The Mekong is home to a few Siamese crocodiles and even fewer Irrawaddy dolphins.

SPIRITUAL OFFERINGS

There's more to drinking *lào-láo* (rice whisky) in a Lao home than just chugging back rocket fuel. Towards the end of a meal the hosts will produce a bottle to honour their guests. The host will first pour one glass onto the floor or a used dinner plate to appease the *phĭi*, or house spirits, that live in every home. He will

CARTLOADS OF FUN FOR CHILDREN IN WAT THAM KRABOK

BOATS AT THEIR SPINDLY MOORINGS ON THE MEKONG RIVER, LUANG PRABANG

down the second himself, in one swift gulp, before sharing the spirit around. Guests are obliged to drink at least once or risk offending the house spirit.

TABOOS

In some remote villages taboos are observed to avoid disturbing the house spirit. In a Katang village, for example, visitors should never enter the owner's bedroom or touch the spirit place, sleep beside a person of the opposite sex (even their spouse) or clap hands in a house without first asking permission

⌃ ADORNED BUDDHA STATUE AT WAT PHU, CHAMPASAK

of the elder (who will then check with the spirit). Breaking a taboo might require the village to make an expensive sacrifice to mollify the spirit, possibly even killing a buffalo.

KARMA

The Lao are famous for being so laid-back they seem to go through life almost horizontal. But there is a reason behind what's often misconstrued as a lack of ambition – karma. In Theravada Buddhism, displaying strong emotions is socially very uncool, and bad karma. And karma is believed to determine one's lot in life, not devotion, prayer or hard work. Which makes keeping cool a wise investment in the future.

ECOTOURISM

Laos is fast becoming the ecotourism capital of Asia. Whether you're trekking through the hills in the Nam Ha National Protected Area, zipping through tree tops at the Gibbon Experience or watching rare Irrawaddy dolphins playing in the Mekong, ecotourism is helping travellers gain experiences and locals make money. Mostly, projects have been well planned and are legitimately low impact.

FUTURE DIRECTIONS

Political change happens at a snail's pace in Laos and despite younger faces appearing in top posts, there's no reason to expect multiparty democracy to emerge any time soon. Economically, the completion of the huge Nam Theun 2 Dam will bring foreign exchange, but for the average Lao agriculture and, to a lesser extent, tourism will be the mainstays for a while yet.

○ **Watching saffron-robed monks silently collect alms in mystical Luang Prabang**

○ **Experiencing the mighty Mekong River from the roof of a river boat**

○ **Realising you don't need electricity to become totally chilled in the islands of Si Phan Don**

○ **Soaking up the sunrise from ancient Wat Phu Champasak**

○ **Meeting the Akha, Lao Huay and Khamu people as you trek in Nam Ha National Protected Area**

○ **Reaching for a Beer Lao to quench the fire of a spicy *láap* (Lao-style meat salad)**

CHINA

Nam Ha National Protected Area • Phongsali
VIETNAM
MYANMAR (BURMA) • Luang Nam Tha
Huay Xai • Luang Prabang • Phonsavan
VIENTIANE ⊕ • Paksan
Tha Khaek •
Savannakhet •
THAILAND Salavan •
Pakse • Sekong (Muang Lamam)
Si Phan Don • • Attapeu (Samakhi Xai)
CAMBODIA

MAP REF // P9

⌃ FRATERNISING STATUES IN XIANG KHOUAN (BUDDHA PARK), VIENTIANE

PHOTOGRAPHER ALAIN EVRARD LONELY PLANET IMAGES

PHOTOGRAPHER SHAUN EDWARDS ALAMY

LAST DIP OF THE DAY IN THE NAM SONG, VANG VIENG »

A RELAXED MOMENT FOR A NOVICE MONK AT WAT XIENG THONG »

THE STATELY PATUXAI AT SUNSET »

TEXT ROBERT REID

MYANMAR

RICHLY BUDDHIST AND ETERNALLY SWEET, MYANMAR SEEMS POISED SOMEWHERE IN THE DISTANT PAST, WITH HORSE CARTS LEADING PAST THATCH VILLAGES AND GOLD-LEAF STUPAS.

CAPITAL CITY PYINMANA   POPULATION 47.4 MILLION   AREA 678,500 SQ KM   OFFICIAL LANGUAGE BURMESE

⌃ A LONG WALK ACROSS THE GLISTENING U BEIN BRIDGE

LANDSCAPE
A bit bigger than France, kite-shaped Myanmar is rimmed with lush mountains and beaches, and sliced by rivers fed by monsoon downpours and melted Himalayan snows. A vast, rice-rich delta stretches south from Yangon towards the Bay of Bengal. North of Yangon, the broad, dusty 'dry zone' fills Myanmar's centre around Bagan and Mandalay. In each direction are mountains: to the north, the rugged Kachin Hills serve as first steps to the Himalayas; the Shan Hills stretch east towards Thailand; and west of the Ayeyarwady (Irrawaddy) River, the Rakhaing Yoma (Arakan Mountains) line the Bangladesh border.

HISTORY IN A NUTSHELL
The 11th-century kingdom at Bagan managed to unify scattered groups in the region, until Kublai Khan invaded in 1287. The next five centuries saw rival kingdoms wrestle for land, Buddhism flourish and the so-called Second Burmese Empire take root in Inwa, outside Mandalay. In the 19th century Britain took Burma in three waves. The country won independence in 1948, but a left-wing army revolt led by General Ne Win deposed the democratic army, and the country's economy crumbled. Following harsh military response to mass protests in 1988, the National League of Democracy (NLD), under the leadership of Aung San Suu Kyi, dominated 'democratic' elections. The military never relinquished control, and Aung San Suu Kyi remains under house arrest. General Than Shwe relocated the government to remote Pyinmana in late 2005.

PEOPLE
Myanmar has 135 ethnic groups; the Bamar majority makes up 68 per cent of the population. Minority groups include the Shan (nine per cent of the population), Karen (seven per cent), Rakhaing (four per cent), Chinese (three per cent), Indian (two per cent) and Mon (two per cent). About 89 per cent of the country is Buddhist, four per cent is Christian, four per cent Muslim and one per cent animist.

MARKETPLACE
Rich in resources, but crippled by its economy, Myanmar is an agricultural nation – about seven out of ten people work on farms, and the scarcity of city jobs means that number is holding steady. The EU and the USA boycott trade with Myanmar, but it trades openly with China, India, Thailand, Singapore and, in recent years, Japan. The average monthly income is about US$140 – about five times less than Thailand.

TRADEMARKS
○ Men in *longyi* (sarong-style lower garments), women with dollops of *thanaka* (make-up made from bark) on their faces
○ Rickshaws, horse carts, stuffed pick-up trucks
○ Friendliness: locals call you 'brother' or 'sister' right off
○ Aung San Suu Kyi, the graceful NLD leader

URBAN SCENE
Rickshaws and horse carts aren't allowed on the busy central streets of Yangon, which was home to the military junta's government until 2005. There are lively Chinese markets and the (supposedly) 2500-year-old Shwedagon Paya, Myanmar's holiest site. Laid-back Mandalay – home to the last Burmese king – is squeak-of-the-bicycle quiet in comparison. A steep climb up Mandalay Hill offers views of the Ayeyarwady, while the city's southern side streets are home to more monks than anywhere else in the country.

RANDOM FACTS
○ Pro-democracy advocates both in and outside of Myanmar have mixed opinions about whether or not individual travellers should support the travel boycott initiated by Aung San Suu Kyi.

THE RECLINING BUDDHA OF THE ZINATHUKHA PAGODA IN MAGNIFICENT REPOSE

THE RIVER

Pick-up trucks and ox carts bounce along muddy roads, but Myanmar moves most smoothly along its rivers, particularly the 2000-kilometre Ayeyarwady, which weaves from the Himalayan foothills to the Andaman Sea. Commuters get to market on open-deck ferries (including some old British ones left over from colonial times) and on simple fishing boats that drift along, but the rivers are more than a way to get around. Locals bathe, clean, drink, fish and exercise in the country's rivers.

SURPRISES

○ At Minbu there's a snake-guarded 'volcano' site made of mounds created by bubbling butane gas.
○ Outside Pyay, the Shwemyetman Paya is home to a spectacled Buddha.
○ A Myingyan monastery is housed in an old British colonial bank – the safe now guards prized Buddha relics (such as hair and teeth).
○ Street markets in many places offer wriggling snacks of larvae to nibble on.
○ The ultimate surprise is how the gravity-defying Golden Rock at Kyaiktiyo keeps from tumbling off the mountain.

TOP FESTIVALS

Myanmar knows how to throw a party. *Nat* (guardian spirit) festivals often lead to spirit possessions, which can be embarrassing if it's Ko Gyi Kyaw (a drunkard *nat*). The Myanmar New Year begins with a splash in April, with a bucket-dunking water fight nationwide. Expect everyone – even monks – to get into the firework action during the full-moon night of Tazaungmon (October or November). Best of all, though, are the impromptu *pwe* (festivals) that mark a birthday, anniversary or funeral.

PHOTOGRAPHER JEFF WILLIS

⌃ AN AREA OF SHWEDAGON PAYA FORBIDDEN TO WOMEN, YANGON

ESSENTIAL EXPERIENCES

○ **Poking around Bagan's 1000-year-old temples to find hidden stairways and peeling murals**

○ **Hiking to Shan villages between Kalaw and Inle Lake or outside Hsipaw**

○ **Paying tribute to Myanmar's 37 *nat* – and a few monkeys – at the spiritual centre of the *nat*, Mt Popa**

○ **Rising with dawn at Shwedagon Paya, Yangon's (and Myanmar's) most beloved Buddhist site**

○ **Bumping along dirt roads in the back of horse or ox cart, Myanmar's quintessential means of transport**

PHOTOGRAPHER JEREMY HORNER / PANOS

⌃ A YOUNG GIRL WEARING *THANAKA* (MAKE-UP MADE FROM BARK)

MAP REF // O9

BEST TIME TO VISIT **NOVEMBER TO FEBRUARY**

SLOW TRAVEL OVER THE ANCIENT TEMPLES OF BAGAN

LABELLING LOGS FOR EXPORT

THE MORNING ROUNDS: NUNS TOUR CENTRAL YANGON IN SEARCH OF ALMS

TEXT SIMON RICHMOND

MALAYSIA

DIVERSITY – IN PEOPLE, CULTURES AND THE NATURAL ENVIRONMENT – IS THE HALLMARK OF THIS RELAXED SOUTHEAST ASIAN NATION.

CAPITAL CITY KUALA LUMPUR   POPULATION 24.4 MILLION   AREA 329,750 SQ KM   OFFICIAL LANGUAGE BAHASA MALAYSIA

LANDSCAPE

Lush jungle cloaks peninsular Malaysia, particularly the mountainous, thinly populated northern half abutting Thailand. On the west coast a long, fertile plain runs down to the sea; this is the most industrialised and urban part of the country, and contains vast oil palm plantations. Mountains descend more steeply to the east coast, which is fringed with sandy beaches and quiet villages. Some 600 kilometres across the South China Sea and occupying the northern part of the island of Borneo is East Malaysia, which comprises more than 50 per cent of the nation's total area. The dense jungle here is sliced through by mighty rivers, and broken by the 4101-metre Mt Kinabalu, Malaysia's highest peak.

HISTORY IN A NUTSHELL

Malay culture has its origins in the golden age of the Melaka Sultanate and the state adoption of Islam in the 15th century. Portugal was the first European power to colonise this strategically important and naturally abundant region. The Dutch and then the British followed, the latter encouraging the immigration of the Chinese and Indians who now make up significant parts of Malaysia's ethnic mix.

Under the British Empire, Malaya (as it was then known) flourished. Still, even before the Japanese stormed in during World War II there were rumblings for independence. *Merdeka* (independence) came on 31 August 1957; the country of Malaysia as it is today, including the East Malaysian states of Sabah and Sarawak, was created in 1963.

PEOPLE

Malays, including aboriginal peoples known locally as Orang Asli, make up around 62 per cent of the population. Chinese make up 24 per cent and Indians seven per cent, and the remaining seven per cent is a mixture. Malays by definition are Muslim, and there's a small percentage of Indian Muslims, too. Most Indians, however, are Hindus; the Chinese population follows a mix of Buddhism, Confucianism and Taoism. A long history of coexistence between these groups has given Malaysia a very multicultural character and a generally tolerant nature. Nevertheless, there have been instances of violence between the races, and even today there remains a level of mistrust and misunderstanding between the dominant Malay population and the other ethnic groups, particularly the economically successful Chinese.

MARKETPLACE

Rich in natural resources including oil, gas, rubber and timber, Malaysia has a strong economy. Since the 1970s the country has embraced manufacturing, particularly electronics and electrical machinery, which now account for around 68 per cent of exports. Seduced by tax incentives, hamstrung trade unions and a very pro-business government, multinationals have poured billions into the Malaysian economy. Even so, Malaysia's per capita GDP of US$10,400 is less than half that of its neighbours Singapore and Brunei.

TRADEMARKS

○ Petronas Towers
○ Longhouses
○ Durians
○ Giant ornamental kites
○ Orang-utans
○ Oil palm trees

NATURAL BEAUTY

Idyllic, palm-fringed, soft-sand beaches characterise the hundreds of islands that are part of Malaysia. There are 104 islands in the Langkawi group alone off

THICK-SKINNED: BODY PIERCING AT THE THAIPUSAM FESTIVAL »

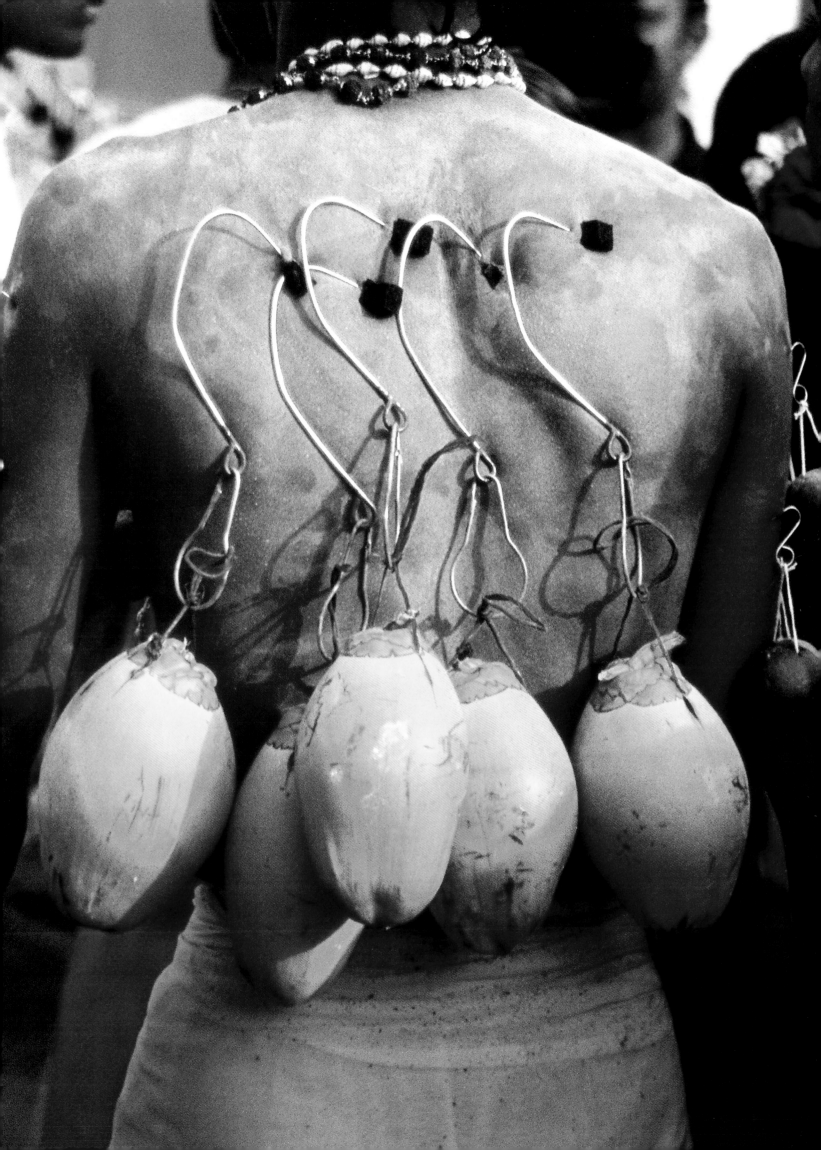

the northwest coast of the peninsula, the largest being stunning Pulau Langkawi. Pulau Tioman, off the east coast, was used by Hollywood as the setting for Bali Hai in the musical South Pacific. Pulau Tiga, the island location of the first series of TV's Survivor, is off the coast of Sabah.

RANDOM FACTS

○ Malaysians who have become famous overseas include shoe-smith Jimmy Choo, who hails from Penang, and the movie actress Michelle Yeoh, born in Ipoh.

○ Malaysia has nine sultans who take turns every five years to be the nation's king.

○ The martial art of silat, which originated in Melaka in the 15th century, has become a highly stylised and refined practice that's akin to modern dance.

○ The 51-kilometre-long Clearwater Cave, in the Gunung Mulu National Park in Sarawak, is the longest cave passage in Southeast Asia.

○ The centre of Malaysian tea production is the cool Cameron Highlands, where the temperature rarely drops below 10°C or climbs above 21°C.

URBAN SCENE

After years spent in the shadow of other go-ahead and more glamorous Southeast Asian cities, Kuala Lumpur is coming into its own as a great place to be. The glittering Petronas Towers anchoring the impressive Kuala Lumpur City Centre (KLCC) development are an obvious draw, but now there's also much-improved public transport, including a zippy monorail, some of the best value five-star hotels in Asia, a fantastic dining scene and vibrant nightlife.

CUISINE

Malaysia's prime attraction for most visitors is its magnificent culinary scene, embracing the food cultures of the Malays, Chinese and Indians. Rice and noodles are the staples and come in a bewildering variety of forms. The fertile land and jungles provide a wealth of exotic fruits and vegetables, while the surrounding seas are rich in seafood. Laksa noodle soups, rich coconut milk–flavoured beef rendang curry, fragrant chicken rice and rojak salad (fruit and vegetables with peanut sauce) are all stand-out dishes.

CULTURE

The Peranakans, also known as Baba-Nonyas, have a hybrid culture found mainly in the old colonial cities of Melaka and Penang. The descendants of the earliest Chinese settlers who intermarried with Malays, they took the names and religion of their Chinese fathers and combined them with the customs, language and dress of their Malay mothers. Peranakan culture is fully expressed in the ornate homes, fashions and distinct style of cooking that were part of the daily life of this generally wealthy merchant class.

WILD THINGS

Malaysia's jungles are believed to be 130 million years old. They support a staggering amount of wildlife, including around 14,500 species of flowering plants and trees, 210 species of mammals, 600 species of birds, 150 species of frogs, 80 species of lizards and thousands of types of insects. Sadly, several of Malaysia's best-known animals – including the Sumatran rhino, Asian elephant, Malaysian tiger and giant leatherback turtle – are seriously endangered.

TOP FESTIVAL

Even though its origins are in Southern India, the Hindu festival of Thaipusam, during which devotees endure seemingly hideous body piercings, has become closely associated with Malaysia. It's most famously celebrated at the Batu Caves on the outskirts of Kuala Lumpur. Crowds numbering up to a million gather for the festival, held usually in late January or early February.

⌃ TURNING ON THE CHARM IN THE TOK SNAKE SANCTUARY, LANGKAWI

ESSENTIAL EXPERIENCES

○ **Exploring Malaysia's premier national park, Taman Negara**

○ **Diving in the Tun Sakaran Marine Park**

○ **Discovering the rich colonial history of Penang and Melaka**

○ **Scrambling atop Malaysia's highest peak, Mt Kinabalu**

○ **Relaxing on the idyllic white-sand beaches of Pulau Perhentian**

○ **Grazing through the street-food feast at night markets and mamak (Indian-Muslim) stalls**

THAILAND

• Kangar

• Kota Bharu Perhentian Islands

• Georgetown Penang
Kuala
• Kangsar
Ipoh • Cameron Taman
Highlands Negara

• Kuala Terengganu

• Kuantan

KUALA LUMPUR
✿
Pelabuhan
(Port) Klang • Gemas

Pulau Tioman

Melaka •
Muar • • Keluang

Johor Bahru
INDONESIA
Sumatra SINGAPORE

Thailand Vietnam
MALAYSIA
Brunei
Singapore
Indonesia

THE PHILIPPINES

Kudat •
Mt Kinabalu
Kota Kinabalu •
Sandakan •
BRUNEI Sabah
Miri •
Tawau •

Bintulu •
Sarawak
Sematan • • Sibu
• Kuching INDONESIA
• Sri Aman Kalimantan

MAP REF S13

BEST TIME TO VISIT **MAY TO SEPTEMBER**

⌃ A RICKSHAW DRIVER TAKES IT EASY

THE MONSTROUS BLOOM OF THE RAFFLEASIA PLANT, THE WORLD'S LARGEST FLOWER »

FROM THE TRAVELLER

While wandering around Georgetown hoping to find some interesting temples, I instead found this neglected mansion from the British colonial era, with a rusty old Morris Minor out the front. To get a good shot, I had to clamber onto the crumbling old wall, which I was sure would collapse at any moment.

GUY HAWKSWORTH » AUSTRALIA

A GAGGLE OF SCHOOLGIRLS, KUALA LUMPUR

SINGAPORE

A TINY ISLAND RENOWNED FOR ITS STRICT SOCIAL RULES AND CONSERVATISM, SINGAPORE IS A DYNAMIC, COSMOPOLITAN CITY-STATE WITH SOME OF THE BEST EATING, SHOPPING AND NIGHTLIFE IN ASIA.

CAPITAL CITY SINGAPORE   POPULATION 4.5 MILLION   AREA 693 SQ KM   OFFICIAL LANGUAGE ENGLISH

☆ THE *CHINGAY* PROCESSION DURING CHINESE NEW YEAR DISPLAYS ALL THE COLOUR OF A TROPICAL REEF

LANDSCAPE

Singapore is very small, very flat and very hot. Less than half the size of London, the island's highest peak towers just 163 metres above sea level and the temperature never falls below 20°C, even at night. But Singapore packs a lot of nature into that tiny space. The centre of the island is given almost entirely to reservoirs and protected forest, surrounded to the north, south and east by urban development.

HISTORY IN A NUTSHELL

Though there are records of Chinese traders visiting the island as far back as the 5th century, the history of Singapore is generally considered to have begun in earnest with the arrival of Sir Stamford Raffles in 1819. Seeking to revive British imperial ambitions in Southeast Asia, Raffles plucked the island away from the Johor empire with some diplomatic sleight of hand, transferred it into the hands of the giant East India Company and masterminded its transformation into a polyglot free-trade port. It remained a vital link in Britain's trading empire until World War II; the Japanese overran the island in 1942. Postwar Singapore elected its first local prime minister, Lee Kuan Yew, in 1954 and joined the new federation of Malaysia in 1963. Kicked out in 1965, the city became an independent nation, but faced a precarious, isolated future. Driven by the relentless vision of Lee Kuan Yew, it transformed itself into an industrial dynamo, melding free-market economics with strict Confucian-inspired social engineering. Lee Kuan Yew's son now leads the country and faces a tough job maintaining Singapore's place in the ruthless global economy.

PEOPLE

Singapore has no indigenous population – though there may be a few Malays who can trace their roots back to the few hundred (or thousand, nobody's sure) people who lived on Singapura when Raffles arrived. The island has, by virtue of numbers, become defined as 'Chinese'. Ethnic Chinese make up three-quarters of the population. Malays and Indians (mainly Tamil) have a 14 per cent and eight per cent share respectively. Within the Chinese population there are Cantonese, Hokkien, Teochew and Mandarin dialect groups, as well as the many Peranakans (a mixed-race Chinese-Malay group often known as Straits Chinese or Baba-Nonya, who have their own distinct dialect and culture). Buddhism is the principal religion, though the government's social policies adhere more to Confucian ideals than Buddhist philosophy.

MARKETPLACE

Singapore rose to 'tiger economy' status on the back of manufacturing, its massive port, oil refining, rig construction and shipbuilding, among other industries. Hit by the 1997 recession, slapped in the face by SARS and loomed over by China and India, Singapore has realised it needs to reinvent itself to be less vulnerable to the vagaries of the global economy. Still, its GDP surpasses that of New Zealand and almost equals that of the UK. It is now focusing on high-tech industries, finance and biomedical research to sandbag the economy against future slumps.

TRADEMARKS

- Singapore Slings
- Chewing gum (the lack of it)
- Raffles Hotel
- Hawker centres
- Singlish, lah

NATURAL BEAUTY

Unlikely as it sounds, this miniature nation boasts some beautiful natural vistas, from pristine rainforests to some of the most diverse mangrove environments in the world and spectacular views of the Indonesian islands from the city's southern hills.

URBAN SCENE

Singapore is at last shaking off its stuffy image and becoming something of an Asian party capital. With its big-name European clubs, long licensing hours, all-night beach parties and some seriously debauched behaviour, it may not be a Bangkok, but it's certainly not boring.

CUISINE

For variety and accessibility, Singapore is the best food city in Southeast Asia. Every kind of Chinese, Malay, North Indian, South Indian and Peranakan cuisine is staple fare in the hawker centres and food courts. The city also brims with upmarket restaurants representing every corner of the globe. Eating is one of the greatest pleasures in this food-obsessed city.

FUTURE DIRECTIONS

Singapore has developed astonishingly fast. It's easy to forget how fast, because so few signs remain of the days when it was a swampy, vice-ridden port town. It has dragged itself, in the words of its founding father, from Third World to First, but now it has to stay there. The country has its sights set on becoming a global city, a hub for everything from aviation and digital media to finance and tourism, to ensure it doesn't fall down as fast as it came up.

⌃ SPIRALLING UPWARDS: INCENSE COILS OUTSIDE WAK HAI CHENG TEMPLE

PHOTOGRAPHER REX BUTCHER GETTY

FROM THE TRAVELLER

At the Singapore Zoological Gardens, a friend and I were enraptured with a huge troupe of hamadryas baboons. The baboons were so humanlike; one overwhelmed mother kept disciplining this little one, who got scolded for disturbing his father. While he was nestled in his mother's fur, a disturbance in the trees above sparked his interest and I snapped this photo.

SEAN PATRICK DOYLE   USA

ESSENTIAL EXPERIENCES

◊ **Tucking into the staggering variety of food at an open-air hawker centre – washed down with a few Tiger beers**

◊ **Nursing your wounded credit card after a hard day in the shopping paradise of Orchard Road**

◊ **Trundling around the hushed Night Safari, only a few metres from nature's most fearsome predators**

◊ **Exploring the city's old ethnic districts: Little India, Kampong Glam and Chinatown**

◊ **Soaking up high culture in some of the region's most impressive museums and concert halls**

◊ **Surrendering to the world of illusion and kitsch that is Sentosa, Singapore's pleasure island**

PHOTOGRAPHER DEMETRIO CARRASCO GETTY

MALAYSIA

● Woodlands

Ji Kayu ●

Changi

Jurong ●   Bedok ●

● Queenstown

SINGAPORE ✪

Jurong

Southern Islands

MAP REF Q13

BEST TIME TO VISIT **OCTOBER TO MARCH**

⌃ CHINESE PRIESTS AT THE FESTIVAL OF HUNGRY GHOSTS

I THINK I CAN: A STREET SALESMAN WITH A HEAVY LOAD

THE MERLION, THE SYMBOL OF SINGAPORE, ILLUMINATED AT DUSK

INTO THE MOUTH OF THE DRAGON, TIGER BALM GARDENS

TEXT TOM PARKINSON

BRUNEI

BRUNEI IS SOUTHEAST ASIA'S MOST ENDURING ANACHRONISM, A TINY HAVEN OF ABSOLUTE MONARCHY AND IMPOSSIBLE WEALTH STILL IMMERSED IN THE LEGACY OF A BYGONE ISLAMIC EMPIRE.

LANDSCAPE

Thanks to the vagaries of colonial politics, Brunei forms a curious lopsided 'W' shape in the middle of the northern coastline of the island of Borneo, bordered by the Malaysian state of Sarawak. Most of the country is still covered by rainforest, tapering into beaches along the low-lying coastal areas and becoming more hilly as you head inland.

HISTORY IN A NUTSHELL

For centuries Brunei controlled the whole island of Borneo and territories as far afield as the Philippines, exerting considerable influence over the South China Sea region. It was only with the arrival of the British that the sultanate's position was seriously eroded, as the embattled sultans ceded progressively more territory in return for economic and military support. Just as Brunei seemed set to vanish from the map entirely, oil was discovered off the coast, securing a prosperous future.

PEOPLE

The Bruneians themselves are a mainly Muslim Malay people (around 70 per cent of the country's modest population), supplemented by a large Chinese minority (15 per cent), smaller groups of indigenous tribes in the interior, and significant numbers of immigrant workers from Malaysia, Indonesia and the Philippines.

CAPITAL CITY BANDAR SERI BEGAWAN (BSB)   POPULATION 379,400   AREA 5770 SQ KM   OFFICIAL LANGUAGE BAHASA MALAYSIA

UPLIFTED SOULS: MOTHER AND DAUGHTERS WASH BEFORE ENTERING THE PRAYER HALL AT OMAR ALI SAIFUDDIEN MOSQUE

MARKETPLACE

Despite some attempts to diversify, Brunei's economy is still very much dependent on oil and gas, which account for roughly half the country's GDP and a massive 90 per cent of state revenue. With supplies dwindling rapidly, however, the government is promoting tourism, Islamic banking and foreign investment as alternative sources of income.

TRADEMARKS
- Hydrocarbons
- Money
- Monarchy
- Politeness
- Islamic law
- Traditional weaving

RANDOM FACTS
- Brunei is one of the most effective welfare states in the world, with no income tax, free health care and a whole range of benefits for its citizens.
- Brunei's ruling dynasty is the longest-surviving royal line in the world, having clocked up over 500 years of continuous rule.
- Logging is prohibited by law, and the country retains 90 per cent of its original forest cover.
- The current sultan technically has two second wives – he divorced his original second wife and married again in 2005.
- Despite the alcohol ban, it's rumoured the sultan has a bar in the palace basement for visiting dignitaries.

IMPORT
- Filipino workers
- British manners
- Gurkha soldiers (to guard the oil wells)
- Malaysian beer and chicken wings (smuggled)
- Diplomatic gifts

EXPORT
- Hydrocarbons
- Prince Jefri (in disgrace after allegedly 'misplacing' US$16 billion)

URBAN SCENE

Bandar Seri Begawan, or BSB, as Brunei's capital is universally known, isn't exactly the most vibrant city in the world. It's home to a mere 22,000 people, and the central waterfront area, where most visitors stay, usually seems completely dead not long after darkness falls. Head out into the suburbs, though, and you'll find out where everyone really is: shopping, eating or just hanging out in one of the city's huge modern malls.

FUTURE DIRECTIONS

After years as a virtual (if largely benevolent) dictatorship, there are signs that Brunei is slowly beginning to change its ways politically. The sultan recently allowed the formation of an opposition party, restored the Legislative Council after a 25-year suspension, and fired his education minister for pushing too much religion in schools – all drastic steps in a country where there hasn't been an election since 1962. At the same time, however, the constitution was rewritten to declare the sultan infallible – it may still be some time before Bruneians see any real change.

- **Hurtling around the 28 water villages that comprise Kampung Ayer in a motorboat taxi**
- **Admiring the upper reaches of the rainforest from the canopy walkway at Ulu Temburong National Park**
- **Taking afternoon tea at the stupendously lavish Empire Hotel**
- **Wandering the semi-deserted pathways of the Jerudong Park Playground amusement park**
- **Taking part in traditional longhouse activities at Kuala Balai**
- **Tracing the fates of some lesser-known monarchs at the Brunei Museum**
- **Watching the sun set behind the dome of BSB's renowned Omar Ali Saifuddien Mosque**

MAP REF // S12

BEST TIME TO VISIT **SEPTEMBER TO MARCH**

A BOY FILLS THE GENERATION GAP AT NOON PRAYER

OMAR ALI SAIFUDDIEN MOSQUE APPEARS EVEN MORE ENCHANTED THROUGH THE HAZE

INDONESIA

THE WORLD'S LARGEST ARCHIPELAGO BOASTS ENOUGH CULTURE, WILDLIFE, LANDSCAPES AND EXPERIENCES TO KEEP THE HEADS OF EVEN VETERAN EXPLORERS SPINNING.

CAPITAL CITY JAKARTA   POPULATION 245.4 MILLION   AREA 1.9 MILLION SQ KM   OFFICIAL LANGUAGE BAHASA INDONESIA

THE VOLCANIC MT BROMO IS A SLEEPING GIANT AT DAWN

LANDSCAPE

Straddling 5000 kilometres of hot and steamy equator, Indonesia encompasses a staggering 18,000-plus islands (several less when the tide's in). Almost two-thirds of its landmass is covered in tropical rainforest, but active and inert volcanoes, swampy mangroves and stretches of coral gardens also feature. Seasons are divided into wet and dry and many of the islands experience near-continuous rains.

HISTORY IN A NUTSHELL

Most Indonesians are of Malay origin, descended from migrants who arrived around 4000 BC. But the dominant influences of Hinduism, Buddhism and Islam arrived between the 1st and 15th centuries when Indonesia became a stopover on the India–China trade route. In the 17th century European powers got in on the action, and the Dutch became a colonial power until Indonesia declared independence on 17 August 1945. United and led by Sukarno, one of the leaders of the freedom struggle, the country was later ruled by the military dictator Soeharto. Democracy was reinstated after the revolution of 1998 and in 2002 East Timor gained independence after decades of bloody conflict. In 2004, vast areas of Aceh and Sumatra were levelled by the devastating Boxing Day tsunami.

PEOPLE

Indonesia's diverse population comprises some 300 ethnic groups. The largest groups are the Javanese (45 per cent), Sundanese (14 per cent), Madurese (seven and a half per cent) and Malays (seven and a half per cent). The country is primarily Muslim (88 per cent), but around eight per cent are Christian. Bali is predominantly Hindu. The Indonesian-Chinese minority is three per cent of the population, and is the wealthiest ethnic group in the country.

MARKETPLACE

Indonesia's economy is built primarily on natural resources: oil, gas, tin, copper, gold and logging. Rice, palm oil, rubber, tea and coffee are the major crops. The average income per capita is US$3600 and government spending is US$57.7 billion, compared with US$34.62 billion for Malaysia or US$240.2 billion for Australia. Indonesia has yet to recover from the 1997 Asian economic crisis and still suffers from high unemployment and crumbling infrastructure.

TRADEMARKS

- Smoking volcanoes
- Mob riots
- Jungle adventures
- Clove cigarettes
- Batik
- Becaks (bicycle rickshaws)
- Bintang, the locally brewed beer

NATURAL BEAUTY

Dense, verdant jungles dominate much of Indonesia's landscape, providing barely penetrable interiors. Mighty rivers course through Sulawesi, Sumatra, Java and Kalimantan; they form the dominant transport routes in the latter. Slumbering volcanoes provide dramatic backdrops on many islands and the size of the archipelago ensures hundreds of sublime beaches; Lombok's Gili islands, Maluku's Banda Islands and Bali's southern coast are among the best. Then there's the underwater world, where the topography rivals that of the terra firma and divers explore dramatic seascapes and sea-creatures.

WILD THINGS

Apes, tigers, elephants, leopards, rhinos, birds, butterflies, bears, dragons and even kangaroos… Indonesia's varied wildlife beguiles animal lovers. Must-sees include the endangered orang-utans of Sumatra and Kalimantan, Nusa Tenggara's famed Komodo dragons and Papua's rare cenderawasih

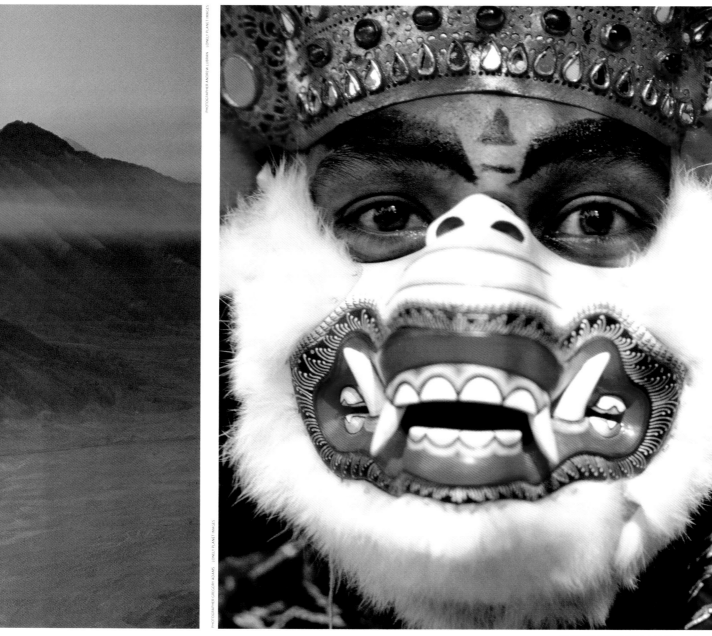

MONKEY BUSINESS: THE MASK OF HANUMAN, THE MONKEY GOD

(bird of paradise). Offshore the sea brims with vivid marine life, particularly in the coral gardens around the Banda Islands and Sumatra's Pulau Weh. Sulawesi's Pulau Bunaken is home to more than 300 species of fish and coral, as well as inquisitive turtles, rays, sharks and dolphins.

CULTURE

Javanese and Balinese culture dominate the artistic life of the country. Both traditions are rooted in Hinduism and include such distinct traditions as elaborately costumed dances and shadow puppetry. With the adoption of Islam, Indonesia also took up many Arabic traditions and heroic religious stories. Periodically, the sensual aspects of Hindu-based art are censored by religious concerns for modesty and monotheism.

RANDOM FACTS

○ Indonesia is the most populous Muslim nation in the world.
○ Indonesia has more active volcanoes (at least 129) than any other nation.
○ In 2006, 20 new frog species and one new bird species were discovered in the Foja Mountain Range.
○ Indonesia is almost three times the size of Texas.

TEXTILE ART

Indonesians have been producing vibrant textiles for centuries. One of the most prominent is *ikat:* intricately patterned cloths made from thread that's painstakingly tie-dyed before being woven together.

Ikat is made in many regions, from Sumatra to West Timor, but it thrives most in Nusa Tenggara. *Ikat* garments come in an incredible diversity of colours and patterns: the spectacular *ikat* of Sumba and the intricately patterned work of Flores (including *kapita,* used to wrap the dead) are the best known.

CUISINE

Indonesian food is diverse, spicy and delicious. The common staple is *nasi* (rice). Spices, sauces and condiments are also constants, and *sambal* (fresh chilli sauce), soy sauce and *kecap manis* (sweet soy sauce) grace virtually every dining table. Specialities vary wildly from region to region and depend largely on the landscape. Delicious barbecued *ikan* (fish) is prevalent in coastal areas on most islands and *sate* (skewered meat with peanut sauce), *nasi goreng* (fried rice), *ayam goreng* (fried chicken) and *gado gado* (vegetables with peanut sauce) have become unofficial national dishes.

MUSIC

The traditional *gamelan* orchestras of Java and Bali are Indonesia's most prominent musical heritage. The orchestra is typically an ensemble of percussive instruments, including drums, gongs, xylophones and *angklung* (bamboo tubes shaken to produce a note). *Dangdut* music is a brew of traditional and modern music, featuring instruments such as Indian tablas and flutes. The result is reminiscent of an Indonesian version of Take That: cheesy love songs with plenty of sex appeal and emotion.

⌃ A GLUM MOMENT FOR AN ORANG-UTAN

⌃ SPRAY-PAINTED CHICKENS – WHAT'S YOUR FAVOURITE COLOUR?

⌃ A FULL HOUSE AT FRIDAY PRAYERS IN ISTIQLAL MOSQUE, JAKARTA

ESSENTIAL EXPERIENCES

Bronzing up, dining out and winding down in Bali

Frolicking with whale sharks and other marine wonders at Sumatra's Pulau Weh

Gaping at the peaks of Borobudur, Java's spectacular monument to Buddha

Hooking up with endangered orang-utans in Kalimantan's Tanjung Puting National Park

Diving the pristine coral reefs off Maluku's Banda Islands

Witnessing elaborate funeral rites in Sulawesi's Tana Toraja

Stalking the gargantuan dragons on Komodo Island

MAP REF ⌐ T14

BEST TIME TO VISIT **MAY TO SEPTEMBER**

SET IN STONE: A BUDDHA AT THE BOROBUDUR COMPLEX IN JAVA

BOYS LISTEN FROM THE LOBBY OF THE MOSQUE IN BANJARMASIN

BIRD HOUSE–LIKE TRADITIONAL MINANGKABAU FARM BUILDINGS IN SUMATRA

EAST TIMOR

THE TINY HALF-AN-ISLAND NATION ONLY JOINED THE UN IN 2002, AFTER A VIOLENCE-PLAGUED INDEPENDENCE REFERENDUM FREED IT FROM INDONESIAN RULE.

CAPITAL CITY **DILI**   POPULATION **1 MILLION**   AREA **15,007 SQ KM**   OFFICIAL LANGUAGES **TETUN, PORTUGUESE**

LANDSCAPE

The terrain is dramatically rugged and beaches dot the north coast where the mountains often tumble straight into the sea. Despite its tiny size, East Timor has higher peaks than anything in neighbouring Australia, which has more than 500 times the area.

HISTORY IN A NUTSHELL

Four hundred years of Portuguese rule ended with the 1974 collapse of Portugal's military government in Europe. The following 24 years of Indonesian rule were often brutal, but the violence reached new depths after the independence referendum in 1999. The UN ushered in independence, only for a fresh cycle of home-grown chaos to hit the new nation in 2006.

PEOPLE

East Timor's population is very diverse: Tetun speakers, the largest local language group, only constitute 25 per cent of the population. A host of other languages are spoken, but Bahasa Indonesia is the nearest thing to a lingua franca. The population suffered disastrous declines during the Indonesian occupation and at the hands of the Japanese during World War II. The vast majority of people are Catholic.

MARKETPLACE

Oil and gas from the Timor Sea is set to transform the country's economy, but otherwise it's dependent upon subsistence agriculture, coffee, a trickle of tourism and a lot of foreign aid.

TRADEMARKS

○ Burnt-out houses from both the post-referendum Indonesian violence and the 2006 internal strife
○ Portuguese colonial remnants, including churches, pousada (traditional inns) and Mateus Rose wine

○ Stunning coral reefs offering tempting scuba diving
○ Touchy relations with Indonesia, despite which Indonesia remains a major trading partner
○ The 'Australian Flag House' in Balibo, a memorial to the five Australia-based journalists killed by the Indonesian invaders in 1975

CATHOLIC INFLUENCE

The Catholic church grew much stronger during the Indonesian period. Dili's huge cathedral and 27-metre-high Christ Statue, strongly reminiscent of Rio de Janiero's Christ the Redeemer figure, are both from the Indonesian period.

RANDOM FACTS

○ Four centuries of Portuguese rule did not extend sealed roads a single kilometre outside of Dili or bridge any major river.
○ The biggest buyer for East Timor's high-quality organically grown coffee is Starbucks.
○ Portuguese is one of the official languages of East Timor, though there are very few fluent speakers apart from the small, old colonial elite.

URBAN SCENE

Dili has some Portuguese flavour and, courtesy of the UN and other international influences, a big variety of restaurants, bars and cafés. Mountains hem the town in against the coast while Atauro Island dominates the horizon offshore.

TEXTILE ART

Tais, the beautiful East Timorese weavings, use the Indonesian *ikat* process, where the threads are dyed before they are woven into the finished cloth. The colours and patterns are so distinctive that an expert can instantly pinpoint the regional origin of a *tais.*

SURPRISES

○ The official currency is the US dollar.
○ East Timor was once an important stepping stone on the old 'hippy trail' between Europe and Australia in the 1960s and '70s.
○ When they first arrived on the island of Timor in the 16th century, the Portuguese established themselves at Lifau in Oecussi, the enclave in West Timor. Their headquarters were not shifted to the modern-day capital of Dili until 1769, more than 200 years later.
○ After the famous mutiny on the Bounty Captain Bligh sailed the length of Timor before making landfall at Kupang on West Timor.

ESSENTIAL EXPERIENCES

○ **Checking out the view to the north and south coasts from the top of Mt Ramelau (Gunung Tatamailau)**

○ **Diving on the north-coast reefs, so close to shore you can swim out to them**

○ **Staying in environmentally sensitive accommodation on Atauro Island and perhaps encountering dolphins or pilot whales on the boat ride back to Dili**

○ **Exploring the island's Portuguese history at old forts like Maubara**

○ **Taking the ferry to the enclave of Oecussi in Indonesian West Timor**

FROM THE TRAVELLER

I came across this gentleman in the *tais* (woven cloth) market in Dili, which is surrounded by a mixture of bombed-out buildings and palm trees. Looking at his lined face it seemed to me to be etched with the troubles that the world's newest nation has been through – despite this, the Timorese people are incredibly friendly. This gentleman hadn't met many tourists and was intrigued that I wanted to take a picture of him.

CHARLOTTE HALL   UK

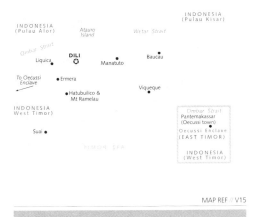

MAP REF V15

BEST TIME TO VISIT **MAY TO NOVEMBER**

PORTRAIT OF AN EAST TIMORESE MAN

A CHRIST STATUE WELCOMES ALL FROM A HILLTOP AT DUSK

SINGING THE BLUES IN MAUBISSA

TEXT GREG BLOOM

PHILIPPINES

THERE'S A QUIRKY SURPRISE AND A NEW ADVENTURE LURKING ON EVERY ONE OF THE PHILIPPINES' 7000-PLUS ISLANDS.

CAPITAL CITY MANILA   POPULATION 89.5 MILLION   AREA 300,000 SQ KM   OFFICIAL LANGUAGES ENGLISH, FILIPINO (TAGALOG)

^ IN THE SWING OF THINGS, BORACAY

LANDSCAPE

An assemblage of tropical isles scattered about like pieces of a giant jigsaw puzzle, the Philippines stubbornly defies geographic generalisation. The typical island boasts a jungle-clad, critter-infested interior and a sandy coastline flanked by aquamarine waters and the requisite coral reef. More populated islands have less jungle and more farmland. Outside of the highlands it's pretty much always hot, but there's plenty of rain to cool things off, especially from June to September.

HISTORY IN A NUTSHELL

Ancient Filipinos stuck to their own islands and social groups until the 16th century, when Ferdinand Magellan claimed the islands for Spain and began the bloody process of Christianisation. Filipinos' waning acceptance of Spanish rule evaporated after the Spaniards executed national hero José Rizal in 1896. They revolted and won, only to have the Americans take over in 1898, whereupon they revolted again and lost. World War II brought much bloodshed, but out of the war's ashes rose an independent republic, albeit one that would soon elect hardliner Ferdinand Marcos as president. Marcos' declaration of martial law in 1972 and the 1986 'People Power' revolution that led to his overthrow are the two defining moments of modern Filipino history. Since 'People Power' the country has remained democratic but its fortunes have barely improved under a string of leaders who have done little to eradicate the paralysing corruption and cronyism of the Marcos years.

PEOPLE

A journey from the northern tip of Luzon to the southern Sulu islands reveals a range of ethnic groups speaking almost 100 different languages. While most Filipinos are related to Malaysians and Indonesians, only about five per cent are Muslim; the vast majority are Roman Catholic. Partially because of the Catholic Church's hard line on 'artificial' birth control, the Philippines' population is growing at one of the fastest rates in Asia. It's also becoming younger and more urban: the median age is only 22.5 and almost a quarter of the population live in or around metro Manila. One other statistic that won't show up in the census is that Filipinos are, according to various studies, among the world's happiest people!

MARKETPLACE

For a number of reasons, including massive corruption, in the last 50 years the Philippines has gone from being Asia's second-richest country to being one of its poorest. Fishing, farming and manufacturing drive the economy, which gets a big lift from the US$10 billion in remittances sent home annually by 'OFWs' (overseas Filipino workers). The government has zealously pursued mining since the Marcos era, but at enormous environmental cost. While plantation and mine owners are enormously wealthy, the incomes of average Filipinos have remained stagnant.

TRADEMARKS

- Jeepneys
- Smiling children
- Bug-eyed tarsiers
- Jollibee restaurants
- Rice terraces
- Tropical islands

NATURAL BEAUTY

The defining image of the Philippines is a dreamy desert island festooned with palm trees and ringed by white sand. The country's beautiful reefs, while threatened by destructive fishing methods and other nuisances, are world famous for their diverse and colourful marine life. Back on terra firma, angry

VIGAN HANDMADE WEAVINGS ADORN DOORWAYS FOR THE *VIVA VIGAN* FESTIVAL, LUZON

AN IFUGAO VILLAGE SET AMID EMERALD-GREEN TERRACES, BANAUE

subterranean forces have sculpted a gloriously crooked landscape of smouldering volcanoes, endless caves, frothy waterfalls and jagged mountains covered by jungle and incredible rice terraces.

ECOTOURISM

With its natural wonders facing a litany of environmental threats, the Philippines is ripe for an ecotourism revolution. Underwater, the revolution has already begun: the growth of scuba diving has led to the creation of protected marine reserves, while in Donsol former dynamite fishermen now earn their crust bringing tourists to snorkel with whale sharks. Alas, there have been few such successes on land, where logging interests thwart forest-protection efforts and tourism officials seem oblivious to the country's potential to become an adventure-tourism mecca. Only a few enterprising individuals offer the spelunking, trekking, rappelling, kayaking and mountain-biking for which the country is tailor-made.

RANDOM FACTS
- The Philippines is the only predominantly Christian country in Asia.
- The most popular sports are basketball and cockfighting.
- The Philippines is the world's biggest producer of coconuts.
- The Guinness Book of World Records once named a Philippine mango the world's sweetest fruit.

CULTURE

The Philippines seems Americanised at first glance, but that's a bit of an illusion. Sure, there are malls and fast-food chains and English is widely spoken, but Filipinos are Asian at their core. That means concepts like 'face-saving', respect for one's elders and fierce loyalty to one's tribe are paramount. Men still possess plenty of Latino-style machismo left over from Spanish colonial times, but what really separates Filipinos from the rest of Asia is their Christianity.

PHOTOGRAPHER OLIVER STREWE LONELY PLANET IMAGES

OLD-STYLE TRAVEL THROUGH CHINATOWN IN MANILA

Visitors will notice how many Filipinos keep numerous religious icons and supernatural talismans close at hand.

IMPORT
- American everything
- Spanish architecture
- Basketball
- Big Brother
- Single Western male retirees
- Roughly US$50 million annually in US military assistance
- Roughly US$1 billion annually in overseas development assistance

EXPORT
- Cover bands
- Electronics
- Nurses, domestic helpers and other OFWs
- Actor Lou Diamond Phillips
- Actress/singer Lea Salonga
- Illegal fishing products (to China and Japan)
- Rattan baskets

STRANGEST RITUAL

Every Good Friday thousands of Catholic worshippers and curious onlookers venture north of Manila to observe the bizarre crucifixion ceremony in the town of San Fernando. Men stroll through town whipping their backs into a bloody pulp. The ceremony culminates with a handful of die-hard devotees being nailed to crosses in the ultimate recreation of Jesus' suffering. Similar ceremonies take place across the country on Good Friday, but San Fernando's is by far the biggest.

ESSENTIAL EXPERIENCES

- **Roaming the rice terraces of the Cordillera Mountains**
- **Sweating out a walking tour of steamy, seamy Manila**
- **Lazing by day and partying by night on sun-splashed Boracay Island**
- **Snorkelling with whale sharks near Donsol or southern Leyte**
- **Getting adventurous on lush, volcanic Camiguin island**
- **Diving among sunken Japanese war ships in Coron Bay**

MAP REF : U11

BEST TIME TO VISIT NOVEMBER TO FEBRUARY

A RICKETY BRIDGE THROUGH BANAUE'S SILVER AND GREEN

PHOTOGRAPHER PETER ADAMS GETTY

COLOURFUL JEEPNEYS AWAIT THEIR PASSENGERS IN MANILA

PERMANENTLY ON WATCH: A WOODEN GUARD IN IFUGAO

MEN OF STRAW AT THE DINAGYANG FESTIVAL

NORTHEAST ASIA

FROM THE RUGGED WILDERNESS OF MONGOLIA TO NEON-LIT TOKYO, NORTHEAST ASIA IS A JARRING, ENCHANTING MIX OF THE TRADITIONAL AND THE MODERN. A JOURNEY THROUGH THIS LANDSCAPE IS A MIND-BOGGLING ENCOUNTER WITH SOME OF THE MOST POPULATED PLACES ON EARTH AND SOME OF THE MOST ENIGMATIC.

China is the key to the entire region. Northeast Asia encompasses societies that were once part of or have been heavily influenced by Chinese culture. Chinese language and script, Confucianism, Buddhism (originally from India), Taoism, and many festivals and arts were exports from early Chinese society, spreading northwards to the Korean Peninsula and then to the island of Japan. These Northeast Asian cultures absorbed Chinese influences and adapted them to local circumstances and traditions.

China's landmass – of which less than 15 per cent is arable land – supports a fifth of the world's population. China's geography resembles a staircase – to the west are the high plateaus of Tibet, which drop sharply towards the east into fertile plains, and the northwest region is a vast inhospitable desert. On the coast are located some of China's greatest cities: vibrant Hong Kong, with its gleaming towers, workaholic business culture and sensational cuisine; cosmopolitan Shànghǎi;

and, at the centre of the Chinese universe, the sprawling inland capital of Běijīng.

China's grip extends across the narrow Taiwan Strait to the 'renegade' (at least according to mainlanders) island of Taiwan, known more for its uneasy relationship with the colossal giant than as a tourist destination. China's territory also includes the former Portuguese enclave of Macau, famous for its glitzy Las Vegas–style casinos and Mediterranean flavour. China is a region of unsettling contrasts, where imperial splendours such as the Great Wall contrast with futuristic skylines and rampant new development.

The island nation of Japan is another dominant player in the northeast. Japan is a dazzling showcase of 21st-century possibilities; a land of über-modern eccentricity and long-held traditions. Where else could manga and punk bands be revered on the same level as swords and *sensei* (teachers)? Despite its frenetic pace, traditional Japanese customs still hold fast – one of the most beloved of holidays is

hanami, when thousands congregate to see the blooming of the country's cherry blossoms.

While China and Japan are fairly familiar to travellers, some regions of Northeast Asia still remain little explored. The 'Hermit Kingdom' of North Korea is perpetually shadowed in secrecy and remains off-limits to most outsiders. South Korea, however, is incredibly hospitable. With abundant natural resources, South Korea also possesses beautiful mountain ranges that make it a terrific hiking destination. Mongolia has only in recent years opened its doors, and its unbroken blue sky, rugged steppes and rich nomadic culture make travel through its unforgettable landscape a unique experience.

Though celebrated, studied and satirised, Northeast Asia nevertheless retains enough secrets and surprises to keep the rest of the world enthralled for centuries to come.

TEXT: JULIE GRUNDVIG

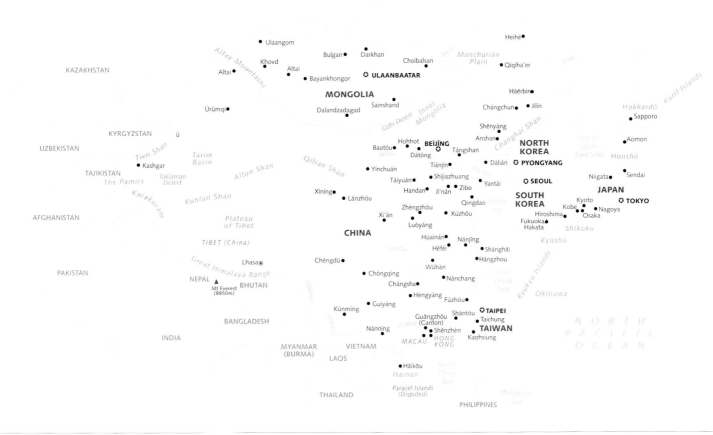

KAZAKHSTAN

Ulaangom

Bulgan   Darkhan

Altay Mountains

Khovd
Altai   Choibalsan
Altai
Bayankhongor   ☼ ULAANBAATAR

Heihé

Manchurian
Plain
Qíqíha'er

MONGOLIA

Ürümqi

Dalandzadagad   Sainshand

Gobi Desert   Inner
Mongolia

Háärbin

Chángchun   Jílín

KYRGYZSTAN   û

UZBEKISTAN

Tien Shan   Tarim
Basin

TAJIKISTAN
Kashgar
The Pamirs   Taklaman
Desert

Altun Shan

Qílían Shan

Shényáng   Anshan

Hohhot   BEIJING
Baotóu   ☼
Dátóng   Tángshan

NORTH
KOREA   ☼ PYONGYANG

Hokkaidō   Kuril Islands

Sapporo

Aomori

Honshū

Karakoram   Kunlun Shan

Xining   Lánzhóu

AFGHANISTAN

Plateau
of Tibet

Yínchuán
Tiánjin   Dálián

Táiyuán   Shíjiazhuang
Handan   Jí'nán   Zibo
Zhéngzhóu   Qingdao
Xi'ān   Xúzhóu
Luóyáng

Yantái

☼ SEOUL

SOUTH
KOREA

Niigata   Sendai

JAPAN

Kyoto   ☼ TOKYO
Kobe   Nagoya
Osaka

TIBET (China)

CHINA

Hiroshima
Fukuoka
Hakata

Shikoku

PAKISTAN

Great Himalaya Range   Lhasa ⊙

NEPAL   ▲
Mt Everest
(8850m)   BHUTAN

Chéngdú

Chóngqíng
Chángsha

Húainán   Nánjing
Héféi   Shánghái
Hángzhou
Wúhàn
Nánchang

Kyūshū

Ryukyu Islands

Okinawa

NORTH
PACIFIC
OCEAN

BANGLADESH

Künming   Guìyáng

Héngyáng   Fúzhóu

INDIA

Nánníng

Guǎngzhóu
(Canton)   Shàntóu   ☼ TAIPEI
Shénzhén   Taichung
MACAU   TAIWAN
HONG
KONG   Kaohsiung

MYANMAR
(BURMA)   VIETNAM

LAOS

Hǎikǒu

Hainan

THAILAND

Paracel Islands
(Disputed)

PHILIPPINES

HONG KONG

HONG KONG BLENDS COMMERCIAL CHAOS WITH A MELLOW CULTURE AND FUTURISTIC HIGH-RISES WITH AN ANCIENT SOUL.

CAPITAL CITY VICTORIA   POPULATION 6.9 MILLION   AREA 1092 SQ KM   OFFICIAL LANGUAGES CANTONESE, ENGLISH

LANDSCAPE

Hong Kong's spectacular cityscape engulfs Hong Kong Island's northern end and Kowloon Peninsula's southern tip. Outside these areas and the growing urban development of the New Territories are 234 islands, ranging from lush Lantau – twice the size and elevation of Hong Kong Island – to uninhabited islets at the furthest reaches of the Outlying Islands.

HISTORY IN A NUTSHELL

The region's early inhabitants, the Yue, had yielded to the Eastern Han Chinese dynasty by the 2nd century AD. Trade with the Portuguese began in the mid-16th century and 150 years later a dozen countries were haggling over tea, silk and porcelain here – including the British, who also discovered a voracious market for opium. A war over the opium trade ensued, resulting in the Chinese ceding Hong Kong Island to the British in 1842. The population grew eightfold over the next 50 years, and by 1950 the financial and manufacturing industries that would dominate Hong Kong's future had sprung up. When a 99-year lease negotiated by the British to secure more real estate expired in 1997, China reclaimed Hong Kong and designated it a Special Administrative Region (SAR).

PEOPLE

Around 95 per cent of Hong Kong's population is ethnic Chinese, with over half born within the SAR. Resident foreigners comprise mainly Filipinos and Indonesians, with only one-third as many American, Canadian and Thai expats. Buddhism and Taoism are the dominant religions; Confucianism and animist beliefs are also represented. Hong Kong also has around 530,000 Christians and 70,000 Muslims.

MARKETPLACE

Manufacturing once accounted for most of Hong Kong's economic dealings, but this industry is now largely based in southern China and local emphasis has shifted to service industries, including banking, retail, telecommunications and tourism. Hong Kong is too busy to look after itself and so imports almost everything it needs, mostly from China.

TRADEMARKS

- Neon-lit skyscrapers
- Cantonese banquets
- Jackie Chan
- Tsim Sha Tsui shops
- Business suits and skirts

RANDOM FACTS

- Kwun Tong in New Kowloon is the most densely populated place on the planet (51,000 people per square kilometre).
- The Tian Tan Buddha isn't the world's biggest Buddha, but it is the world's tallest, seated, bronze, outdoor Buddha – so there.
- Most people think of Hong Kong as one big city, but over 75 per cent of its 1103 square kilometres remains undeveloped.

NATURAL BEAUTY

Scattered across Hong Kong's myriad landscapes are lush woodlands, steep-sided mountains and dozens of beaches. The view from Victoria Peak out across an island-studded swath of the South China Sea can foster an appreciation of the region's environmental diversity. Hiking trails crisscross islands such as Lantau and wend their way deep into the New Territories, climbing over mountain ridges and descending to remote sandy strips. Protected habitats such as Mai Po Marsh reveal numerous bird species, while Hong Kong's coastal waters are home to creatures such as the Chinese white dolphin (which is actually pink).

CULTURE

Hong Kong's culture is difficult to pin down, because of the dilution of long-standing Chinese beliefs by 150 years of British rule, plus the entrepreneurialism of the past half-century. The spiritual demands of Buddhism and Taoism are tempered by what some would call the city's true religion, work, which is not confined by weekday office hours. One ongoing tradition is superstition, with many Chinese paying respectful attention to feng shui, numerology and the Chinese zodiac, while fortune-tellers ply their trade in places such as the wonderful, incense-wreathed Man Mo Temple. The six floors of the Hong Kong Museum of Art offer a formal introduction to Chinese art.

ON FILM

Top Hong Kong films:

- *Enter the Dragon* (1973) teamed Bruce Lee with Hollywood.
- *Infernal Affairs* (2002) was the first in a trilogy about post-Triad life.
- *The World of Suzie Wong* (1960) follows a woman's path from Wan Chai prostitute to fashion icon.
- *In the Mood for Love* (2000) depicts a stylish love quadrangle.

MYTHS & LEGENDS

Chinese religion is replete with deities that look after different aspects of everyday life, from study to the running of pawn shops. One of the most popular deities, whose name is associated with over 60 temples throughout Hong Kong, is Tin Hau. The 'Queen of Heaven' looks after seafaring folk, so it's understandable that a place surrounded by water would want to keep her happy. Stanley's Tin Hau temple is Hong Kong's oldest building.

CUISINE

The Cantonese cuisine that dominates Hong Kong meal times applies subtle, elaborately prepared sauces to the freshest of produce, such as recently expired chickens, pigeons and sea creatures. Innovation is paramount in a place as entrepreneurial as this, so few dishes are prepared exactly the same way every time. Similarly, Hong Kong's busy pace of life is reflected by the inclination to cook foodstuffs rapidly over high heat. The Chinese eat regularly throughout the day, with the most conviviality reserved for dinners and weekend afternoon teas.

TOP FESTIVAL

The Yue Laan (Hungry Ghost) festival is celebrated on the 14th night of the seventh moon, sometime during August/September. It's during this lunar month that 'hungry ghosts' emerge from hell to seek sustenance. Food offerings are made to these spirits and 'hell money' and other paper votives, often in the shapes of cars and houses, are burned to appease them.

↟ FEELING CHIRPY AT A BIRD MARKET OFF PRINCE EDWARD ROAD

↟ THE CENTRAL SKYLINE LOOMS OVER THE HARBOUR FERRY

↟ BRIGHT LIGHTS, BIG CITY, TSIM SHA TSU

> ## ESSENTIAL EXPERIENCES
>
> - **Bobbing across Victoria Harbour on the Star Ferry**
> - **Lying back and enjoying the ride on the steep Peak Tram**
> - **Losing all sense of time bar-hopping in Lan Kwai Fong**
> - **Haggling over fashion rip-offs at Temple Street Night Market**
> - **Making a pilgrimage to see the Tian Tan Buddha**

Shenzhen
• Lo Wu
Ping Chau
• Shekou
Yuen Long • Kam Tin
New Territories
• Tuen Mun
Sha Tin
Sai Kung •
• Pak Tam Chung
Chek Lap Kok
Kowloon
Peng Chau **VICTORIA** ✪
Lantau Island
Aberdeen •
Hong Kong Island
Tung Lung Island
Cheung Chau
• Stanley
Outlying Islands
Lamma Island
Po Toi Islands

MAP REF   S9

BEST TIME TO VISIT **OCTOBER TO DECEMBER**

PHOTOGRAPHER ROLAND NEVEU / ON ASIA

BUG-EYED CHILDREN AT A SWIMMING POOL IN KOWLOON

PHOTOGRAPHER GREG ELMS / LONELY PLANET IMAGES

THE ENORMOUSLY SERENE TIAN TAN BUDDHA, LANTAU

A FINE BALANCE OVER THE SKYSCRAPERS OF HONG KONG

TEXT PAUL SMITZ

LANDSCAPE

Central Macau's streets zigzag across the Macau Peninsula, which is fringed by lagoons and coloured by patches of greenery such as the shady Lou Lim loc Garden. Three bridges, ranging from 2.2 to 4.5 kilometres long, stretch south from the peninsula to the sleepy villages and beaches of Taipa and Coloane Islands, which are connected to each other by an artificial isthmus.

HISTORY IN A NUTSHELL

Chinese farmers had Macau Peninsula to themselves until the Portuguese established a trading post in 1557 and set about erecting ornate villas and baroque churches, using the proceeds of trade brokered between China and Japan. China signed Macau over to the Portuguese in 1887, but by this time Hong Kong controlled regional trade, and Macau's economic pendulum swung towards gambling instead. Portugal negotiated the return of the now-unwanted territory to China in 1999, sweetening the deal by tackling Triad control of local casinos. Over the past decade Macau has undertaken some massive construction projects, including a US$12 billion airport and a planned bridge that will link it with Zhūhǎi and Hong Kong.

MACAU

A GAMBLING ADDICTION CAN'T TAKE THE SHINE OFF MACAU'S COLONIAL SPLENDOUR AND ATTRACTIVE CIVIC DEVELOPMENTS.

POPULATION 453,130   AREA 28 SQ KM   OFFICIAL LANGUAGES CANTONESE, PORTUGUESE

IN THE BELLY OF THE BEAST

PEOPLE

Macau's Chinese residents are mostly devoted to either Buddhism or Taoism. However, thanks to around 450 years of Portuguese influence, about six per cent of the population is staunchly Christian. Macau has a Portuguese minority (two per cent of the total population) and an equal number of Macanese, who are of mixed Chinese, Portuguese and/or African blood.

MARKETPLACE

Tourism tops up Macau's coffers, thanks to cashed-up visitors from China, Hong Kong, Japan and the USA. But most of the region's income is derived from the gambling that takes place in its 20-odd casinos. Some manufacturing industries still eke out a living here by exporting textiles, toys and clothing.

TRADEMARKS

- Spinning roulette wheels
- Portuguese colonial villas
- Christian churches and Chinese temples
- Vinho verde (green wine)
- Cobbled backstreets

CULTURE

Macau is enlivened by a mixture of traditional Chinese culture, with belief systems revolving around the tenets of Taoism and Buddhism, and a Portuguese culture flavoured with Spanish, Italian and French influences. The traditions of the Macanese are also

distinctive – they speak a dialect called Patuá, and have their own festivals and a cuisine that mixes and matches Chinese, Indian and African cookery.

SURPRISES

- There's an abundance of parks and gardens on Macau Peninsula.
- Macau hosts the world's biggest fireworks display.
- Casinos have dress codes: no shorts, sandals or thongs.
- There are live bands playing Latin and African music.

ARCHITECTURE

Macau contains several dozen skyscrapers, including the 338-metre Macau Tower, one of the world's tallest buildings. But far more striking are the Portuguese structures that decorate the city. To see how wealthy traders lived, visit the grouping of fine Macanese villas comprising Taipa House Museum. The memorable style of Portuguese civic buildings is showcased by the Leal Senado, the former Senate, while Macau's wonderful churches include the baroque Church of St Dominic and the Church of St Lawrence.

RANDOM FACTS

- Gambling taxes generate one-third of Macau's GDP.
- Macau receives 12 million visitors annually, around 25 times its population.
- Macau's historic centre was awarded Unesco World Heritage status in 2005.

MYTHS & LEGENDS

Macau is named after A-Ma, the goddess responsible for seafarers – 'A Ma Gau' (Bay of A-Ma) is apparently what the Portuguese were told when they enquired about the name of the place. The legend of A-Ma is that she asked various wealthy junk owners to take her to Guǎngzhōu, but they all refused, and it was left to a poor fisherman to provide passage. A storm sank all the junks except the one carrying A-Ma, who upon returning to Macau ascended to heaven from Barra Hill. The famous A-Ma Temple was subsequently erected nearby.

SLOPING UP TO THE RUINS OF ST PAUL'S CATHEDRAL

Kun Iam Temple

Luís de Camões Grotto & Gardens

Sun Yatsen Memorial Home

Ruins of the Church of St Paul

Chapel of St Michael

Fortaleza de Monte

Leal Senado

Jorge Alvares Statue

St Francis Garden

A-Ma Temple

Barra Hill

Ponte Governador Nobre de Carvalho Macau-Taipa Bridge

MAP REF   S9

BEST TIME TO VISIT OCTOBER TO DECEMBER

DOING THE DOG-PADDLE: LEADING GREYHOUNDS THROUGH THEIR TRAINING

TEXT CHRISTOPHER PITTS

CHINA

CHINA IS ALL ABOUT SENSORY OVERLOAD: IT'S A HIGH-DECIBEL, NONSTOP ROLLER COASTER RIDE THROUGH URBAN CHAOS, CACOPHONIC BANQUETS, IMPERIAL REMAINS AND SACRED MOUNTAINS.

CAPITAL CITY BĚIJĪNG   POPULATION 1.3 BILLION   AREA 9.6 MILLION SQ KM   OFFICIAL LANGUAGE STANDARD MANDARIN

LANDSCAPE

China is one of the largest countries in the world and stretches from Siberian taiga and Mongolian steppe in the north through the wheat belt (the northern plains) to the rice bowl (the Yangzi Basin) and on to tropical rainforests. The Chinese word for landscape is *shanshui,* meaning 'mountains and rivers' – the two dominant features of a country that comprises less than 15 per cent arable land. Major waterways include the Yangzi, Yellow and Pearl Rivers. Elevation ranges from a towering 8611 metres (K2) down to 154 metres below sea-level (Turpan Basin) in between the Taklamakan and Gobi deserts.

HISTORY IN A NUTSHELL

The key to understanding China's long history lies in the country's name for itself, which translates as 'the Middle Kingdom'. An agricultural society surrounded by powerful nomadic groups, China was intrinsically at odds with its neighbours and viewed itself as the civilising force of the universe. Arrogance aside, the impact of traditional Chinese culture in East Asia was undeniable. Nevertheless, the empire was ill prepared when the colonial powers came knocking in the 18th century. The resulting struggle to redefine itself as a

modern nation was full of tragedy, from the Opium War (1839–42; when the British forced opium upon China) up to the human catastrophes under Mao Zedong (the Great Leap Forward and Cultural Revolution). This is why China today is so desperate to forget its past – most people just want to get on with living a life that they believe can only get better.

PEOPLE

China is comprised of 56 ethnic groups, the largest being the Han Chinese, who make up 92 per cent of the population. Most other ethnic groups live in the border regions; others were assimilated into Chinese culture long ago. The country's official language is based on the four-tone Běijīng dialect, though Chinese can be broken down into 10 main dialects (such as nine-tone Cantonese), and further divided into many regional subgroups. Religion in China has always been a healthy mix of Confucianism, Taoism and Buddhism, each complementing the other. There are also small populations of Muslims and Christians.

MARKETPLACE

No-one knows exactly where the Chinese economy is going, but wherever it goes, there's very little doubt

that it will irrevocably change the world. Western governments already face massive trade imbalances and Běijīng holds nearly US$820 billion in foreign exchange reserves. And despite all this, the country still can't seem to create enough jobs to keep up with its vast and rapidly changing society. The demons of the past – drought, floods and corruption – continue to threaten China's peasants, while new problems – such as inadequate social security and health care – keep cropping up at every turn. The gap between rich and poor keeps on growing, but then again, so does the middle class. As Mao Zedong once predicted, 'the bourgeoisie is right inside the Communist Party itself'.

TRADEMARKS

○ Acupuncture
○ Chinese characters
○ Dust storms
○ Firecrackers
○ Giant pandas
○ Green tea
○ Mao
○ Martial arts
○ One-child policy

⌃ RICE TERRACES BLUR THE DISTINCTION BETWEEN LAND, WATER AND SKY IN YUANYANG, YÚNNÁN PROVINCE

⌃ ALL DOLLED UP: LONG HORN MIAO GIRLS IN TRADITIONAL COSTUME TO CELEBRATE THE FLOWER DANCE FESTIVAL

⌃ THE BASE OF THE ORIENTAL PEARL TV TOWER IN FUTURISTIC SHÀNGHǍI

HIS CUPS OVERFLOWETH: A MAN RECEIVES TRADITIONAL CUPPING TREATMENT

THE CYCLE OF LIFE CONTINUES: TIÁNÁNMÉN SQUARE AND THE FORBIDDEN PALACE

FROM THE TRAVELLER

This is a reconstructed section of the Great Wall north of Beijing. Within the courtyard behind the wall there were tourist amenities and a general sense of artificiality. This prayer tree seemed the most visible symbol of traditionalism I saw in China. Whatever the state of spirituality or religion there remained an understated and genuine expression of tradition.

SHAMUS BRENNAN   USA

URBAN SCENE

Shànghǎi is the fastest-growing city in the world. It's an intense, high-octane metropolis that lives for glitz, glamour and money. Běijīng, however, remains the country's political and cultural heart. It cooks up the propaganda, sends out the directives, allocates the funds and even nurtures artistic communities – albeit not intentionally.

WILD THINGS

Despite a growing list of major environmental problems and a continuously shrinking wilderness, China still has some of the most diverse ecosystems on the planet. There are over 30,000 species of plants, and a number of fascinating – though unfortunately endangered – animals. Tigers, monkeys, yaks, pandas, leopards and camels are the most popular mammals, but don't forget the cranes, ibis and other birds.

MYTHS & LEGENDS

One legend whose echoes continue to resound is the story of the mythic sage-king, Yu the Great (?–2061 BC). Yu spent 13 years of his life travelling the countryside, building dykes and dredging silt, in an attempt to end the Yellow River's devastating floods. The controversial Three Gorges Dam is essentially a 21st-century adaptation of Yu's legendary undertaking – harnessing nature is a critical part of every ruler's job description.

CUISINE

Chinese cuisine is generally broken down into four schools: northern (Běijīng duck, hotpot), eastern (braised seafood), western (lots of chillies) and southern (dim sum). Rice is the main staple, though in the north, noodles and dumplings are more prominent. Food is central to Chinese life: one common greeting is, 'Have you eaten yet?'

WRITING

Chinese characters originated over 3500 years ago as symbols written on turtle shells used for divination. During the Qin dynasty (221–206 BC) the script was standardised, effectively unifying a country that spoke mutually unintelligible dialects. After the communists came to power in 1949, they simplified the writing system, greatly improving the country's literacy rate. There are nearly 50,000 known characters; you need to know a minimum 3000 to read a newspaper.

FUTURE DIRECTIONS

China is the world's fastest-rising superpower, which worries a great many people. No-one wants an authoritarian, one-party system with a record of human rights abuses to start calling the shots. Many developed nations also fret over the country's growing appetite for natural resources – who's going to provide all the power necessary for 1.3 billion people anyway? But to be fair, Běijīng has a long way to go before it can throw its weight around like Washington does. China's future will be dictated by its massive population: its greatest resource, but also its greatest challenge.

ESSENTIAL EXPERIENCES

- **Turning your legs to jelly while tramping along the Great Wall**
- **Picking up tai chi tips at dawn in Běijīng's Temple of Heaven**
- **Staining your favourite shirt trying to dip dumplings**
- **Immersing yourself in traditional art in the Shànghǎi Museum – then stepping outside to meet China's future head on**
- **Climbing into a landscape painting on the misty crags of Huang Mountain**
- **Bargaining for Mao memorabilia**
- **Coming face-to-face with the imperial past at the Terracotta Army**
- **Trying to outsmart monkey bandits on sacred Emei Mountain**

PHOTOGRAPHER BRADLEY MAYHEW – LONELY PLANET IMAGES

△ LABOUR OF LOVE: AN ELDERLY WOMAN WRITES BUDDHIST SCRIPTURES

MAP REF   O6

BEST TIME TO VISIT APRIL TO MAY, SEPTEMBER TO OCTOBER

A CLOAK OF SNOW COVERS THE VILLAGE OF ZHŌNGDIÀN

PHOTOGRAPHER NORMAN NG, ON ASIA

TWO KUNG FU STUDENTS GET THEIR KICKS INSIDE THE SHAOLIN TEMPLE, HÉNÁN

A PANDA CUB DISPLAYS ITS SENSE OF FUN AT A RESEARCH CENTRE

MONGOLIA

THE BROCHURES DON'T LIE: DESPITE CHAOTIC MODERNISATION, MONGOLIA REMAINS ASIA'S MOST HOSPITABLE AND HUMBLE DESTINATION.

CAPITAL CITY **ULAANBAATAR** POPULATION **2.8 MILLION** AREA **1.5 MILLION SQ KM** OFFICIAL LANGUAGE **MONGOLIAN**

ROOM FOR THE WHOLE FAMILY: THE MOTORBIKE IS BECOMING THE VEHICLE OF CHOICE IN MANY MONGOLIAN HOUSEHOLDS

LANDSCAPE

Vast and empty, Mongolia stretches for 2500 kilometres across the plains of northern Asia. Biologists consider it one of the most pristine landscapes anywhere, citing its lack of fences, infrastructure and people. But there is a reason for this vacuum of development: Mongolia has a harsh landscape with little water or arable land, which is compounded by brutal weather conditions.

HISTORY IN A NUTSHELL

Long before the Mongols came on the scene, Turkic-speaking tribes occupied what is now Mongolia. When not fighting each other, they banded together, headed south and terrorised China. The Chinese thought building a really big wall would keep them out, but the barbarians simply bribed the guards. Around the year 1206 a Mongol chief named Genghis Khan (Chinggis Khaan) united the tribes and declared himself 'the leader of all those who lived in felt tents'. Over the next hundred years he and his grandsons forged an empire that stretched from Korea to Hungary. The empire eventually collapsed, as empires do, and the Mongols retreated, later adhering to more sedentary pursuits such as Buddhism. China occupied Mongolia for a while before the Soviets arrived in the

early 20th century, bringing with them their own brand of communism, marked by the banning of religion, an overthrow of the aristocracy and a genocide that killed around 27,000 Buddhist monks. In 1990 peaceful demonstrations ended communist rule and Mongolia has since embarked on a path of free markets and democracy.

PEOPLE

Mongolia is a largely homogeneous society, with Mongols making up around 94 per cent of the population. The largest minority group comprises around 100,000 ethnic Kazakhs, who live in the Altai Mountains of western Mongolia. Shamanism is the oldest religion in Mongolia, followed by Tibetan-style Buddhism, which has dominated since the late 1600s. Since 1990 Christian missionaries, mainly from the US and Korea, have converted unknown thousands.

MARKETPLACE

Mongolia's traditional income rests on the backs of around 30 million cattle, sheep, horses, goats and camels (the five snouts). But devastating winter storms in 2001 and 2002 killed millions of animals and forced many nomads off the steppes and into the cities, where they've joined the ranks of the

urban poor. Mining is now big business, accounting for half of the country's industrial output. Tourism is another growing sector, although it remains limited by a lack of infrastructure and the short summer tourist season.

TRADEMARKS

- Gers ('yurts' to you)
- Half-wild horses
- The Gobi Desert
- Genghis Khan
- Subarctic winters

NATURAL BEAUTY

Think about the country as one enormous golf course. A few years back an American man had this sentiment and managed to golf his way across Mongolia in six months. Further south, the Gobi Desert remains a significant and foreboding obstacle, renowned for its summer heat, winter freeze and spectacular sandstorms. Along the northern border of Mongolia is a strip of Siberian taiga, complete with stubby mountains, alpine lakes and bear-infested forests. The biggest mountains are the majestic Altai, which soar to a height of 4374 metres near the Russian and Chinese borders.

CORRECT WEIGHT: YOUNG JOCKEYS AFTER A HORSE RACE AT THE ANNUAL NAADAM FESTIVAL

RANDOM FACTS

A recent DNA study of various populations in Asia indicates that there are more than 17 million blood-linked descendents of Genghis Khan.

Mongolia became the world's second communist country in 1924.

Mongolia is the world's only UN-recognised 'nuclear-free zone'.

With 1.4 people per square kilometre, Mongolia has the lowest population density on earth.

WILD THINGS

For millennia, wild animals grazed peacefully on the open steppe, which once supported huge herds of gazelles, wild horses, argali sheep, bears, camels and an array of winged creatures. Since the destabilisation of the country in 1990, and the general absence of laws, many animals have come under the threat of poaching. Concerned biologists are battling to save several endangered species, notably gazelles and falcons. The good news story concerns the Przewalski (takhi) horse, which was extinct in the wild by the late 1960s but was reintroduced by European zoos in the early 1990s.

CULTURE

Despite a veneer of Buddhism, Mongolian culture is more deeply rooted in nomadic traditions and shamanism. The history of movement, use of horses and life inside the *ger* has shaped the character and world view of Mongols. Herders generally take pity on city folk forced into the concrete jungle of Ulaanbaatar. No matter where they live, all Mongolians have a deep respect for nature and a naturally guided awareness of their environment.

CUISINE

If you've come to Mongolia in search of a good barbecue you'll be sorely disappointed. The 'Mongolian barbecue' familiar back home is a modern Chinese creation which never existed in Mongolia. An authentic 'Mongolian barbecue' consists of a gutted marmot stuffed full of scalding hot rocks and singed from the outside with a blowtorch. Be careful: in autumn (late August through September) marmots carry the bubonic plague. Less adventurous dishes include boiled mutton soup, meat dumplings, dried cheese and yak milk tea blended with salt.

MUSIC

Throat singing, or overtone singing, has become somewhat fashionable in Western music circles, but it all began in western Mongolia and the neighbouring province of Tuva. The horsehead fiddle – so-called because the top portion is carved into the shape of a horse's head – is Mongolia's national instrument, and often accompanies 'Mongolian country music', which speaks of mothers, horses and the beauty of nature.

TOP FESTIVAL

Naadam, a sort of Olympics for nomads, is Mongolia's iconic festival. Featuring wrestling, horse racing and archery, it displays the qualities necessary to win an empire. Indeed, the games began centuries ago among the warring tribes of Genghis Khan. The national Naadam in Ulaanbaatar is something of a commercial event these days, so try seeing a countryside version. Visitors should be careful – they may be asked to make up the numbers in the wrestling tournament!

MONGOLIAN BOOTS MADE FOR WALKING

LUNCH FOR PIGEONS, GANDAN KHIID MONASTERY, ULAANBAATAR

MASTER BUILDER: A CHILD ASSEMBLES HIS FAMILY'S *GER*

ESSENTIAL EXPERIENCES

- **Horse trekking across the steppe**
- **Polishing off a bottle of vodka before 9am**
- **Getting stranded in the wilderness with a broken-down Russian jeep**
- **Eating boiled sheep guts in the company of a nomad family**
- **Digging for dinosaur fossils in the Gobi**

RUSSIA

- Ulaangom
- Olgii
- Tavanbogh National Park
- Amarbayasgalant Khiid
- Mörön
- Sükhbaatar
- Darkhan
- Bulgan
- Choibalsan
- Uliastai
- **ULAAN BAATAR**
- Altai
- Kharkhorin
- Öndörkhaan
- Bayankhongor
- Arvaikheer
- Baruun Urt
- Mandalgovi
- Sainshand
- Dalandzadagad

CHINA

MAP REF P4

BEST TIME TO VISIT JUNE TO SEPTEMBER

MEN GO HEAD TO HEAD DURING THE NAADAM FESTIVAL

TRADITIONAL MONGOLIAN DANCERS IN A BLUR OF GOLD

TEXT MARTIN ROBINSON

SOUTH KOREA

SOUTH KOREA IS AN UNDISCOVERED COUNTRY, WHERE YOU CAN TRAVEL FOR A WEEK AND NEVER SEE A WESTERN FACE, AND THE LANGUAGE, CULTURE AND CUISINE ARE UNIQUE – RECOGNISABLY ASIAN BUT WITH A VERY KOREAN TWIST.

CAPITAL CITY SEOUL   POPULATION 48.8 MILLION   AREA 98,480 SQ KM   OFFICIAL LANGUAGE KOREAN

SPECIAL WARFARE COMMAND SOLDIERS DO IT TOUGH IN THE SNOW, HEONGGYE

LANDSCAPE

Eighty per cent of South Korea is forest-covered mountains and hills, which are studded with brightly painted wooden Buddhist temples. The southwestern plains are the country's food basket, with small orchards, polythene greenhouses and irrigated rice fields patrolled by white egrets. Hundreds of hilly islands, mainly scattered off the southern coast, are rural idylls inhabited by fisherfolk and farmers.

HISTORY IN A NUTSHELL

A Confucian, slave-based monarchy ruled until it collapsed in 1910, when Japan colonised the country. In 1945 independence arrived, following the Japanese defeat in World War II. But Korea was soon divided into North and South, and a devastating civil war (1950–53) was sparked off by an invasion from the North. Since 1953 the South has achieved miraculous economic development and is now the world's 10th largest economy.

PEOPLE

South Koreans pride themselves on their mono-ethnic identity, although international marriages are increasing, particularly in the countryside. A quarter of the population are Buddhist; another quarter are Christian, mainly Protestant, making Korea one of the few Asian countries with a significant number of Christians. Politics often sees the eastern provinces pitted against the western provinces. In general, Koreans are hard-working, usually in a rush and great believers in education.

MARKETPLACE

After a setback in the late 1990s caused by a financial crisis, the South Korean economy continues to power ahead, boosted by rising exports of semiconductors, mobile phones, ships, cars and just about everything else. Expat English teachers earn over US$2000 a month and also receive free accommodation and other benefits.

TRADEMARKS

- Samsung and Hyundai
- A divided country
- Tae kwon do
- Ginseng, the wonder root
- Kimchi, a spicy cabbage side dish
- Dog restaurants
- Examination hell and intense competition for university places
- Reaching the World Cup soccer semifinals in 2002

RANDOM FACTS

- Traffic rules are not enforced.
- Many Koreans love raw food, especially raw fish and seafood.
- For most of its history Korea was a slave-owning aristocracy-cum-monarchy.
- Only foreigners are allowed into Korean casinos.
- Korean gays are still in the closet.
- Korea has more saunas than Finland.
- There is no tipping in Korea.
- All Korean men must serve two years in the armed services.

NATURAL BEAUTY

Green forest-covered mountains and hills, indented with streams and lakes, take on glorious red and yellow hues in autumn, and are crisscrossed by trails enjoyed by a multitude of jolly hikers. Ancient Buddhist temples and monasteries are hidden away in remote valleys. The country's 20 national parks are still home to a few bears, antelopes and roe deer. South Korea's coastline has many unspoilt offshore islands, where a relaxing rural lifestyle still prevails – except on the sandy beaches, which become crowded in the hot, humid summer months of July and August.

PHOTOGRAPHER JOSE FUSTE RAGA / CORBIS

PHOTOGRAPHER CHUNG SUNG-JUN / GETTY

ON FILM

Local movies cover every genre, have improved greatly in recent years and now challenge Hollywood for box office supremacy in Korea.

○ *The President's Last Bang* (2005) takes a highly satirical look at the 1979 assassination of Park Chung Hee.

○ *Marathon* (2005) stars a very amusing young autistic man and his long-suffering mother.

○ *JSA* (2001) is a taut thriller about a friendship across the Demilitarised Zone (DMZ) between soldiers from South and North Korea.

○ *My Sassy Girl* (2001) tells the humorous story of a girlish guy and his bossy girlfriend.

○ *Untold Scandal* (2004) is a stylised historical drama about a pleasure-loving Confucian nobleman and a virtuous Catholic woman.

CUISINE

Many meals are accompanied by rice, soup (spicy or bland, hot or cold) and side dishes such as anchovies, salad, radish and fiery *kimchi*. Besides the well-known on-your-table barbecues of beef or pork (often served with lettuce and sesame leaf wraps), tofu and bean curd stews are popular. Because of their hectic lifestyles, families do not usually eat together except perhaps on Sunday.

IMPORT

↗ Pizza
↗ Bakeries
↗ Beds
↗ Soft pillows
↗ Sit-down toilets
↗ Democracy
↗ Dutch soccer coaches
↗ American baseball and basketball players
↗ English teachers
↗ Vietnamese wives for Korean farmers

EXPORT

↗ Movies, TV dramas, pop music and fashions to all of Asia
↗ Park Ji-Sung to play for Manchester United football club
↗ IT products
↗ Three million cars a year
↗ Students

PHOTOGRAPHER JEREMY WOODHOUSE | GETTY

↗ TRAFFIC AROUND THE NAMDAEMUN GATE IN SEOUL

○ Package tourists
○ Orphans adopted by US parents

TOP FESTIVAL

The South Korean festival that foreigners enjoy most is the midsummer mudness of the Boryeong Mud Festival, held over seven days in late July at Daecheon Beach on the west coast. Bring out the child within with mud slides, mud softball, mud wrestling, mud skin treatments and mud massages. You can even buy mud soap.

ESSENTIAL EXPERIENCES

○ Stepping into Korea's feudal past in Seoul's impressive and varied Confucian palaces

○ Exploring the relics of the ancient Silla dynasty around Gyeongju in Gyeongsangbuk province

○ Dancing the night away in Seoul in Hongik's student clubs or Itaewon's expat nightclubs

○ Feeling the chill of the Cold War on a tour of Panmunjeom, where communist and capitalist armies still face off across the DMZ, 55 kilometres north of Seoul

○ Touring the spectacular volcanic scenery of Jejudo, Korea's southerly honeymoon island, with its scenic craters, giant lava tubes, black-sand beaches and the country's highest mountain, Hallasan (1950 metres)

○ Hiking around the World Heritage 18th-century fortress wall that stretches for over five kilometres in Suwon city, just south of Seoul

○ Experiencing a 'roof of the world' feeling atop Ulsanbawi in Seoraksan National Park in Gangwon province

○ Relaxing body and mind in one of the many *jjimjilbang*, luxury hot-spring spas with varied saunas

○ Getting lost in the alleyways of Jeonju Hanok Village, which recreates the lost world of aristocratic Confucian scholars

○ Climbing inside a captured North Korean submarine near Jeongdongjin on the east coast

NORTH KOREA
Seoraksan National Park
● Janggok
● Gangneung
✿ SEOUL
● Korean Folk Village
Songnisan National Park
● Buyeo   Yeongdeok ●
● Gunsan
Daegu   ● Pohang
● Gyeongju
● Gwangju   Masan ●
● Mokpo   ● Busan
JAPAN
Jeju-si
Jejudo

MAP REF | V6

BEST TIME TO VISIT MID-SEPTEMBER TO MID-NOVEMBER, MID-APRIL TO MID-JUNE

PHOTOGRAPHER CHUNG SUNG-JUN | GETTY

↗ A TIGER POPS UP TO SAY HI IN A SEOUL SAFARI PARK

PHOTOGRAPHER: CHUNG SUNG-JUN GETTY

I took this picture during an overnight trip to a temple in the town of Paju. At 4am we got up for morning prayers with the monks, after which we went to eat. I spied this dog taking a nap under the bell which is rung prior to evening meditation. The monks ring the bell for the living things in nature. Apparently, some living things use the bell for other purposes!

JASON JARVIS   SOUTH KOREA

RING OF FIRE: SPINNING FIRE CANS AT HAN RIVER IN SEOUL, PART OF A DAEBOREUM FOLK ART FESTIVAL

A CHEEKY CHARACTER AT A MARCH FOR WOMEN'S DAY IN SEOUL

NORTH KOREA

ASIA'S MOST SECRETIVE COUNTRY AND SOLE 'AXIS OF EVIL' MEMBER, NORTH KOREA ALLOWS IN A TRICKLE OF HIGHLY REGIMENTED TOURISTS EACH YEAR WHO ARE SHOWN EXACTLY WHAT THE GOVERNMENT WANTS THEM TO SEE IN THIS FASCINATING COMMUNIST TIME CAPSULE.

CAPITAL CITY PYONGYANG   **POPULATION** 23. 1 MILLION   **AREA** 120,540 SQ KM   **OFFICIAL LANGUAGE** KOREAN

LANDSCAPE

North Korea is an extremely mountainous country, large swaths of which are inaccessible by roads even if foreigners were permitted to make their way off the beaten track. Biodiversity is greater here than in South Korea, because of the varying climate zones that are home for subarctic, alpine and subtropical plant and tree species.

HISTORY IN A NUTSHELL

Born out of the anti-Japanese struggle at the end of World War II, North Korea was supported by the Soviet Union, whose Red Army finished off the Japanese presence on the peninsula in 1945. Simultaneously, the US moved into the south of the peninsula and plans for one Korea became hostage to Cold War tensions – both North and South declared themselves independent republics in 1948 and nothing significant has changed in the North since then. The 'Great Leader' Kim Il-sung was worshipped as a living god until his death in 1994. The communist world's first dynastic succession then occurred when his son Kim Jong-il became the country's leader, a position he retains today.

PEOPLE

The population in the North – possibly several million fewer than the official total of 23.1 million – is ethnically almost uniform. Traditionally North Koreans practise Buddhism and Confucianism, although religion has been strongly discouraged by the state and largely replaced by the apotheosis of its political leaders. A smattering of traditional temples remains but they're for show rather than for locals to worship at.

MARKETPLACE

The self-declared 'Juche' principles of autarchy that made North Korea seem a relatively viable economy in the 1960s have proved since to be a complete joke – since an economic slump in the 1970s the country has gone from one benefactor to another in its search for aid (the Soviet Union, China, the UN, the US and even South Korea). The economy remains backward, centrally planned and in desperate need of reform.

TRADEMARKS

○ Portraits of Kim Il-sung and Kim Jong-il everywhere
○ Richly painted propaganda posters adorning every street corner
○ Vast monolithic architecture in concrete and steel designed to impress and intimidate
○ Shy locals who will wave or smile at your passing bus but will never speak to you

WORKERS' PARADISE

In North Korea, two official guides accompany tourists everywhere outside their hotels. This is the only way to see the country, and so to reduce costs most people go on an organised tour. Travellers can expect to be kept busy by enthusiastic guides showing them monuments, museums and performances extolling the virtues of the regime.

AMERICAN DREAM

There has been a ban on Americans visiting North Korea since the end of the Korean War (the North Koreans accuse the US of atrocities during that time), but this has been somewhat relaxed in recent years, with Americans now able to join three-day tours of the country for the annual mass games, a vast gymnastic show performed by tens of thousands of people between August and October in Pyongyang.

RANDOM FACTS

○ Kim Jong-il, despite leading the country for over a decade, has only ever spoken in public once, and even then it was a handful of words.
○ The International Friendship Exhibition consists of two massive vaults in the mountains where Kim Il-sung and Kim Jong-il's gifts from foreign leaders are displayed.
○ When the lights go out in the frequent power cuts, North Koreans typically shout 'Blame America!'
○ Kim Jong-il loves basketball. Madeleine Albright presented him with a ball signed by Michael Jordan on her visit there in 2000.

FUTURE DIRECTIONS

Rumours from the 'hermit kingdom' occasionally escape to the west suggesting things are slowly changing – but so far every time a major change has been on the cards nothing happens. The country is Asia's (and perhaps the world's) biggest enigma, and visiting it doesn't get you much closer to the truth!

ESSENTIAL EXPERIENCES

○ **Paying homage to the 'Great Leader' Kim Il-sung at his massive bronze statue in Pyongyang – it's obligatory!**

○ **Going eyeball to eyeball with South Korean soldiers at the scary DMZ**

○ **Hiking North Korean style in the mountains: climbing concrete steps through lush forests**

○ **Swimming on a North Korean beach at Nampo or playing a round of golf in Pyongyang – who can say they've done either in North Korea?**

○ **Trying to decide whether the busy 'commuters' on the Pyongyang metro are just actors or not**

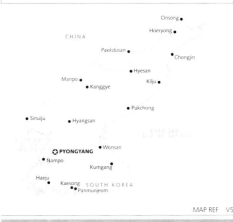

MAP REF   V5

BEST TIME TO VISIT MARCH TO JUNE, SEPTEMBER TO NOVEMBER

지의 위대한 승리 만

ONWARD AND UPWARD: ONE OF NORTH KOREA'S UBIQUITOUS PROPAGANDA POSTERS

BESIDE THE SEASIDE AT WONSAN BEACH

A DANCE TROUPE IN THE CHILDREN'S PALACE, PYONGYANG

PHOTOGRAPHER MARTIN SASSE/LAIF   AURORA PHOTOS

PHOTOGRAPHER ALAIN NOGUES   CORBIS

JAPAN

JAPAN IS A HIGH-WIRE ACT, BOUND BY TRADITION YET RELENTLESSLY MODERN, AS EXOTIC AS IT IS SAFE, A LAND OF BIG CITIES THAT TREASURES ITS COUNTRYSIDE.

CAPITAL CITY TOKYO   POPULATION 127.4 MILLION   AREA 377,840 SQ KM   OFFICIAL LANGUAGE JAPANESE

LANDSCAPE

Japan's four main islands sit between the Pacific Ocean to the east and the Sea of Japan to the west, stretching about 1900 kilometres from end to end. Hokkaidō, the northern island, is dominated by a soaring national park at its centre and fertile coastlines around its perimeter. Honshū is the largest island; its spine is the Japan Alps mountain range, while the Tokyo-to-Osaka megalopolis is home to over 60 million people. Rural, mountainous Shikoku lies across the glorious Inland Sea, while southern Kyūshū is home to rice farming, aquaculture and bamboo crafts.

HISTORY IN A NUTSHELL

The earliest indications of civilisation in Japan date back about 10,000 years, in the form of Jomon pottery. By about AD 300, most of the Japanese archipelago was unified under the Yamato clan, which claimed the title of emperor on the basis of its descent from Amaterasu, the sun goddess of Japan's native Shinto religion. Buddhism arrived in the mid-6th century, and with it the Chinese writing system. From 794 to 1185 the nation's capital was in Heian-kyō (now Kyoto), after which there were centuries of conflict among emperors, *shōgun* (military rulers),

daimyō (regional feudal lords) and their subordinate samurai warriors. The unification of the nation around 1600 under the Tokugawa *shōgun,* based in Edo (now Tokyo), ushered in 250 years of peace and isolation from the rest of the world, but in 1853 the American 'Black Ships' cracked this isolation; under the emperor Meiji, Japan modernised and Westernised rapidly. Japan also studied war, culminating in incursions and wars in Asia and Russia and ultimately World War II, which ended when Japan became the only nation in history to endure an atomic bombing. Postwar Japan saw breathtaking economic expansion.

PEOPLE

Of Japan's more than 127 million people, about 75 per cent live in urban areas. The Tokyo metro area is the world's largest, with 33.4 million inhabitants. Ethnic Japanese comprise 99 per cent of the population, but notable minority groups include ethnic Koreans and the Ainu (the indigenous people of Hokkaidō). Religion in Japan can be confusing to those who are used to practising one religion exclusively; many Japanese find it perfectly normal to have Shinto rites at birth, a Christian wedding and a Buddhist funeral. Japan has one of the world's oldest

populations, with 20 per cent aged 65 or older. The birth rate of around 1.4 children per woman is far below replacement level (around 2.1 children).

MARKETPLACE

The world's second largest economy, Japan is a leading producer of motor vehicles, electronics, machine tools and metals. GDP per capita is around US$31,500. With few natural resources and little arable land, Japan grew strong on trade and manufacturing. Yet the last two decades were not kind: a real estate bubble burst in the late 1980s, plunging Japan into a trenchant recession from which it was slow to emerge.

TRADEMARKS

- Sushi
- *Kabuki*
- The *shinkansen* (bullet train)
- Geisha
- *Anime* and manga
- Sumo wrestlers
- *Ikebana* (flower arranging)
- Mt Fuji
- Astro Boy
- *Sakura* (cherry blossoms)

A YOUNG WOMAN DESCENDS THE RED STAIRWAY AT THE NAKANO SUN PLAZA HALL, TOKYO

TWO SUMO WRESTLERS VIE FOR TOP SCORES AT A PACHINKO PARLOUR, TOKYO

PHOTOGRAPHER BOB CHARLTON . LONELY PLANET IMAGES

弱冷房車

AS JAPANESE AS IT GETS: LAKE KAWAGUCHI AND CHERRY BLOSSOM

THE SUITS SQUEEZE IN AT RUSH HOUR, UENO STATION

PHOTOGRAPHER: CATHERINE KARNOW   CORBIS

PHOTOGRAPHER: KEVIN CRUFF   GETTY

BATHERS WALKING TO MINERAL HOT SPRINGS UNDER A CANOPY OF BLOSSOMS

PHOTOGRAPHER: TIBOR BOGNÁR   CORBIS

LANTERNS ILLUMINATE THE TIERS OF A PAGODA, TOKYO

FROM THE TRAVELLER

Tokyo still contains pockets of peaceful traditional Japanese culture. This is a shot of a Japanese (torii gate) in front of a small Shinto shrine in a residential area just a few minutes' walk from Shinjuku station, one of the busiest train stations in the world. After a day of fervent sightseeing, you can take a moment of tranquillity and catch your breath here.

DAVID REDFERN   AUSTRALIA

○ There are 450 varieties of fish and seafood traded daily at the Tsukiji Fish Market in Tokyo, the largest such market in the world.

○ Some devout Buddhists make a 1400-kilometre trek taking in 88 temples on the island of Shikoku. The most devout travel on foot, wearing special white costumes.

○ If you go to a baseball game in Japan, take earplugs. The fans engage in riotous chanting enhanced by horns and drums.

○ Noodles are served piping hot in a large bowl of broth. When eating them, slurping is *de rigueur*: it cools the noodles and enhances the flavour.

NATURE IN PERFECTION

Japanese temple gardens are not just pretty arrangements of plants, rocks and waterways but a representation of an ideal world. Ideal worlds don't just happen – watch as a gardener plucks pine needles one by one. Flowers are clumped just so, and the placement of a stone can change the entire meaning of the garden path.

URBAN SCENE

Tokyo is everything you'd expect: high-energy, stylish and always ahead of the curve. Kyoto is also undeniably modern, but as the former capital it also has its share of World Heritage List structures. One only-in-Japan urbanity is 'cos-play' (short for 'costume play'): teens dressing in outrageous get-ups from satin-Goth-babydoll to their favourite comic book characters.

SURPRISES

○ *Sake* (rice wine) is Japan's national beverage, but it ranks third in sales, behind beer and *shōchu*, a spirit distilled from anything from sweet potatoes to sugar cane.

○ In the mountains of central Honshū, snow monkeys live around certain hot springs.

○ Vending machines in Japan sell everything, ranging from drinks (cold and hot) to underthings, beer and pornography.

IN IMAGES

Ukiyo-e (Japanese wood-block prints) didn't start out as high art. Subjects included images of everyday life, characters in *kabuki* plays, and scenes from the 'floating world' pleasure quarters of old Edo; great examples include Hiroshige's *53 Stations of the Tokaido Road* and Hokusai's *36 Views of Mt Fuji*. In the 19th century, after Japan ended its isolation, *ukiyo-e*'s vivid colours and novel composition influenced the work of some of Europe's great impressionists and post-impressionists.

CUISINE

Japanese cuisine – healthful, delicious and handsomely presented – has transformed the way the rest of the world eats. Try to imagine life without sushi, wasabi mashed potatoes, miso-glazed cod or green tea ice cream. Enjoy small plates of grills in an *izakaya* (pub) or sit down to *kaiseki*, the pinnacle of Japanese cuisine, where each tiny dish is chosen to suit the morsel inside it.

TURN, TURN, TURN...

Japanese culture is deeply keyed into the seasons. Even in the big city, you won't have to look far to notice seasonal reminders: plum blossoms in February, cherry blossom–viewing parties in spring, oysters, persimmons and cold noodles served at their peak of flavour, and the display of *mikan* (mandarin oranges) and *mochi* (cakes of pounded rice) leading up to New Year.

CULTURE

If there's one characteristic that defines Japanese culture, it's looking out for one's peers. Once let into a group, you always consider the others in your words and deeds: watching what you say, gift-giving, avoiding conflict. Yet although relationships are extremely important, the idea that all members of a social set *think* identically is absurd.

IMPORTS
↗ Buddhism
↗ Chinese writing system
↗ Classical music
↗ Coffee (the good kind)
↗ *Fiddler on the Roof*
↗ French patisseries
↗ Korean soap operas
↗ Prussian schoolboy outfits
↗ *Sunflowers* by Van Gogh
↗ Tofu

EXPORTS
↖ Comme des Garçons
↖ Green tea
↖ Hello Kitty
↖ Just-in-time manufacturing
↖ Minimalism
↖ Sony, Panasonic, Toyota, Nintendo, Nissan, Honda, Toshiba…
↖ *Spirited Away*
↖ Sudoku
↖ The Suzuki method
↖ Tofu

ESSENTIAL EXPERIENCES

○ **Facing rush hour on the Tokyo subway, cheek to jowl to elbow to newspaper with your neighbours**

○ **Pausing for a bowl of whisked green tea, to put yourself only in that moment**

○ **Beholding the great Buddha of Nara**

○ **Taking that first 'Ah, too hot!' slurp from a steaming bowl of ramen, followed by inevitable ecstasy**

○ **Turning a corner in Kyoto to catch a fleeting glimpse of a geisha**

○ **Understanding the meaning of good hospitality in an elegant *ryokan* (traditional Japanese inn)**

○ **Viewing a sky full of stars from a *rotemburo* (open-air bath)**

○ **Marvelling at crafts, from ceramics to paper-making, gold-leaf appliqué to weaving, bamboo basketry to kimono dyeing**

○ **Beholding the future of technology, fashion and pop culture as they unfold before your eyes**

PHOTOGRAPHER RICHARD I'ANSON · LONELY PLANET IMAGES

↖ SUMO WRESTLERS THROWING THEIR WEIGHT AROUND

MAP REF / X6

BEST TIME TO VISIT APRIL TO EARLY JUNE, LATE SEPTEMBER TO NOVEMBER

SWANS ORNAMENT THE GLASS-LIKE POND AROUND MATSUMOTO CASTLE

A GEISHA EXHIBITS HER MUSICAL SKILL

TAIWAN

WITH ITS SOARING MOUNTAINS, HOSPITABLE PEOPLE AND OUTSTANDING CUISINE, THE 'BEAUTIFUL ISLAND' IS A SHOWCASE OF NATURAL ATTRACTIONS AND CULTURAL TREASURES.

CAPITAL CITY **TAIPEI**   POPULATION **22.5 MILLION**   AREA **35,560 SQ KM**   OFFICIAL LANGUAGE **MANDARIN CHINESE**

A WOMAN LAYS OUT PAINTED PAPER UMBRELLAS TO DRY IN THE MID-AFTERNOON SUN, MEILUNG

LANDSCAPE

Taiwan is roughly shaped like a tobacco leaf, 394 kilometres in length and a mere 144 kilometres across at its widest point. Fifteen offshore islands bob in the frothy waters along the east and west coasts. The spiny backbone of the Central Mountain Range runs from north to south, dividing the island in half, with Yushan (Jade Mountain) standing tall near the island's centre. Western Taiwan, a fertile region of plains and basins, is densely populated; the east coast, with its rocky coastline and towering cliffs, has fewer people.

HISTORY IN A NUTSHELL

Taiwan has been inhabited since around 10,000 BC by people thought to be from Austronesia. China and Taiwan have had contact since at least the 1400s, when boatloads of Fujian immigrants washed up on the island's shores seeking refuge from political instability on the mainland. Mass migration continued from southern China over the course of several hundred years. It was in the 16th century that the Europeans showed up – first the Portuguese arrived, dubbing the island *Ilha Formosa* or 'beautiful island', then the Dutch came and established Taiwan as a trading centre, until they were driven out by China's Ming loyalist Koxinga in 1661. China's Qing government established control over the island and ruled half-heartedly until losing the Sino-Japanese War of 1894. In 1895 Taiwan was ceded to Japan and endured Japanese occupation until the end of World War II. After the communists took power in China in 1949, two million nationalists, led by Chiang Kai-shek, fled to Taiwan and established a government. The nationalists established a strong central government and enforced martial law, which ended in 1987. In 2000 the nationalist grip on power finally ended and the Democratic Progressive Party, led by Chen Shuibian, took control. President Chen was re-elected in 2004, despite accusations of vote tampering. Tensions between China and Taiwan about possible reunification remain strong and it's uncertain what's in store for the future.

PEOPLE

About 98 per cent of Taiwan's inhabitants are Han Chinese, a diverse mix of ethnic and linguistic groups, including Hakka, Cantonese and Fujianese, who came from China's southern coast. Taiwan's other two per cent are from one of the nine indigenous tribes, which are scattered throughout the island but largely concentrated along the east coast and in the Central Mountain Range.

MARKETPLACE

Taiwan is an economic dynamo, with the third-largest foreign reserves in the world. It's a top producer of plastics, computer chips and chemicals and leads the world in the production of notebook computers. Agriculture contributes only two per cent to the economy, while its service sector comprises 69 per cent of its GDP.

TRADEMARKS

CUISINE

Taiwanese proudly boast that their island has the best Chinese cuisine in Northeast Asia. It's hard to argue with them. Mainland Chinese immigrants brought with them to Taiwan the diverse cooking styles of their homeland. You'll find everything from the fiery flavours of Sichuan to the delicate seasonings of Guangdong. The Taiwanese eat communally and an entire family gathered around the dinner table is a symbol of peace and prosperity.

AN INVITATION TO ENTER THE DRAGON AT THE SPRING AND AUTUMN PAVILION, KAOHSIUNG

A FLYING LEAP FOR A ROC SOLDIER, MATZU ISLANDS

NATURAL BEAUTY

Taiwan's most breathtaking scenery is along the east coast, with miles of plunging granite cliffs that gradually give way to fine sand beaches and rice paddies. A close second for beauty is the rugged, mountainous interior. Alishan in central Taiwan is carpeted with dense forests of pine and cypress, while further south the South Cross-Island Highway dives through some of Taiwan's wildest mountain terrain.

MYTHS & LEGENDS

Matsu, goddess of the sea, is the most revered deity of Taiwan. Legend has it that Matsu was once a real person named Lin Mo, born to fisherfolk on Meizhou Island in Fujian, China. It is said that Lin Mo loved the sea and would often stand on the seashore and guide ships safely to shore. On a stormy night, Lin Mo drowned while saving a sailor and her body washed up on the shores of Nankan Island, Matsu, where she was buried by the villagers. Temples were built to honour the young woman and her popularity eventually spread as far as Japan and Southeast Asia. Today there are over 500 temples dedicated to her around Taiwan.

CULTURE

Traditional Chinese culture shapes Taiwanese society, with influences from Japan and its indigenous peoples. Despite the island's modern veneer, ancestor worship and folk religions, along with Taoism, Confucianism and Buddhism, all remain strong. Temples are colourful and vibrant, redolent with incense and packed with worshippers. The Taiwan Folk Village is a living museum of traditional architecture and arts.

GLOVE-PUPPET THEATRE

One of Taiwan's most endearing art forms is glove-puppet theatre. Drawing on Chinese fables and martial arts epics, televised puppet shows are incredibly popular among both children and adults and were even banned in the 1960s because they were allegedly distracting people from work. Nowadays, puppets are back on the air with a vengeance, and politicians even compare themselves to puppet heroes.

FUTURE DIRECTIONS

Where Taiwan is headed is anyone's guess. Cross-strait relations with China remain tense, but with a strong economy, political and economic reforms and improved trade ties, it's certain that this energetic island has no intention of slowing down.

⌃ A WOMAN SELLS SCENTED BLOSSOMS AT TAIPEI'S LUNG SHAN TEMPLE

PHOTOGRAPHER RON WATTS   CORBIS

PHOTOGRAPHER CHRIS STOWERS   PANOS

⌃ FOR A RAINY DAY: STUDENTS WEARING THE NATIONAL COLOURS

ESSENTIAL EXPERIENCES

○ Marvelling at the wonders of the National Palace Museum, Taipei, home to the world's finest collection of Chinese art

○ Exploring the remote, windswept islands of the Matsu Archipelago, just off the coast of mainland China

○ Admiring the jagged cliffs and rocky coastline of the awe-inspiring Suao–Hualien Highway

○ Hiking through the spectacular marble-walled canyons of Taroko Gorge

○ Soaking in the peaceful hot springs of Chihpen, surrounded by lush vegetation, temples and waterfalls

PHOTOGRAPHER CHRIS STOWERS   PANOS

⌃ A CAN-CAN ROUTINE IN MAKUNG

⊹ TAIPEI
● Hsinchu
● Miaoli
T'aichung ●　　● Tienhsiang
Changhua ●　　Taroko Gorge　● Hualien
Penghu Islands
Alishan ●　　　● Shihtiping
● Makung
Anping ●● Tainan
　　● Maolin
　● Taitung
Kaohsiung ●　　Green Island
Liuchiu Island　● Tungkang
　● Fengkang
　● Oluanpi　Lanyu

MAP REF   T9

BEST TIME TO VISIT **OCTOBER TO NOVEMBER**

A PARADE OF PORTRAITS: THE IMAGE OF SUN YAT-SEN IS HELD ALOFT DURING A NATIONAL DAY PARADE

ILLUMINATED BUDDHA STATUES

A BUDDHIST TEMPLE COMMANDS A STUNNING LOCATION IN TAROKO GORGE

THE INDIAN SUBCONTINENT & THE HIMALAYA

THIS REGION HAS A DISTINCT IDENTITY THAT TRANSCENDS THE ARTIFICIALITY OF POLITICAL BORDERS. SCREENED OFF FROM THE REST OF THE WORLD BY THE HIMALAYA, IT RESTS ON A SINGLE TECTONIC PLATE AND ITS COMMON GEOGRAPHY HAS, OVER THE YEARS, BUILT A SHARED HERITAGE.

If you were to traverse the Indian subcontinent from north to south, you would start from the world's highest city, Lhasa in Tibet, and cross the Himalaya mountain range. These mountains are truly magnificent in their scale: the world's 14 peaks exceeding 8000 metres are all located here (the next highest, the Aconcagua in the Andes, is a mere 6962 metres). The Indus, the Brahmaputra (the holy river created from a drop of water squeezed out of Lord Shiva's matted locks) and the Yangzi rivers have their origins here, with their combined watershed extending over the subcontinent from the Arabian Sea to the Bay of Bengal. No wonder the ancient Indian poet Kalidasa wrote: 'Linking the oceans on the east and the west, He (the Himalaya) cuts across the earth like a scale kept to measure it.'

Move further south and you reach the Deccan plateau, on either side of which are the slivers of coastline that border peninsular India. The verdant island of Sri Lanka drops off like a tear from the south coast of India. And then you reach the Maldives, the world's 'flattest' country, with a maximum elevation of just 2.4 metres.

The Indus Valley civilisation – a contemporary of the ancient Egyptian and Sumerian cultures – existed here 4500 years ago. The subcontinent has seen the birth of four religions, still practised: Hinduism, Jainism, Buddhism and Sikhism. Christianity was established in South India in the 1st century by St Thomas, long before it arrived in Europe. Islam was brought in by Arab invaders in the 8th century; and the Dalai Lama today influences Tibet from his home in exile in India. The subcontinent was under British control till the middle of the 20th century, and 25 years later the eastern portion of Pakistan broke away to form an independent Bangladesh.

This is a stunning and varied region. You can trek through the mountains in Pakistan, Tibet, Nepal, Bhutan or India. Rest those aching muscles on a beach holiday in Cox's Bazaar in Bangladesh (the longest stretch of beach in the world), or in Goa. Whitewater raft on the Brahmaputra or the Ganges, riding rapids with names like Roller Coaster, Wall or Double Trouble... If you prefer, scuba dive off the coast of Galle in Sri Lanka or in the Maldives. Track the royal Bengal tiger in the Sundarbans (Bangladesh) or bottle-feed a baby elephant at the Pinnewala Elephant Orphanage in Sri Lanka. Then kick-start the brain cells by exploring the sites of the Indus Valley civilisation, the magnificent forts of Rajasthan, or ancient palaces all over India. Check out the acoustics of the Golgumbaz (Bijapur), the second largest dome in the world after St Peter's. Or rejuvenate yourself with the wonders of *ayurveda* in Kerala.

One sees here an intermingling of lifestyles and cultures across borders, but also differences within the same country. There is a greater similarity between South Indians and Sri Lankans than there is between the South Indians and the Punjabis of North India, who have more affinity with their counterparts in Pakistan. In fact, this similarity of identity across borders is reflected in the ambiguity of the political status of Kashmir, with both Pakistan and India continually bickering over it. Otherwise, the relationships between the countries of the region are cordial, though rather unequal, with India taking on the role of big brother in most international forums.

TEXT: DEVIKA RAJAN

INDIA

IT HAS BEEN SAID THAT THERE ARE TWO TYPES OF PEOPLE IN THE WORLD, THOSE WHO HAVE BEEN TO INDIA AND THOSE WHO HAVEN'T – WHAT'S CERTAIN IS THAT NO-ONE WHO VISITS THIS NATION OF JUNGLES, TEMPLES AND TIGERS EVER FORGETS IT.

CAPITAL CITY NEW DELHI POPULATION 1.1 BILLION AREA 3.2 MILLION SQ KM OFFICIAL LANGUAGES HINDI, ENGLISH, BENGALI, TELUGU, MARATHI, TAMIL, URDU, GUJARATI, MALAYALAM, KANNADA, ORIYA, PUNJABI, ASSAMESE, KASHMIRI, SINDHI, SANSKRIT

LANDSCAPE

India is the world in one nation. From the dizzy heights of the Himalaya, the landscape plunges down towards the plains, passing lush green hills, jungles, deserts and grassland on its way to the palm-fringed beaches of Goa and Kerala. Indians divide their nation into the Hills (encompassing the foothills of the Himalaya and the southern highlands) and the Plains, which sprawl south towards the tip of the subcontinent. The steamy south of India is almost another country – jungle-covered, beach-fringed and inundated by rivers and streams.

HISTORY IN A NUTSHELL

The earliest recorded Indian civilisation appeared in the Indus Valley around 3500 BC, but the native Dravidians were driven south by Aryan tribes from the north in around 1500 BC. Over the next two millennia, Buddhism and Hinduism became the dominant religions in the subcontinent. From the 8th century AD onwards, northern India faced wave after wave of Muslim invaders, eventually falling to the Mughals, who ruled until the rise of European colonialism in the 18th century. Although the Portuguese and French established small trading colonies, most of

India was incorporated into the British Empire. Mahatma Gandhi finally marched India to independence in 1947. The nation was immediately torn apart by sectarian conflict – the majority Muslim states were snipped off to create Pakistan and East Pakistan (now Bangladesh) and hundreds of thousands died in the crossfire. India and Pakistan remain locked in an ongoing cat-and-mouse game over the disputed region of Kashmir.

PEOPLE

With 800 spoken languages and 2000 regional dialects, India has one of the most diverse populations on the planet, as well as one of the largest. Indians are broadly defined by their religion; around 80 per cent are Hindu, 13 per cent are Muslim, two per cent are Christian and two per cent are Sikh. Other important communities include the Buddhists, hidden away in the foothills of the Himalaya, and the Adivasis, India's tribal peoples, found in pockets across the country.

MARKETPLACE

The Indian economy is growing exponentially. Within a few decades, India could rival China as an economic

superpower. Although 60 per cent of Indians work in agriculture, new industries like information technology and outsourcing are swelling the nation's coffers. India currently has the 12th-largest economy in the world based on GDP, though wealth is unevenly distributed and the average wage is just US$1.60 per day.

TRADEMARKS

○ Red-hot curries
○ Multi-armed deities
○ Elephants and tigers
○ Yoga and meditation
○ Chai (Indian tea)
○ The Holy River Ganges
○ Ganja

WILD THINGS

The royal Bengal tiger is one of India's most endangered animals. Just 3000 wild tigers survive, most of them in the national parks of the central plains and the Sunderbans in West Bengal. Elephant-back safaris offer the best chance of seeing these magnificent creatures up close; you may also bump into rhinos, bears, deer, wild elephants and monkeys.

PORTRAIT OF A PROUD FATHER AND HIS LITTLE PRINCES IN SAMODE PALACE, JAIPUR

↗ MEDITATING ON THE MAJESTY OF AMRITSAR'S GOLDEN TEMPLE

↗ A PRIEST SENDS PRAYERS UP IN SMOKE DURING THE NIGHTLY *PUJA*, VARANASI

A WOMAN PLAYS PEEKABOO BEHIND CARPET YARN, KASHMIR

COLOUR AND RITUAL: A WOMAN AT THE *CHURA* CEREMONY PRIOR TO HER MARRIAGE, NEW DELHI

THE BEGINNING OF THE DAY'S BUSTLE ON THE GANGES IN VARANASI

FROM THE TRAVELLER

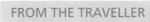

On the balcony of my hotel in Varanasi one morning, I noticed this scene in the river below. A *sadhu* was standing on the river edge doing some stretches and brushing his teeth with the water of the Ganges. All the while, a herd of buffalo circled around him. To me it summed up Varanasi to a tee – all forms of life, in whatever stage of incarnation, competing for a little space and sharing the holy water in peace.

DAVID MACPHEE   CANADA

NATURAL BEAUTY

With so much scenery to choose from, the only
problem is where to start. Perhaps the most striking
landscapes are found in the foothills of the Himalaya,
soaring above the plains but dwarfed by the snow-
covered peaks. In the lowlands are dense and steamy
jungles, endless rice fields and deserts plucked
straight from the Arabian Nights, while the south is
famous for its brochure-perfect beaches.

URBAN SCENE

India's cities are some of the most populated places
on the planet. Based on current trends, Mumbai looks
set to top 25 million residents by 2011. Despite the
crowds, the atmosphere of India's cities is legendary –
rickshaws, ox-carts, bicycles, taxis, trams, buses,
trucks, pedestrians and cows compete for space in
the streets and the noise and chaos is unrelenting.
Some travellers are invigorated by the energy; others
find it utterly overpowering.

MYTHS & LEGENDS

Perhaps the most popular Indian legend is the story of
Rama and Sita, hero and heroine of the Ramayana.
Rama was the rightful heir to the throne of Ayodhya,
but he was cruelly banished to the jungle, where his

wife, Sita, was kidnapped by the demon king of Lanka
(thought to be modern-day Sri Lanka). After scouring
the earth to find Sita, Rama joined forces with the
monkey god Hanuman, besieging the island with an
army of monkeys to rescue his bride. Although parts of
the story are fanciful, Rama was a real historical figure.

CUISINE

India has probably the most recognisable cuisine on
the planet. The word 'curry' comes from the Tamil
word *kari*, meaning sauce, but most Indian dishes are
named for their ingredients, the style of cooking, the

town where they originated, or the *masala* (spice
mix) used in their preparation. The north of India is
famous for its meaty tandoori dishes, which are
cooked in a traditional clay oven, while the south is
renowned for its spicy vegetarian *thalis* (plate meals),
which are commonly prepared with searing
quantities of chilli.

FUTURE DIRECTIONS

The future is bright. The future is Indian. At least,
that's what the politicians say. If India continues its
meteoric rise, it stands to be one of the world's top
five economies by 2020. The shift from agrarian
economy to industrialised nation is well underway
and service industries such as banking,
telecommunications and IT are creating a new Indian
middle class, with Western aspirations and plenty of
disposable income. One thing that could puncture
the bubble, however, is overpopulation. There are
many more people than opportunities, and the
growing rift between haves and have-nots is
threatening social cohesion across the country.

ESSENTIAL EXPERIENCES

- Feasting on India's famous cuisine, quite
  possibly the spiciest on the planet
- Touring terrific temples – hundreds of
  thousands are dotted right across the
  Indian landscape
- Trekking in the mighty Himalaya,
  straddling the border between India,
  Nepal and Tibet
- Exploring jungles by jumbo in India's
  fabulous national parks
- Practising yoga by the River Ganges or
  meditating at mountain monasteries
- Riding the rails – India has the largest rail
  network in the world

MAP REF K9

BEST TIME TO VISIT OCTOBER TO FEBRUARY
(MAY TO OCTOBER IN THE MOUNTAINS)

PHOTOGRAPHER MARK HENLEY / PANOS

SPRAY-PAINTED JAUNDICE AT A HINDU FESTIVAL

SHORE TEMPLE AGAINST THE SUNSET, MAMALLAPURAM »

A FORMER SERVANT OF THE BRITISH RAJ HOLDS ONTO HIS SALUTE, VARANASI »

TEXT SARINA SINGH

PAKISTAN

WITH ITS KALEIDOSCOPE OF TRIBAL CULTURES, ANCIENT RUINS, JAW-DROPPING MOUNTAINSCAPES, RAMBUNCTIOUS BAZAARS AND LEGENDARY TREKKING ROUTES, THERE'S A WHOLE LOT MORE TO PAKISTAN THAN THE MEDIA CLICHÉS WOULD HAVE YOU BELIEVE.

CAPITAL CITY **ISLAMABAD**   POPULATION **165.8 MILLION**   AREA **803,940 SQ KM**   OFFICIAL LANGUAGES **URDU, ENGLISH**

⌃ A SLITHERY SILVER SEA OF FISH BEING GRADED

LANDSCAPE

Wedged between India to the east, Iran to the southwest, Afghanistan to the northwest and China to the northeast, Pakistan consists of six topographic regions: the northern mountains, northern plateau, western mountains, Balochistan plateau, southeast desert and the Indus plain. Coursing through it all like a 2500-kilometre artery is the Indus River – rising in Tibet, flowing northwest and around Nanga Parbat, dropping south out of the mountains to water a populous flood plain, and emptying through an immense delta into the Arabian Sea. Pakistan lies in the collision region between the Eurasian and Indian tectonic plates, making it prone to seismic instability; the last major earthquake occurred in October 2005.

HISTORY IN A NUTSHELL

Pakistan's history is peppered with intermittent bouts of military government and democratic rule. Created after India's independence from Britain in 1947, Pakistan was born amid intense controversy and sectarian carnage. The partition of the subcontinent into Hindu-dominated India and Muslim-dominated Pakistan resulted in a frenzied mass movement of humanity which left over 500,000 people dead. At the time of partition, Pakistan was comprised of two parts, East and West, over 1000 kilometres apart. However, in 1971 East Pakistan broke away, becoming Bangladesh. The dispute over Kashmir, a territory claimed by both Pakistan and India, has remained unresolved since independence, resulting in two major wars and ongoing artillery exchanges.

PEOPLE

With a melange of ethnic communities, Pakistan has six native languages, each spoken by an eponymous ethnic group: Punjabi (from the Punjab region), Sindhi (Sindh), Mohajir (Sindh), Pashtun (Balochistan and North-West Frontier Province), and Baluch and Brahui (Balochistan). Other noteworthy groups include the Kalasha (North-West Frontier Province), Burusho, Wakhi and Balti (Northern Areas) and the Gujar (North-West Frontier Province and Northern Areas). Pakistan is also home to over three million Afghan refugees. Punjabis grab the biggest chunk of the population pie (44 per cent), followed by Pashtuns (15 per cent) and Sindhis (14 per cent). Although Urdu is championed as the 'national language', it's spoken by only eight per cent of the population, with the most widely spoken dialect being Punjabi (45 per cent). Around 97 per cent of Pakistan's population is Muslim, with the majority being Sunni (77 per cent). An estimated 32 per cent of the population lives below the poverty line.

MARKETPLACE

Agriculture has long been the cornerstone of Pakistan's economy, accounting for approximately 24 per cent of GDP and almost 45 per cent of the labour force; major crops include rice, wheat, cotton and sugar cane. In recent years textile production has emerged as the country's largest foreign-exchange earner, comprising roughly 65 per cent of total exports. Other prominent industries include cement, steel, tobacco and machinery.

TRADEMARKS

- Mind-bending mountain treks
- Mosques
- Burkas and *shalwar kameez* (a traditional dress-like tunic-and-trouser combination with styles for both men and women)
- Time-honoured Islamic traditions
- Fabled bazaars

SUFIS

Seeking spiritual emancipation, Pakistan's Sufis wobble and whirl at breakneck speed, coaxed to holy

A TRUCK INTERIOR'S VISUAL OVERLOAD

heights by the hypnotic beating of a *dhol* (traditional two-sided drum). This ancient ritual takes place at various shrines throughout the country, each drawing a crush of captivated onlookers who watch in awe as the spinning Sufis relinquish themselves to a higher force.

NATURAL BEAUTY

Northern Pakistan has some of the world's most phenomenal mountain ranges, and trekking features on most travellers' itineraries. One of the country's most enigmatic regions is the rugged North-West Frontier Province. It stretches for 700 kilometres along the border with Afghanistan, astride the Khyber Pass and other historical gateways that lead to India from Persia and Central Asia, and embraces some of Asia's most impenetrable mountains.

CUISINE

Unlike vegetarian-dominated India, most Pakistani dishes revolve around meat, with a hearty array of Mughlai-style barbecue creations, from yoghurt-and-mint-marinated lamb kebabs to spice-swamped chicken tikkas. Pork, however, is taboo for Muslims. Traditional bread such as *chapati*, *paratha* and *naan* accompany most meals, with rice-based dishes such as fragrant *biryani* and *kabuli pilau* also commonly eaten. Meals are a family affair, with guests afforded extra special attention.

URBAN SCENE

Islamabad may be Pakistan's capital, but Lahore wins hands down as the country's cultural, artistic and intellectual hub. With its eclectic art galleries, formidable mix of architecture – from mighty Mughal monuments to the crumbling legacies of the British Raj – and dynamic performing arts scene, this buzzing metropolis offers a scintillating window into Pakistani culture and history.

CAPTIVATING QAWWALI

Qawwali, Islamic devotional singing, is widely performed in Pakistan, traditionally taking place at a *mehfil* (gathering), with a lead singer, back-up vocalists and an ensemble of percussionists. The lead singer whips up the audience with powerful poetic verses, dramatic hand gestures and religious phrases, as the back-up voices weave in and out. The internationally renowned Nusrat Fateh Ali Khan (1948–97) has been dubbed the most innovative Qawwali performer of all time.

TOP FESTIVAL

Heralding the onset of spring (late February/March), the colourful Basant Festival is marked by the enthusiastic flying of kites. Kite 'battles' are mostly done in good fun, however in recent years some over-zealous revellers have clandestinely coated kite-strings with glass shards, inflicting nasty flesh wounds upon fellow kite-flyers. A government ban on kite-flying – specifically to curb the spiralling injuries – has failed to quash the much-loved tradition.

△ DUCKING DOWN A NARROW ALLEY IN MULTAN

PHOTOGRAPHER ROBERT HARDING; GETTY

ESSENTIAL EXPERIENCES

○ **Trekking in Baltistan and beyond, where the Karakoram ruptures the earth's crust in an unequalled display of lofty peaks and twisting glaciers**

○ **Spinning out with Sufis and catching the Qawwali vibe in Lahore**

○ **Glimpsing the fading traditions of the Kalasha in their remote Hindu Kush valley strongholds**

○ **Gaping at the sublime shrines and tombs of Multan and Uch Sharif**

○ **Cheering with pumped-up patriots at the fantastical Pakistan–India border-closing ceremony at Wagah**

○ **Rambling among the ruins of Moenjodaro, one of the most remarkable cities of the ancient world**

○ **Crossing the Khunjerab Pass, a geographical and cultural watershed, in a modern replay of an ancient passage between empires past**

CHINA

• Khunjerab Pass

• Chitral

AFGHANISTAN   Peshawar ● ✪ **ISLAMABAD**
● Rawalpindi

Lahore ●

● Quetta   ● Multan
Bahawalpur ●

IRAN   Sukkur
Moenjodaro ●

INDIA

Hyderabad ●
● Karachi

MAP REF : I8

PHOTOGRAPHER MEL McVEIGH

◁ WEIGHING UP AT A STREET MARKET IN PESHAWAR

WHO NEEDS A BUS? A ROAD TRIP IN THE HUNZA REGION

A SHIP OF THE DESERT ON CLIFTON BEACH, KARACHI

THE SHEER EDIFICE OF THE TOMB OF MOHAMMED ALI JINNAH, KARACHI

NEPAL

A DISNEYLAND FOR BACKPACKERS, TREKKERS AND MOUNTAINEERS, NEPAL IS ONE OF THE MOST PERENNIALLY POPULAR DESTINATIONS IN ASIA.

CAPITAL CITY KATHMANDU   POPULATION 28.3 MILLION   AREA 147,180 SQ KM   OFFICIAL LANGUAGE NEPALI

LANDSCAPE

Nepal is famously draped along the icy heights of the Himalaya. Though it's most renowned for these mountains, Nepal actually has an incredible variety of scenery, including the sweltering jungles of the Terai as well as the glacial ice fields of the Khumbu. In between these extremes lie the Middle Hills, a more hospitable area which is home to the bulk of Nepal's population – and is largely shaped by human hand. The trans-Himalayan regions of Mustang and Dolpo, in the far north of the country, closely resemble the arid Tibetan plateau.

HISTORY IN A NUTSHELL

The stunning architectural and artistic heritage of medieval Kathmandu, Patan and Bhaktapur date from the golden age of the Malla kings in the 14th to 16th centuries. In 1760 the brilliant general Prithvi Narayan Shah unified Nepal and ushered in the Shah dynasty, whose lineage has continued from that time right up to the current king, Gyanendra Bir Bikram Shah Dev, with the exception of a century of Rana rule. The 'People's War' between the government and Maoist rebels has claimed around 13,000 lives throughout the last decade.

PEOPLE

The ethnic groups of Nepal are almost as numerous as its mountain valleys. Broadly speaking, the country is the meeting place of the Tibeto-Burmese peoples from the Himalaya and the Indo-Aryans from the Indian subcontinent. The country's mountains are shared by Rais and Limbus, the Tibetan-related Bhotiyas, entrepreneurial Thakalis and Manangis from the Annapurna region, the Tamangs north of Kathmandu and the Sherpas of the Everest region. The Newars, who live in the Kathmandu Valley, have been famous as craftspeople and traders for centuries. As well as these indigenous groups, significant numbers of Tibetan refugees live in Nepal. Hinduism is the country's predominant religion, but there are important pockets of Buddhists, including Tibetan Buddhists. In practice, however, Nepalis tend to combine the two faiths, and temples attract worshippers from both.

MARKETPLACE

Nepal is one of the poorest countries in Asia, with a GDP of only US$220 per person. Foreign aid is a significant industry, along with hydroelectricity and tourism, though agriculture remains predominant and accounts for 40 per cent of Nepal's GDP. Economic growth has stalled during the last decade of political uncertainty.

TRADEMARKS

○ Yaks and yetis
○ Trekking lodges
○ Everest base camp
○ Maoist rebels
○ The Himalaya

MYTHS & LEGENDS

Hinduism in Nepal is tightly wrapped up in dozens of colourful legends. Perhaps the most popular deity in Nepal, Ganesh, is easily recognisable because of his elephant's head. The story goes that Ganesh's father, the mighty Shiva, came home from a long trip to discover his wife Parvati in bed with a young man. In a fit of rage he lopped off the young man's head, not thinking to consider that his son Ganesh might have grown up a little during the years of his absence. Parvati forced Shiva to bring his son back to life, but he could only do so by giving him the head of the first living thing he saw, which just happened to be an elephant.

READING, WRITING AND REALLY LONG HORNS: A NOVICE MONK AT SHEDRUPLING MONASTERY, KATHMANDU

⌃ FLOWER SELLERS SIT AMID A RIOT OF COLOUR AT THE BUSY JUNCTION OF ASIAN TOLE, KATHMANDU

⌃ A *SADHU* CURLED UP WITH A GOOD BOOK AT THE PASHUPATINATH TEMPLE COMPLEX

PHOTOGRAPHER RICHARD I'ANSON | LONELY PLANET IMAGES

⌃ THE CHILL BEAUTY OF THE FIRST LAKE, GOKYO LAKE REGION

A *SADHU* PAUSES TO SAY HELLO, KATHMANDU

BHAIRAB AND GANESH (THE GODDESS KUMARI'S CONSORTS) AND FRIENDS LOOK ON DURING THE INDRA JATRA FESTIVAL

THE NAGARJUN STUPA, THINLY VEILED BY WEATHERED PRAYER FLAGS

NATURAL BEAUTY

Whether you're watching kingfishers while rafting down the jungle-clad Sun Kosi or Karnali rivers or savouring Himalayan views over a gin and tonic from the hill towns of Nagarkot or Daman, the beauty of Nepal is never far from sight. Tightly terraced hillsides, the last rays of sunset catching the peaks of Machhapuchhare, and the stark glacial beauty of the high mountains all rank highly. But most stunning of all are the views from the Gokyo Valley in the Everest region, which just have to be seen to be believed.

WILD THINGS

Top of the food chain is the Bengal tiger, which, with luck, can be spotted at Royal Chitwan National Park, along with one-horned rhinos, Indian elephants and various crocodiles. Bird spotting is fantastic at Koshi Tappu Wildlife Reserve, home to over 400 species of birds. The foothills of Mt Kanchenjunga to the east are famous for their spectacular rhododendron displays. Langurs and rhesus macaques are seen everywhere.

CULTURE

Over 85 per cent of Nepalis live in rural areas. The Nepali view of the world is dominated by *puja*, prayer and ritual. Perhaps the dominant cultural concepts are those of caste and status, which create a strictly defined system of hierarchy and deference. Nepalis are admirably flexible, pragmatic and, above all, tolerant – there is almost no religious tension in Nepal. Arranged marriages remain the norm.

RANDOM FACTS

○ The most common Nepali greeting is *Namaste*, which in literal translation means 'I greet the divine inside of you'.
○ The World Elephant Polo Championships are held every year near Royal Chitwan National Park.

○ Ten members of Nepal's royal family were gunned down by a drunk and unhinged Prince Dipendra in June 2001, who then killed himself. The massacre was reportedly caused by a marriage dispute.
○ Sherpas actually do very little portering, focusing mostly on high-altitude expedition work.
○ Nepal boasts 10 of the world's 14 highest peaks.

CUISINE

The standard Nepali dish is *daal bhaat tarkari*, literally 'lentil soup', 'rice' and 'curried vegetables', though Tibetan *momo* (meat dumplings) are also popular, as are a variety of sticky Indian-style sweets. Backpacker restaurants in Kathmandu and Pokhara offer a wide variety of foreign cuisines, from Mexican burritos to lemon meringue pie. *Tongba* is a Himalayan brew made by pouring (and re-adding) boiling water into a bamboo tube of fermented millet. As with all fine beers, it's generally drunk through a straw.

MUSIC

Nepali music is dominated by the *bansari* (flute) and *sarangi* (four-stringed lute) and moves to the rhythms of the tabla and madal drums. A good introduction to popular Nepali folk music is the trio (flute, sitar and tabla) Sur Sudha, Nepal's de facto musical ambassadors, whose evocative recordings will take you back to the region long after you've left.

TOP FESTIVAL

Nepal is home to some truly epic chariot festivals, during which time huge, creaking three-storey chariots are pulled through the towns of the Kathmandu Valley. Some are so large that the army has to be brought in to move them. The spectacular Bisket Jatra chariot festival in Bhaktapur ushers in the new year in mid-April and features a huge tug-of-war between the east and west halves of town. The Rato Machhendranath festival in

April/May in Patan also features a chariot procession and ends in the unveiling of a sacred vest. It's attended by the king of Nepal.

ECOTOURISM

Tourism, in particular trekking, has had a deep environmental impact in Nepal. Trees have been felled to provide firewood for heating and cooking in trekking lodges, and trekkers have left behind mountains of non-recyclable water bottles and camera batteries. Luckily, several excellent ecotourism programmes in the Annapurna and Everest regions have slowed the trend, partly by providing lodges with fuel-efficient stoves and solar heating and setting up purified-water stations along popular trails. Organisations such as the Kathmandu Environmental Education Project (KEEP; www.keepnepal.org) educate trekkers on the best ways to travel lightly through Nepal's fabulous mountains.

FUTURE DIRECTIONS

Mass demonstrations in April 2006 brought about a dramatic change in government and drastically diminished the powers of the unpopular King Gyanendra. What happens next is still largely up in the air. Maoist rebels are still in negotiations with the new government and it's hoped that this could usher in an end to the decade-long insurgency.

ESSENTIAL EXPERIENCES

○ **Trekking along the Annapurna Circuit or Everest Base Camp routes**

○ **Wandering the alleys of medieval Bhaktapur, a Unesco World Heritage Site**

○ **Tracking tigers on elephant-back in Royal Chitwan National Park**

○ **Dodging traffic en route to the fantastic temples and pagodas of Kathmandu's Durbar Square**

○ **Chowing down on a yak steak in relaxing Pokhara after days of *daal bhaat***

○ **Pondering the nature of existence at Lumbini, birthplace of the Buddha**

○ **Experiencing a full-on adrenaline rush rafting the Bhote Khosi or canyoning near the Tibetan border**

○ **Joining the Tibetan pilgrims on a circuit of Bodhnath's great stupa**

PHOTOGRAPHER RICHARD I'ANSON | LONELY PLANET IMAGES

⌃ A MAN CONCENTRATES ON A GAME OF CAROM

MAP REF : L8

BEST TIME TO VISIT **OCTOBER TO NOVEMBER, MARCH TO APRIL**

TENTS FEEBLY IMITATE THE PEAKS OF TAWACHEE (LEFT) AND CHOLATSE (RIGHT) ON THE EVEREST TREK

PHOTOGRAPHER JILL GOCHER GETTY

A NICE PIECE OF WORK: A MONK PAINTS A *THANGKA* (TIBETAN RELIGIOUS PAINTING) FOR THE VILLAGE MONASTERY, DZON

BUDDHIST *LAMA* DECKED OUT FOR THE TEEJI FESTIVAL, MUSTANG

TEXT LINDSAY BROWN

BHUTAN

TUCKED INTO A CORNER OF THE MIGHTY HIMALAYA AND SHROUDED IN MYSTIQUE, THE TINY BUDDHIST KINGDOM OF BHUTAN CHERISHES TRADITION, VENERATES NATURE AND CAUTIOUSLY CONCEDES TO THE INTRUSIONS OF THE 21ST CENTURY.

CAPITAL CITY THIMPHU   POPULATION 673,000   AREA 47,000 SQ KM   OFFICIAL LANGUAGE DZONGKHA

A YAK HERDER PLAYS IT COOL ON THE BHUTAN–TIBET BORDER

LANDSCAPE

From foothills to peaks, this mountainous kingdom ranges in altitude from 100 metres to over 7500 metres, with the topography of a scrunched-up newspaper. To the north and west, beyond the sacred summits, traditional trade routes lead to the Tibetan plateau and the Chinese border. Several mighty rivers flow south from the snowbound heights; cutting deep valleys, they roar through forests of green oak, red rhododendron and white magnolia to weave past terraced hills under the gaze of strategic fortresses. As the rivers leave the foothills of the eastern Himalaya they also leave Bhutan, spilling abruptly onto the great plain of India.

HISTORY IN A NUTSHELL

The spread of Tibetan influence and Bhutan's early history are chronicled in Buddhist scriptures and steeped in a wondrous mythology. In the 1600s Zhabdrung Rinpoche, builder of the great *dzong* (fort-monasteries), emerged as the first recognised national leader of Bhutan. The expansion of the East India Company led to a series of skirmishes and treaties and a shrinking of Bhutan's borders. Emerging from this unrest, Ugyen Wangchuck, the first *Druk Gyalpo* (Dragon King), was crowned in 1907. The present king, the fourth *Druk Gyalpo*, continues the controlled modernisation and promotion of national identity introduced by his father.

PEOPLE

The predominantly Buddhist population of Bhutan numbered 673,000 in 2005, and comprised three main ethnic groups. The Sharchops, or 'people of the east', are recognised as the original inhabitants of Bhutan, although where they migrated from and when is uncertain. The Ngalop are descendants of Tibetan immigrants who arrived in the 9th century and settled in western Bhutan. The Sharchops and Ngalops account for about 65 per cent of the population and are collectively known as Drukpas. The third group, the Lhotshampas, includes the people of Nepali descent who moved into southern Bhutan in the 19th century. Several smaller groups, many with their own language and customs, form about one per cent of the population.

MARKETPLACE

In March 2006 Bhutan's per capita income was estimated at US$1321, placing Bhutan firmly in the 'developing nation' category. This statistical picture is due to the high percentage of subsistence farming and belies the good nutrition and housing enjoyed by most Bhutanese. Foreign currency is earned through a handful of industries, a small amount of agricultural export, and the burgeoning tourism sector. Hydroelectricity is Bhutan's single biggest export earner; electricity sales to India represent 40 per cent of government revenue. India is also Bhutan's primary aid donor, helping develop infrastructure such as roads, dams and power stations.

TRADEMARKS

- Gross National Happiness, the holistic measure of development and progress
- Plaid *gho* (traditional dress for men), woollen socks and well-polished shoes
- Majestic *dzong* and maroon-swathed monks
- Bamboo bows and arrows
- Large red phalluses painted beside doors to ward off evil

URBAN SCENE

Thimphu is not one of Asia's most dynamic cities. Not one traffic light exists in the entire city. The popular traffic police were once replaced by a set of lights, but the ensuing outcry that they were ugly and impersonal saw the return of the snappily dressed, ever-alert, arm-waving cops.

A WHIRLWIND OF RELIGIOUS DANCERS

NATURAL BEAUTY

Thanks to its mountainous terrain, small population and Buddhist outlook, much of Bhutan is forested and great tracts are protected in reserves. In spring, the forests are ablaze with rhododendron blossom, and high-altitude trekking routes provide spectacular Himalayan vistas. Bhutan is also blessed with wildlife: it boasts 675 species of birds, including the rare and graceful black-necked crane, which figures in religious paintings. There are also elephants, tigers, snow leopards and more, but the bizarre takin, an awkward-looking mammal that defies taxonomists' sense of order, reigns as national animal.

RANDOM FACTS

- To the Bhutanese their country is *Druk Yul*, 'Land of the Thunder Dragon'.
- The imposing *dzong* of Bhutan were built without plans and without nails.
- Sakten Wildlife Sanctuary is widely held to have been created to protect the yeti.

MYTHS & LEGENDS

One of Bhutan's favourite legends is that of Lama Drukpa Kunley, 'the divine madman', who travelled the country outraging the clergy and challenging social conventions that he believed obscured the true Buddhist message. His sexual exploits are legendary and he is honoured with the huge phalluses painted on houses and hanging from roof corners.

A DANCER IN ELABORATE TRADITIONAL COSTUME AT PARO TSECHU

TOP FESTIVAL

The Bhutanese calendar is full of festivals, the most notable being the *tsechu*, a series of dances in honour of Guru Rinpoche. Most *dzong* and many monasteries have an annual *tsechu*, and those of Thimphu and Paro have become drawcards. The lively dancers are magnificently and vibrantly robed and masked. During the dances, red-masked *atsara* (clowns) perform routines and brandish large wooden phalluses, with which they harass and bless the audience. Towards the end of the festival a *thondrol*, a massive religious image, is unfurled and all who gaze upon it have their sins expunged.

CUISINE

The national dish, *ema datse*, is simply fiery red chillies in a cheesy sauce, and it can be found on any table, be it in a restaurant or a home. The staple carbohydrate is steamed rice, usually the local red rice, fluffy and pink. Mushrooms are well liked, and, along with fresh greens such as asparagus and *nakey* (fern fronds), are often smothered in the familiar salty cheese. Energy-stacked pork fat and fried or steamed *momo* (meat- or cheese-filled dumplings), are popular everyday snacks, while yak meat is a winter speciality.

FUTURE DIRECTIONS

Bhutan emerged warily from self-imposed isolation in the 1960s and has closely managed the introduction of global trends. In a bold move, not entirely welcomed by his adoring subjects, the well-liked King Jigme Singye Wangchuck has elected to move from an absolute monarchy to a parliamentary democracy upon the succession of his son in 2008.

ESSENTIAL EXPERIENCES

- **Weaving through the heaving throng at the Paro *tsechu* (a series of dances in honour of the Guru Rinpoche)**
- **Climbing to the amazing cliff-side perch of the Buddhist monastery Taktshang Goemba**
- **Trekking beneath the sacred and solid-white bulk of Jumolhari**
- **Capturing the good vibrations of harmonious chants at the fort-monastery Punakha Dzong**
- **Marvelling at the skill and antics at a Thimphu archery tournament**

CHINA

- Laya   Lunana
- Gasa
                    Bumthang   Kurtoe
        Punakha
Paro •   • Wangdue Phodrang   • Jakar
Ha •   **THIMPHU**
                    Kheng   Mongar •   • Trashigang

• Chhukha   • Damphu   • Pemagatsei
                              Samdrup
• Samtse   Sarpang •   Jongkhar

INDIA

MAP REF   N8

BEST TIME TO VISIT **OCTOBER TO NOVEMBER**

THE LIMPET-LIKE TIGER'S DEN MONASTERY

BOYS MARCH AT A FESTIVAL CELEBRATING THE KING'S BIRTHDAY

PHOTOGRAPHER MATTHIEU PALEY / GETTY

A DIFFERENT KIND OF HOUSE PAINTER DECORATES A BHUTANESE DWELLING TO WARD OFF EVIL SPIRITS AND BRING GOOD FORTUNE ⤢

TWO MONKS PLAYING HORNS IN JAKAR ⤢

TIBET

THE 'LAND OF SNOWS', TIBET IS A UNIQUE PLACE OF BREATHTAKING BEAUTY, LITERALLY AND FIGURATIVELY ON A HIGHER PLANE.

CAPITAL CITY LHASA   POPULATION 2.7 MILLION (TIBET AUTONOMOUS REGION)   AREA 1.2 MILLION SQ KM   OFFICIAL LANGUAGES TIBETAN, MANDARIN CHINESE

THE WIND WHIPS PRAYER FLAGS INTO WIDE ARCS ON THE HILLS ABOVE LHASA

LANDSCAPE

Shaped by the continental collision between Asia and India, Tibet is a high-altitude desert fortress with an average elevation of around 4000 metres, buttressed to the south by the Himalaya and to the north by the Kunlun Mountains. The Amdo region, to the north of the country, is mainly high-altitude grasslands, while Kham, to the east, is a land of dramatic peaks cut by the fast-flowing headwaters of Asia's greatest rivers.

HISTORY IN A NUTSHELL

The early Yarlung Valley kings unified central Tibet. The greatest of these was the 7th-century Songtsen Gampo, who, as head of one of Asia's greatest armies, married both Nepali and Chinese princesses to form political alliances. Buddhism took root in the area in the 8th century, eventually supplanting the native Bön religion and transforming the face of Tibet. The Gelugpa school became dominant with the rise of the Dalai Lamas. Tibet's modern history has been dominated by its relationship with China. The British invaded Tibet in 1903, but far more serious were the 1950 Chinese invasion, the 1959 Tibetan uprising, the flight of the Dalai Lama and subsequent Chinese rule of the plateau.

PEOPLE

There are large regional differences between central Tibet and the regions of Amdo (the northeast) and Kham (far east), but wherever you go, Tibetans are among the easiest people to get along with in Asia. Chinese immigration is a hot-button issue, however: it's believed that Tibetans now make up less than half of Lhasa's population, a form of ethnic dilution that the Dalai Lama has termed 'cultural genocide'. There are actually more Tibetans outside Tibet than in it.

MARKETPLACE

China's drive to develop its western regions has had a dramatic effect in Tibet. The Chinese have invested billions of yuan in transport projects in recent years, including a technologically miraculous new railway link, Tibet's first, which many people fear will speed up environmental degradation and Chinese immigration. Tibet's natural resources include gold, lithium, oil, gas and uranium.

TRADEMARKS
- Yaks
- The Dalai Lama
- Monks in maroon robes
- Prayer flags

TRADEMARKS
- Yak-butter tea
- Sky burials
- High altitude, low oxygen
- Chinese oppression

NATURAL BEAUTY

Everything looks beautiful at 4000 metres. The huge inland seas of Nam-tso, Yamdrok-tso and Lake Manasarovar are mesmerising, as are the epic northern grasslands, which stretch to a frozen horizon of snowy 7000-metre peaks. Sacred Mt Kailash, in the far west, is quite detached from the mountains around it and has beguiled for millennia. The views of Everest from the Tibet side blow away anything that you'll see from Nepal. Then there are the alpine peaks and lakes in the far east of Kham, the surreal sand dunes around Samye, the lush layered greens of the road down to Nepal and the Himalayan views from almost any pass in the country. And we're just getting started…

WILD THINGS

You'll see plenty of yaks in Tibet, though most of these are dzo: crosses between a yak and a bull. In the northern Changtang or along the road to Mt Kailash you are likely to see herds of wild asses, antelopes and Tibetan gazelles. Less easily spotted are the

SNOW FIELDS AND THE PEAK OF AMA DABLAM IN THE EVEREST REGION

STURDY MONKS KNOWN AS *GEKO* ARE RECOGNISABLE BY THEIR DISTINCTIVE ATTIRE

endangered chiru antelopes, red pandas, snow leopards, blue sheep, ibexes and black-necked cranes.

CUSTOMS

Sky burial is one of Tibet's most dramatic and unusual customs. After a period of prayer and reflection, the body of the deceased is carried up to a sky burial site, chopped into pieces and fed to a brooding pack of ill-tempered vultures. The bones are then smashed, pounded and mixed with barley flour, and the paste is again fed to the vultures. This very graphic disposal of the body encourages Tibetans to face death squarely and reflect on the impermanence of life.

RANDOM FACTS

- The new train line to Tibet, opened in July 2006, is the highest in the world, topping out at over 5000 metres.
- The Tibetan epic *Gesar of Ling* is the world's longest epic poem and takes over a year to recite.
- Tibetan yak-tail hair was the main material used to produce Santa Claus beards in 1950s America.
- The 'thumbs up' gesture is a sign for begging in Tibet.

BELIEFS

Tibetan Buddhism shapes the Tibetan view of the world. Belief in rebirth, karma and the notions of suffering, desire and non-attachment find expression through daily acts of pilgrimage, prayer and prostration. The pre-Buddhist religion of Bön, with its belief in mountain spirits and demons, has also maintained great relevance.

IN ART

- *Kundun* (1997), an excellent film by Martin Scorsese, depicts the life of the Dalai Lama.
- Seven Years in Tibet (1997) is also a decent film, portraying the German POW Heinrich Harrer, who walked to Tibet during World War II and lived there for well over a year.
- *Lost Horizon*, a novel by James Hilton, kicked off the whole Shangri-La obsession and is really a must-read, despite several cheesy film versions.
- *Tibet*, written by Chöyang Liu (the) and Steve Tibbetts, is a wonderful musical interpretation of Tibet by Tibetan nuns.

TOP FESTIVAL

Losar is the Tibetan New Year festival, held sometime in February. Extravagantly dressed pilgrims pour into Lhasa to visit holy sites and watch Tibetan opera. Two weeks later, huge yak-butter sculptures are displayed as part of the Lantern Festival – which is itself a prelude to the Mönlam Festival, when an image of Maitreya is paraded around the central Barkhor circuit. Despite the cold, this is a great time to be in Lhasa.

A HUGE THANGKA UNFURLED ON A HILL AT THE MONLAM FESTIVAL

MONKS SILHOUETTED IN A PASSAGEWAY AT SAKYA MONASTERY

A PONY'S PROGRESS ON THE FRIENDSHIP HIGHWAY FROM TIBET TO NEPAL

ESSENTIAL EXPERIENCES

- Breathing in the heady smells of yak-butter lamps and juniper incense at one of Tibet's incredible monasteries, such as Tashilhunpo in Shigatse

- Staring open-mouthed at the awesome sheer north face of Mt Everest from Rongphu Monastery

- Gazing up through the fog of an altitude headache at the towering Potala Palace in Lhasa

- Following the shuffling, mumbling pilgrims through the shrines of the sacred Jokhang Temple

- Washing away your sins on a four-wheel drive trip out to Mt Kailash, Asia's most sacred mountain

CHINA

Xinjiang

CHINA

Qinghai

Under administration of China

Gertse

Sichuan
CHINA

Amdo

Mt Kailash
6638m

Chamdo

Shigatse
Sakya
LHASA
Gyantse

NEPAL

Mt Everest
8848m

BHUTAN

INDIA

MYANMAR

MAP REF M7

BEST TIME TO VISIT APRIL TO OCTOBER AND TIBETAN NEW YEAR (FEBRUARY)

PROSTRATE PRAYER AT POTALA PALACE IN LHASA

TWO WOMEN SHARE GROOMING TIPS

NONPLUSSED LAMBS PROVIDE BODY WARMTH FOR TWO YOUNG WOMEN, SHIGATSE

TEXT MARIKA MCADAM

BANGLADESH

SHAPED BY THE FLOW OF WATER AND THE TIDE OF HISTORY, BANGLADESH REMAINS ONE OF ASIA'S LAST FRONTIERS OF GENUINE CULTURAL EXCHANGE.

CAPITAL CITY DHAKA **POPULATION** 147.4 MILLION **AREA** 144,000 SQ KM **OFFICIAL LANGUAGE** BANGLA (ALSO KNOWN AS BENGALI)

LANDSCAPE

Bangladesh's terrain is surprisingly varied. The stark blue of the ocean along the coast contrasts vividly with the tea plantations further north. The land gets soggy down south: dissolving into the Bay of Bengal via the mangrove forest of the Sundarbans – a backdrop for nomadic peoples, fisherfolk, bandits, otters, monkeys, dolphins and tigers. Talking about the weather in Bangladesh is not polite chitchat so much as a discourse on human endurance. The cold season is hot, the hot season is wet and the wet monsoon season is deadly.

HISTORY IN A NUTSHELL

When a Muslim home state was partitioned from India in 1947 it was divided into two sections on opposite sides of the subcontinent: West Pakistan and an eastern section (later known as East Pakistan), which was administered by West Pakistan. Tensions between East and West Pakistan (particularly over language) were compounded by the latter's deficient response to the devastating 1970 cyclone in the east. After years of genocidal bloodshed by West Pakistan, the Indian army mobilised in support of the East's independence. East Pakistan became Bangladesh in 1971.

PEOPLE

Around 80 per cent of Bangladeshis are Muslim; most of the rest are Hindu. Tensions between Hindus and Muslims are not as prevalent as in other parts of the world, largely because of the unity fostered during the independence struggle. However, the colourful tribal groups of the Chittagong Hill Tracts face policies of Islamisation, which threaten the country's diversity.

MARKETPLACE

Bangladesh is one of the poorest countries in the world. Two-thirds of the population is employed in agriculture, and the land is frequently devastated by floods and cyclones. Some 45 per cent of Bangladeshis live below the poverty line and only 43 per cent are literate. The garment industry and investment by foreign corporations offer some hope for alternative means of development, but this will depend on decreased corruption and increased governance.

TRADEMARKS

- Poverty
- Natural disasters
- Cricket fervour
- Crowds
- Rickshaws

CULTURE

The flow of water is part of the cycle of life in Bangladesh. Rivers shape not only terrain but the lives of people; while local inhabitants are displaced by the rising waters, they also benefit from the rejuvenation of the land. The 'Char people' of the Brahmaputra River see this force of nature as both a curse and a blessing, making life both arduous and possible. While floods force them to migrate between shifting sandbanks, they are rewarded afterwards with the 'Golden Time', when the land is at its most fertile.

RANDOM FACTS

- More water flows through Bangladesh than through Europe.
- A one-metre rise in sea level would displace 15 million people here.
- Bangladesh is the eighth most populous country, but has only the ninety-third largest land area.
- Bangladesh-born Rabindranath Tagore became Asia's first Nobel Laureate when he won the prize for literature in 1913.

IN ART

In 1971 George Harrison and Ravi Shankar organised a concert to raise money for Bangladesh's war relief effort. Some 40,000 people attended the event in New York's Madison Square Gardens. In the same year, beat generation icon Allen Ginsberg also put his talents behind the cause when he penned 'September on Jessore Road' – a poem that decried the lack of foreign aid for Bangladesh and vividly described the horrors the country was enduring.

FUTURE DIRECTIONS

The social and political activism that gave birth to the country continues today. In Dhaka's New Market, books about development are sold next to livestock

and burkas. University students keep one foot in school and the other planted in the political process; some have even been elected to parliament. The bomb attacks and violence at mass political protests in recent years have been disconcerting, but widespread public participation shows that Bangladeshis are resolutely pursuing their own development.

ESSENTIAL EXPERIENCES

- **Riding the *Rocket* (a leaky paddle-wheel boat) through the countryside**
- **Exploring the canals of the Sundarbans, the world's largest coastal mangrove forest**
- **Escaping to the tea plantations of Sylhet**
- **Taking a rickshaw ride through the chaotic laneways of Old Dhaka**
- **Swimming fully clothed at Cox's Bazaar, allegedly the world's longest beach**
- **Gaping at the superbly decorated Kantanagar Temple**
- **Tracking down ancient sites at Bagerhat**

MAP REF N9

BEST TIME TO VISIT OCTOBER TO FEBRUARY

A FISHERMAN SETS HIS NETS IN AN AMBER EVENING

RICKSHAWS MAROONED BY FLOODS

WOMEN UNLOAD BASKETS FULL OF SEEDS TO DRY, TANGAIL

SRI LANKA

FINE BEACHES, VERDANT TEA HILLS AND MAGNIFICENT ANCIENT MONUMENTS WOULD MAKE SRI LANKA A TRULY MAGICAL TROPICAL PARADISE, WERE ITS SOCIETY NOT SO SHATTERED BY ONE OF THE WORLD'S MOST TRAGICALLY POINTLESS ETHNIC CONFLICTS.

CAPITAL CITY **COLOMBO**   POPULATION **22.2 MILLION**   AREA **65,610 SQ KM**   OFFICIAL LANGUAGES **SINHALA, TAMIL**

WATCHING THE WORLD GO BY FROM THE WINDOW OF THE KANDY-TO-NUWARA ELIYA TRAIN

LANDSCAPE

Colombo's dynamic if formless urban sprawl seeps down the west coast towards golden, tourist-friendly beaches and isolated patches of animal-rich jungle at Sri Lanka's southern end. Inland, the land tilts steeply up to cool, tea-groomed highlands, above which soar scattered mountain tops, including the sacred Adam's Peak. The lowlands beyond are spiced with abrupt rocky outcrops that are home to ancient Buddhist hermitage caves, such as those at Dimbulagala. The flat, ragged landscapes of the war-ravaged far north dissolve into convoluted lagoons and a flurry of mesmerising islets.

HISTORY IN A NUTSHELL

For much of the island's history it has been divided into mutually antagonistic sub-kingdoms with frequently shifting capitals, most notably at Anuradhapura, Polonnaruwa, Jaffna and Kandy. Colonising Portuguese were swiftly superseded by Dutch and then British overlords. During the early 19th century, the Brits finally brought the last sub-kingdoms of Jaffna and Kandy into an all-island administration, then known as Ceylon. Independence in 1948 went smoothly, but reckless politics in the 1956 election stirred up an unstoppable wave of Sinhalese nationalism. Sinhala replaced English as the national language, effectively making second-class citizens of the Tamil-speaking minority. This sowed the seeds for an appalling ethnic conflict that steadily intensified into the 1990s. A shaky ceasefire was agreed between the government and Tamil Tiger rebels in early 2002. However, the November 2005 elections suggested that leaders on both sides were keen to resume hostilities – much to the horror of the general population. In mid-2006 clashes in the north and east began escalating, potentially towards a renewed, if low-profile, civil war.

PEOPLE

Sri Lanka's major 'ethnic' differences are in fact linguistic and religious. The majority Sinhalese (78 per cent) speak Sinhala and are Buddhist or Christian. Minority Tamil-speakers (18 per cent) might be Hindu, Muslim or Christian, but those who follow Islam (officially around eight per cent but growing rapidly) are locally categorised as a separate ethnic group. Sri Lankan Tamils see themselves as distinct from the so-called Indian Tamils (around five per cent), who mostly arrived during the 19th century to work colonial-era tea plantations. A small but economically important group of English-speaking Burghers trace their ancestry to mixed marriages with the colonial Europeans, most notably the Portuguese. In just a very few isolated villages the Veddahs, Sri Lanka's aboriginal tribes, retain elements of their ancient hunter-gatherer culture.

MARKETPLACE

Textiles and garment production generate much more export revenue than Sri Lanka's traditional plantation products, tea and rubber. Remittances from around a million Sri Lankan workers abroad constitute an estimated five per cent of GDP. Tourism once formed an important element of the economy, but this industry has been undermined by the unresolved Sinhalese–Tamil conflict. The December 2004 tsunami caused massive loss of life and infrastructure, from which the economy of the east coast is yet to recover.

A DELICATELY PERCHED STILT FISHERMAN

ELEPHANTS ON PARADE

Elephants lope about in several of Sri Lanka's national parks, but if you dawdle at dusk beside the Peace Pagoda in Ampara, you're almost assured to see a little troupe sidle past as though on cue. Keep your distance: they're genuinely wild despite their good timekeeping. There are working elephants around Kandy – the peak of pachyderm preening comes at that city's utterly magnificent Esala Perahera mid-summer festival. Over 50 jockeyed elephants are decorated from tusk to toe in splendid colours. The finest, shaded by canopies, carries the nation's holiest Buddhist relic on its annual outing.

TEA TIME

Sri Lanka's most archetypal scene is of emerald-green tea hills manicured into abstract topiary, a scene produced through systematic plucking by colourfully dressed women wearing vast wicker baskets on their unfathomably strong backs. Yet the island's world-famous tea plantations only took off in the 1870s, following a disastrous 'rust' blight that wiped out the formerly dominant coffee crop.

BATTLING FOR BUDDHISM

Sri Lanka has preserved, nurtured and exported Theravada Buddhism for over two millennia. Several excellent Buddhist-based retreats on the island allow visitors to learn the techniques of meditation in a wonderfully spiritual environment. However, elsewhere on the island, it's possible that the historical Buddha would be horrified by the formalistic religion that now uses his name and image. Perhaps most jarring for a philosophy valuing nonviolence is the pseudo-religious reverence given to Dutugemunu, a 1st century BC Sinhalese warrior whose military victories against the Hindu-Tamil king Elara are depicted in many Sri Lankan Buddhist temples.

WHAT A GEM?

Sri Lanka has produced some of the world's finest sapphires and moonstones and there's a major gem industry around Ratnapura. Tourists can expect endless whispered invitations to 'invest' in sparkly stones. These can be entertaining or financially ruinous, according to your attitude or gullibility. Most offerings are flawed to the point of worthlessness or complete imitations, so everyone but genuine experts should keep their wallets in check.

ON PAPER

Sri Lanka's complex social mores and intercommunal tensions offer fertile soil for some truly stimulating, often heart-rending fiction. Reading *Cinnamon Gardens* (Shyam Selvadurai), *July* (Karen Roberts) and *Anil's Ghost* (Michael Ondaatje) can offer more insight into contemporary history than slogging through a pile of heavy textbooks.

CUISINE

Hoppers aren't little jumping creatures but crispy hemispherical pancakes made from rice-flour and coconut milk. They make a delicious accompaniment to the fruity curries that constitute the mainstay of Sri Lanka's strangely underrated cuisine. Beach villages offer a tempting wealth of excellent fresh seafood, while in the far north the sombrero-sized *masala dosa* are more typical of southern India.

> LOTUS STEM PILLARS SUPPORT ONLY SKY AT MANDALAGIRI VIHARA

PHOTOGRAPHER TOMAS VAN HOUTRYVE | CORBIS

PHOTOGRAPHER CHRISTINE NIVEN | LONELY PLANET IMAGES

< THE PRISTINE WHITE SEATED BUDDHA IN MIHINTALE

ESSENTIAL EXPERIENCES

○ **Climbing Sigiriya's surreal rock-citadel during a cacophonous jungle dawn**

○ **Zipping through manicured emerald-green tea plantations on a moped**

○ **Gaping at the swirling pageantry of Kandy's extraordinary Esala Perahera festival**

○ **Joining a meditative Buddhist retreat or colourful Hindu *puja***

○ **Watching wild elephants stroll nonchalantly by at Bundala or Ampara**

INDIA

Jaffna
Kilinochchi
Mullaittivu
Mannar
Vavuniya
Trincomalee
Anuradhapura
Puttalam
Dimbulagala
Dambulla
Batticaloa
Negombo
Kandy
Nuwara Eliya
COLOMBO
Ella
Ratnapura
Ambalangoda
Tissamaharama
Weligama
Tangalla

MAP REF   L12

BEST TIME TO VISIT NOVEMBER TO MARCH

LEGAL OFFICES MAKE THEIR PRESENCE KNOWN IN KANDY

A NICE LONG SOAK AT THE PINNEWALA ELEPHANT ORPHANAGE

PUSH ME, PULL YOU: CHILDREN PLAY ON A SWING IN KALUANCHIKOLI SURIYAPARUM

MALDIVES

THE UNMATCHED BEAUTY OF THESE DAZZLING CORAL ATOLLS MAKES THEM THE ULTIMATE IN LUXURY FOR TRAVELLERS, WITH THEIR STUNNING BEACHES, WARM AND FRIENDLY PEOPLE AND SUPERB DIVING.

CAPITAL CITY MALE'   POPULATION 359,000   AREA 300 SQ KM   OFFICIAL LANGUAGE DHIVEHI

GRACEFULLY CURVED *DHONIS* AT THEIR MOORINGS

LANDSCAPE

The Maldives' coral atolls total only 300 square kilometres, making the country smaller than even tiny Andorra in land area. The Maldives is also the lowest-lying country in the world, with its highest point just 2.4 metres above sea level. Tragically, the country is expected to disappear by the end of the century if sea levels continue to rise unchecked.

HISTORY IN A NUTSHELL

Little is known about the Maldives before its conversion to Islam in 1153. The pre-Islamic civilisation here was probably Buddhist, but the evidence is hazy. Since 1153 the Maldives has struggled to retain its independence in the face of relentless foreign intervention. The Portuguese, the Malabars and the British all had colonial influence over the country, which remained a British protectorate until 1965. Since 1965 the country has developed enormously, largely as a result of establishing a huge tourism industry under the rule of dictator Maumoon Abdul Gayoom. This dictatorship continues today, despite the presence of a vocal pro-democracy movement. Sadly, it's not quite paradise after all – the movement has been violently repressed.

PEOPLE

The Maldivian people are fairly homogeneous and are descended from Dravidian and Sinhalese people who came south from India and Sri Lanka. Over the centuries, however, there's been lots of intermarriage with Arab and African traders, making the Maldives a real mix of cultures. Islam is taken extremely seriously here (far more so than in most Muslim countries) – officially 100 per cent of the population is Sunni Muslim and no other religions are tolerated.

MARKETPLACE

Tourism, fish and ships sum up the Maldives' economy. The development of nearly 100 island resorts throughout the country and their increasing expansion onto uninhabited islands make this by far the country's biggest industry. Fish are also big business: mainly tuna that is canned here and exported around the world. Shipping, based almost exclusively in Male', is another significant industry, due to the Maldives' great need for imports.

PARADISE ON EARTH

Maldivian beaches are famous, and the great news is that they really do look like the photos. Almost anywhere in the country has amazingly white beaches, lapped by cobalt-blue water and dappled by the shade of coconut palms set amid lush vegetation. Most islands have beautiful lagoons too, ideal for swimming and snorkelling. Wth year-round sun, it's one of the world's best beach holiday destinations.

ECOTOURISM

Preserving the Maldives' fragile environment has been a cornerstone of the development of the local tourism industry. Development is very tightly controlled: no building on any resort island can be taller than the highest palm tree, and waste is

RANKS OF RESORT ACCOMMODATION, OLHUVELI

processed carefully and not released into the water. Some resorts offer lessons in marine biology, others have conservation projects visitors can take part in involving turtles and sharks, and still more are growing their own coral.

MYTHS & LEGENDS

Magic and superstition abound here; despite the officially Muslim creed, most Maldivians in the more remote atolls believe very strongly in *jinni*, or evil spirits. They are said to come from the sea, the air or the land; to combat their work the local *hakeem* (medicine man) creates *fandhita* (spells and potions) – to help women conceive, to banish illness or to improve the fishing catch, for example.

URBAN SCENE

Male' is one of the world's most unusual capital cities: tens of thousands of people live side by side on a tiny island just a few kilometres across. Coming here gives travellers the best introduction to the country and a

far more genuinely Maldivian experience than can be found at any of the tourist resorts. Male' is also one of the few inhabited islands of the Maldives that you're allowed to visit independently as a tourist (the segregation of foreigners and tourists is intentional here, to protect the local culture from the frivolity of western liberalism). Male' boasts impressive mosques and an interesting national museum, while daily life holds its own perpetual fascination at the city's fish market.

THE SUBMARINE WORLD

The Maldives is actually made up of the tips of some of the world's tallest mountains, just poking their head above water from miles below. Between them, in the lagoons and channels that divide the atolls, is an incredible array of marine life, including some of the world's most impressive corals (on the road to recovery since 1998's disastrous coral bleaching) and a stunning array of tropical fish, massive moray eels, various species of shark, whales, sting and manta rays, dolphins and tuna.

FUTURE DIRECTIONS

The death knell has hopefully sounded for the reign of the Maldives' dictator Maumoon Abdul Gayoom, who is now in his third decade of iron-fisted rule. Pro-democracy demonstrations (many of which have been violently put down) finally forced Gayoom to announce (achingly slow-moving) plans to introduce democracy. However, while police brutality against human rights activists continues, the organisation Friends of the Maldives (www.friendsofmaldives.org) is promoting a very valid boycott of certain government-owned resorts that all visitors should be aware of.

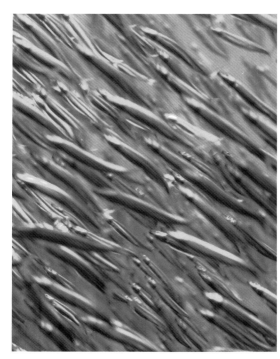

↗ A SCHOOL OF ANCHOVIES SHOOTS PAST LIKE SILVER BULLETS

ESSENTIAL EXPERIENCES

- **Coming in to land at Male' – the view of the atolls as you descend is stunning**
- **Being served cocktails by the infinity pool**
- **Going on a sunset dolphin-watching cruise to the beat of *bodu beru* drums**
- **Checking out the tiny but fascinating Maldivian capital, Male'**
- **Diving with turtles, friendly sharks, manta rays and conger eels all over the country**
- **Finding your own pristine white beach and realising that you really are in paradise**

Haa Alifu ● Dhidhdhoo
Haa Dhaal ● Kulhuduffushi
Funadhoo ● Shaviyani
Noonu
Ugoofaaru ● ● Manadhoo
Raa Lhaviyani
Naifaru
Baa ● Eydhafushi
● Kaafu
Alifu ✦ MALE'
Mahibadhoo ●
● Felidhoo
Vaavu
Magoodhoo ●
Faafu ● Muli
Kudahuvadhoo Meemu
Dhaalu
Veymandhoo ●
Thaa Laamu
● Hithadhoo
Gaaf Alif
● Viligili
Thinadhoo ●
Gaaf Dhaal
Gnaviyani ● Fuamulaku
Seenu ● Hithadhoo

MAP REF J13

BEST TIME TO VISIT **DECEMBER TO APRIL**

↗ AFLOAT ON A HOLIDAY IDYLL

BOLDLY COLOURED MODERN ARCHITECTURE

A RECENTLY SUBMERGED SNORKELLER

A BEACHED FISHING BOAT NESTLES ITS NOSE AMONG THE PALMS, KUDA BANDOS

CENTRAL ASIA

CENTRAL ASIA IS A REGION OF HUGE SKIES AND ENDLESS GRASSY STEPPE. THOUGH SPARSELY POPULATED AND LITTLE VISITED IN THE 21ST CENTURY, IT HAS PLAYED A HUGE ROLE IN WORLD HISTORY.

This is the centre of the Silk Road, the route that carried goods, people and ideas between East and West for centuries: it helped spread the young religion of Buddhism and gave the world one of its greatest travel writers in Marco Polo. Genghis (Jenghiz) Khan also tore along the route, ripping through kingdoms from his Mongolian homeland until he reached the gates of Europe.

Great cities grew up along the Silk Road, a route whose mystery continues to inspire adventurous travellers. The fabled caravanserais and mosques of Samarkand, Bukhara and Khiva in modern Uzbekistan are among the region's greatest attractions, along with Herat in Afghanistan and Turkmenistan's ruined city of Merv.

While the old trading cities lived off the open plains, the region is bounded by some of the world's most formidable mountains. From the south, the Hindu Kush rises through Afghanistan until it meets the mass of the Pamirs. These great peaks clash at a real geopolitical hotspot, where the borders of Afghanistan, Pakistan, China, Tajikistan and Kyrgyzstan constantly push and pull against each

other. The mountains and their high plateaus dominate the latter two countries almost completely, making them superb but little-known trekking destinations. Kyrgyzstan is working hard to develop itself as a regional centre of community tourism, offering horse riding and homestays amid its peaks and lakes.

Natural riches of another kind dominate Kazakhstan and Turkmenistan: oil and natural gas. The richest of the 'Stans' that made up Soviet Central Asia, they have found themselves major players in the energy business. This has done little good for the people of either country, with Kazakhstan blowing its money on a new capital city in the middle of nowhere, and Turkmenistan's president creating a personality cult to rival that of Kim Jong-il in North Korea.

The rush for these new energy supplies has been dubbed the 'New Great Game', echoing the old imperial rivalry between Russia and Britain that was played out in the region's mountain passes and icy steppe in the 19th century. Moscow's disastrous invasion of Afghanistan in 1979 helped bring on the

demise of the Soviet Union, but the Union lives on in spirit in the region's autocratic regimes and bureaucratic border controls.

Nevertheless, Central Asia is increasingly open to travellers ready to explore Silk Roads of their own. The region is as far off the beaten track as Asia gets, with a face rarely turned to the outside world. For those that make it here, Central Asia is a truly gripping destination.

TEXT: PAUL CLAMMER

TURKMENISTAN

THIS DESERT KINGDOM IS WHAT YOU WOULD EXPECT TO FIND IF NORTH KOREA AND QATAR GOT MARRIED AND HAD A SLIGHTLY ODD SON.

CAPITAL CITY ASHGABAT   **POPULATION** 5.04 MILLION   **AREA** 488,100 SQ KM   **OFFICIAL LANGUAGE** TURKMEN

LANDSCAPE

Turkmenistan is a desert kingdom, with around 90 per cent of its area eaten up by the Karakum desert. The Kopet Dag range forms the southern boundary with Iran, while the border with Uzbekistan is marked by the Amu-Darya river. To the west is the Caspian Sea, which gave the region its former name, Transcaspia.

HISTORY IN A NUTSHELL

Over 2000 years ago the Parthians set up their capital at Nissa. The spotlight went off again for 1000 years until the Seljuq Turks built Merv, the Islamic world's second-greatest city until it was destroyed by the Mongols in 1221. Russian tsarist forces later massacred thousands of the slave-trading Turkmen at Goek Tepe, built a railway and introduced cotton, before the Soviets took over. In 1991, independence was forced on Turkmenistan and since then President Niyazov (also known as Turkmenbashi, the 'Leader of the Turkmen') has kept a tight grip on power.

PEOPLE

Around 85 per cent of Turkmenistan's citizens are Turkmen, descendants of Turkic nomads, giving it the highest proportion of the titular nationality in any Central Asian republic. There are also small numbers of Turkmen in Iran. The largest of the hundred or so Turkmen clans are the Yomud, Tekke and Ersari. Since independence, many of Turkmenistan's Russians have left, as life is becoming increasingly difficult for those without a command of the Turkmen language.

MARKETPLACE

Turkmenistan's gas reserves rank among the world's largest – natural gas, electricity and water are free in Turkmenistan. During Soviet times cotton was a major export, but it's no longer cultivated to the same extent. Planned new pipelines under the Caspian Sea to Turkey and southeast to Afghanistan will be essential to Turkmenistan's economic development.

TRADEMARKS

- The bizarre personality cult of Turkmenbashi
- Bukhara carpets
- Big furry hats
- Fat-tailed sheep
- Political repression
- 'Halk, Watan, Turkmenbashi!' (People, Nation, Turkmenbashi!)

TOP FESTIVAL

Independence Day (27–28 October) is the big day out, with epic parades, song and dance performances and much praise of the president. Navrus is the main family holiday. Other wacky festivals include Melon Day, Carpet Day, Bread Day, Good Neighbourliness Day and 'Drop of Water is a Grain of Gold' Day.

RANDOM FACTS

- Air temperatures in the Karakum desert regularly exceed 50°C.
- Merv is Turkmenistan's only World Heritage Site.
- The 1100-kilometre-long Karakum Canal that crosses Turkmenistan's Karakum desert was one of the main reasons for the drying up of the Aral Sea.
- Ashgabat has the largest mosque in Central Asia.

WILD THINGS

The country's most famous equine ambassador is the beautiful Akhal-Teke, one of the world's most valued horse breeds and a favourite gift for visiting heads of state. Camels can be found on the edge of every town, but significantly rarer are the endemic zemzem (desert crocodile), zheyrans (goitred gazelles) and a host of nasties – tarantulas, cobras, vipers and scorpions.

SURPRISES

- Most top-end hotel rooms in the capital Ashgabat are bugged.
- The Berzengi district of Ashgabat has a strip of opulent Las Vegas–style hotels and malls that claim to have the highest fountain in the world.
- The president's bizarre book Ruhnama (Book of the Soul) has been translated into 11 languages, including Zulu. All prospective university students must pass a Ruhnama exam.
- Every year the Turkmen government dons tracksuits and sets out for an eight-kilometre 'Walk of Health'.
- If you want to marry a Turkmen citizen you'll have to pay a US$30,000 tax.

CULTURE

Turkmen clan ties run deep here and are reflected in regional dress, dialect and even the patterns woven into the famous Turkmen gillam (carpets). Turkmen men wear the shaggy Rastafarian-esque hats known as telpek; the Turkmen language is an archaic form of Turkish, close to Azeri. Sufism is very strong here.

ESSENTIAL EXPERIENCES

- **Staring in disbelief at the 12-metre-tall gold revolving statue of President Niyazov in Ashgabat**

- **Haggling for Bukhara carpets in the capital's Tolkuchka Bazaar**

- **Tracking dinosaur footprints at Kugitang Nature Reserve**

- **Touring the remains of Merv and Konye-Urgench, pulverised in the 13th century by Genghis Khan**

- **Staying at a traditional yurt in the Karakum (Black Sands) desert, within sight of the perennially blazing Darvaza gas craters**

MAP REF   G5

BEST TIME TO VISIT MARCH TO MAY, SEPTEMBER, OCTOBER

ONE OF THE INNUMERABLE STATUES OF TURKMENISTAN'S SELF-APPOINTED GOLDEN BOY, PRESIDENT NIYAZOV (TURKMENBASHI)

VENDORS BEHIND A WALL OF FISH

BUSY AND COLOURFUL TOLKUCHKA BAZAAR, ASHGABAT

UZBEKISTAN

STRETCHING OVER THE ANCIENT SILK ROAD, UZBEKISTAN HAS LAYERS OF HISTORY AND HOSPITALITY DEVELOPED DURING CENTURIES OF WELCOMING STRANGERS.

CAPITAL CITY TASHKENT   POPULATION 27.3 MILLION   AREA 447,400 SQ KM   OFFICIAL LANGUAGES UZBEK, RUSSIAN

HERE COMES THE BRIDE, KHIVA

LANDSCAPE

Uzbekistan is an arid, oddly shaped country, double-landlocked in Central Asia. Its most populated region is in the far east, the Fergana Valley, where fruits and vegetables grow in abundance. Soil fertility declines the further west you travel, culminating tragically at the Aral Sea. The sea has been shrinking since the 1960s, thanks to the diversion of source water to grow cotton. The exposed lake bed, subsequently poisoned by residual pesticides, is now the source of toxic dust clouds that periodically engulf nearby villages.

HISTORY IN A NUTSHELL

Though the history of Central Asia is often one of nomads and movement, the inhabitants of what is now Uzbekistan always preferred a more settled existence. Uzbekistan sits at a key crossroads between East and West; Alexander the Great was but one of many conquistadors to pass through here. In the 13th century Genghis (Jenghiz) Khan ravaged the region, paving the way for the rise of Timur (Tamerlane), who built a magnificent capital at Samarkand. In the late 1800s it was Russia that made inroads, placing Central Asia under its colonial administration. In 1924, the Soviets drew a few lines on a map and created the Uzbek Soviet Socialist Republic. Moscow liked the place, grew a lot of cotton and moved in settlers from Russia and Korea. In 1991 Uzbekistan reluctantly declared independence and has been ruled ever since by ex-Soviet bureaucrat Islam Karimov. His benevolent dictatorship has become increasingly unpopular among both ordinary Uzbeks and Western governments.

PEOPLE

Around 80 per cent of the people living in Uzbekistan are ethnic Uzbeks. Russians make up over five per cent of the population; there used to be many more, but around two million Russians fled the country after 1991. About five per cent are Tajik by ethnicity, including most of the people who live in Samarkand and Bukhara. There are also small numbers of Kazakh, Karakalpak and Tatar peoples. Around 88 per cent of the country adheres to Islam – the Sunni variety – while others practice Christianity.

MARKETPLACE

Lying on the Silk Road, Uzbekistan has a long history of trade between East and West. But it also has a few home-grown goods, namely silk, ceramics and knives produced in the Fergana Valley. Cotton is the major export commodity – Uzbekistan is the world's second-largest producer of cotton after the US. Uzbekistan also has a few goodies under its soil, including significant deposits of gold, natural gas, oil and silver.

TRADEMARKS

- The Registan
- Timur
- Bukharan rugs
- Boats without a port (in Moynaq)
- The Silk Road

NATURAL BEAUTY

Uzbekistan undulates magnificently across Central Asia. In the east are the Chatkal Mountains – folds of green and brown that rise to 4000 metres and receive significant snow in winter. The juniper trees that cover its slopes protect white-claw bears, Siberian ibex and the elusive snow leopard. Somewhat starker in its beauty is the Kyzylkum desert, where the red sands merge with the blue sky, and you can imagine the Silk Road camel caravans plodding into the distance.

URBAN SCENE

The Golden Road to Samarkand, as it was described by writer James Elroy Flecker, has been tempting travellers for centuries. They come to see what was once considered the greatest city on earth, Timur's

LOAFING ABOUT: WOMEN SELL UNLEAVENED BREAD AT THE SUNDAY MARKET, SAMARKAND

Samarkand, built to reflect the ideals of its megalomaniac creator. Master craftspeople decorated the city with every shade of blue – Timur's favourite colour. Centuries on, most of the blue has faded away, but there's enough of the ancient town left to give the modern visitor a sense of Samarkand's ancient glory.

CULTURE

Among all the peoples of Central Asia, it was the Uzbeks who emerged from communism with their culture most intact. Thousands of years of settled history helped to ground their traditions, and today Uzbek architecture, music, language and art are still alive. Many traditions were enriched by exchanges from East and West. During their country's time as a Silk Road way-station, the Uzbek people learned to tolerate visitors, wayfarers and wanderers, making hospitality as important as a good cup of tea.

MYTHS & LEGENDS

In 1941, Russian scientist Mikhail Gerasimov exhumed the body of Timur. On 22 June 1941 he opened the tomb and found an inscription: 'Whoever opens this will be defeated by an enemy more fearsome than I.' Hours later, Hitler invaded Russia. Two years later Gerasimov returned the body to its tomb, and within five weeks Nazi Germany was defeated.

CUISINE

Uzbek food is varied, plentiful and delicious. The staples are *shashlyk* (chunks of mutton barbecued over charcoal), *plov* (rice pilaf), and *choy* (green tea) – the Uzbek version of a Big Mac, fries and a coke. One of the tastiest treats is the amazing *nan* (bread), always baked fresh in tandoor ovens, and best eaten hot. Other local treats include *samsa*, a flaky pastry stuffed with meat, and *laghman*, boiled noodles which Uigur traders brought over on the Silk Road centuries ago.

MUSIC

Sometime in the late 16th century, musicians in Bukhara developed *shashmaqam*, now regarded as Uzbek classical music. Its structure is similar to classical Persian music and includes Sufi poetry throughout. One of Uzbekistan's most recognised international musicians is Sevara Nazarkhan, winner of the Best Asian Artist award from BBC Radio 3 in 2004. Nazarkhan plays the *dutar*, a type of lute, and fuses the sounds of Central Asia with Western pop music.

THE IMPOSING KUKHNA ARK FORTRESS, KHIVA

DIVINE LIGHT IN TILLA KARI MEDRESSA, SAMARKAND

ESSENTIAL EXPERIENCES

- Watching the moon rise over historic Khiva
- Haggling over carpets in Bukhara's market
- Gazing at the spectacular architecture of Samarkand's Registan
- Enjoying a stack of hot *nan* (bread) fresh from a tandoor oven
- Getting the shakedown from a policeman in a Tashkent subway station

MAP REF H5

BEST TIME TO VISIT MAY TO JUNE, SEPTEMBER TO NOVEMBER

THE KALEIDOSCOPIC CARPET MARKET IN BUKHARA

A CRESTFALLEN LENIN WAITS TO BE RECYCLED AS SCRAP, TASHKENT

THE DIMPLED ROOF OF KALON MOSQUE, BUKHARA

AN ABANDONED SHIP RUN AGROUND AT WHAT WAS ONCE THE EDGE OF THE ARAL SEA

AFGHANISTAN

STILL STRUGGLING TO EMERGE FROM OVER 25 YEARS OF WAR, AFGHANISTAN CONTINUES TO TEMPT A FEW INTREPID VISITORS WITH ITS SUBLIME MOUNTAIN LANDSCAPES AND FAMOUS HOSPITALITY, BUT SECURITY IN MUCH OF THE COUNTRY WILL REMAIN PROBLEMATIC FOR THE IMMEDIATE FUTURE.

CAPITAL CITY KABUL   POPULATION 31 MILLION   AREA 647,500 SQ KM   OFFICIAL LANGUAGES DARI, PASHTO

BOOK GROUP: YOUNG GIRLS STUDY THE QURAN WITH THE IMAM AT A MOSQUE, ISTALIF

LANDSCAPE

Afghanistan is a country dominated by high mountains and sweeping plains. The flat north and west open out onto the grassy plains of the Central Asia Steppe and the Iranian Plateau, while the south is a barren desert that looks more towards the Indian subcontinent for its climate and inspiration. In the middle of this, the massive spine of the Hindu Kush mountains bisects the country, extending to the far northeast and the thin tongue of the Wakhan Corridor, where it becomes part of the tangled knot of the Pamirs.

HISTORY IN A NUTSHELL

Often known as 'the crossroads of Asia', Afghanistan has hosted many of the great conquerors of history – Alexander the Great, Genghis (Jenghiz) Khan, Timur (Tamerlane), the Moghuls and the British army. Not all of them stayed for long, but most were given a bloody nose at some point: Afghanistan is a notoriously difficult country to conquer. An independent state since the 18th century, Afghanistan's most recent usurpers were the Soviets, who invaded the country in 1979. This kicked off a bloody 10-year freedom struggle, followed by an even more vicious civil war that lasted until the

Taliban took control in 1996. Their brutal and insular rule gave sanctuary to Islamists such as Osama bin Laden, but following the 9/11 attacks in the USA the Taliban's days in power were suddenly numbered. Now with an elected president and parliament, Afghanistan is still enduring the birth pangs of democracy.

PEOPLE

The Pashtuns are Afghanistan's dominant group, and have traditionally provided its rulers, including the current president Hamid Karzai. The Pashtuns are a hardy mountain people; their lands straddle the border with the unruly Tribal Areas of Pakistan. Tajiks make up a quarter of the country's population, followed by the Hazaras (who claim descent from Genghis Khan's hordes), Uzbeks and Turkmen. Afghans follow a traditional form of Islam – Sunni Islam is the dominant strand, although the Hazaras are Shiite.

MARKETPLACE

Traditionally an agrarian country, Afghanistan's economy has been shattered by war. The government is heavily dependent on foreign aid, which accounted for a short-lived boom following the ousting of the

Taliban. The real growth economy lies elsewhere though – in uncertain times many farmers have turned to opium as a reliable source of income. Opium comprises around 40 per cent of Afghanistan's official GDP, with the country exporting 90 per cent of the world's heroin.

TRADEMARKS

◊ Rugged mountains
◊ Proud hospitality
◊ Women in burkas
◊ 'Pancake' *pakul* hats
◊ Chronic instability

CULTURE

The Taliban practised a harsh version of Islam that was alien to the majority of Afghans. Nevertheless, this is a conservative and shell-shocked country, where tribal traditions prevail. Even foreign women need to wear a headscarf, and men need to avoid showing bare arms.

NATURAL BEAUTY

Afghanistan's landscape is harsh but beautiful. The bare peaks of the Hindu Kush and the khaki earth contrast strongly with silver-braided mountain rivers,

TO PROTECT AND TO SERVE: A LOCAL POLICEMAN FROM THE SULEIMAN KHEL TRIBE IN THE VILLAGE OF WAZAKHWA

the electric green of narrow fields, and the rich mineral blue of the isolated Band-e Amir lakes. In the northwest, the Dasht-e Leili (Desert of Tulips) blooms red every year with the spring rains.

RANDOM FACTS

- Afghanistan's lapis lazuli mines have been worked for over 7000 years, and provided the stone for Tutankhamun's funeral mask.
- Zoroastrianism, the world's first monotheistic religion, was founded in Afghanistan.
- Around US$50 billion worth of arms were imported by all sides during the Soviet war.
- The burka was once seen as status symbol for women – wearing it demonstrated that a woman did not have to do manual labour.

ON PAPER

Whether it's the scenery, the culture or the people, Afghanistan has long inspired some of the best travel writers in the business. Outstanding travel books include Robert Byron's *The Road to Oxiana,* Eric Newby's *A Short Walk in the Hindu Kush,* Peter Levi's *The Light Garden of the Angel King* and *An Unexpected Light* by Jason Elliot.

TOP FESTIVAL

March 21 is *Nawroz* (Navrus), the traditional New Year held on the spring equinox. The day is marked with picnics, kite-flying, and the giving of *jelabi,* a festive sweet. The largest celebrations are held at the Shrine of Hazrat Ali in Mazar-e Sharif.

MYTHS & LEGENDS

While most Muslims contend that Ali, son-in-law of the Prophet Mohammed, is buried in Najaf in Iraq, Afghans would have you believe his tomb is in Mazar-e Sharif, carried there on his death by his favourite camel. A shrine was built there in the 12th century, and despite a sacking by Genghis Khan, grew to be the country's most important pilgrimage site.

FUTURE DIRECTIONS

Afghanistan's post-Taliban reconstruction has been a case of one step forward, one step back. While the political process has resulted in elections, the physical process of rebuilding has been rather ineffectual, leading to some disillusionment among a populace sick of war and poverty. While the 'foreign guests' of NATO and the US Army are still largely welcomed, a failure to provide adequate security has led to the resurgence of opium trafficking and the Taliban in the restive southern provinces. Afghanistan still has a long walk back to stability.

ON THE ROAD TO PANJSHIR VALLEY

THE INTRICATE SPLENDOUR OF THE BLUE SHRINE, MAZAR-E-SHARIF

ALL DRESSED UP, GHOWR PROVINCE

ESSENTIAL EXPERIENCES

- Dipping your toes in the lapis-blue waters of the Band-e Amir lakes
- Enjoying the cool peace of Herat's immaculately tiled Friday Mosque
- Seeing the new glass buildings – and bombed-out ruins – of post-Taliban Kabul
- Reflecting on Afghanistan's living and lost beauty at the site of the destroyed Buddhas of Bamiyan
- Standing well back from the touchline at a wild *buzkashi* match (a polo-like game played with a headless goat or calf carcass)
- Heading deep into the mountains in search of the fabled Minaret of Jam

MAP REF   H7

BEST TIME TO VISIT APRIL TO JUNE, SEPTEMBER TO NOVEMBER

WAR TOYS: CHILDREN AT THE NAWABAD REFUGEE CAMP

BAND-E ZULFIQAR, ONE OF THE FIVE BAND-E AMIR LAKES

TRUST IN TROUBLED TIMES: A SHEEP HERDER TENDS HIS FLOCK NEAR THE WAR-RAVAGED DARULAMAN PALACE IN KABUL

TEXT BRADLEY MAYHEW

TAJIKISTAN

ONE OF THE MOST REMOTE CORNERS OF THE FORMER SOVIET UNION, TAJIKISTAN OFFERS CUTTING-EDGE CENTRAL ASIAN ADVENTURE WITH SOME OF THE GRANDEST MOUNTAIN SCENERY ON EARTH.

CAPITAL CITY DUSHANBE   POPULATION 7.3 MILLION   AREA 143,100 SQ KM   OFFICIAL LANGUAGE TAJIK

⌃ CATHEDRAL SPIRES PRICK THE BLOOD-RED SKY IN DUSHANBE

LANDSCAPE

It's all about the mountains in Tajikistan. Half the country lies above 3000 metres and the highest peaks dwarf anything outside Nepal. The western third of the country is a hot, dusty plain, from which rise the remote valleys of the Zeravshan, Hissar, Turkestan and Fan ranges, all spurs of the mighty Tian Shan. Further east, the Pamir plateau, known locally as Bam-i-Dunya (Roof of the World), makes up almost half of Tajikistan's land mass, with dozens of peaks over 7000 metres.

HISTORY IN A NUTSHELL

With roots in ancient Bactria and Sogdiana, modern Tajikistan traces itself back to the Samanids, a 10th-century Persian empire that stretched from Iran to China, with a capital in the Tajik city of Bukhara. Later centuries saw these lands squeezed between the Emirate of Bukhara in Uzbekistan to the west, the Oxus River (Amu-Darya) and Afghanistan to the south, and the Pamirs to the east. The Pamirs were the highest arena of the Great Game, the 19th-century rivalry between the Russian and British empires, before it was closed to foreigners for the next century. Following independence in 1991, the country collapsed into a bloody six-year civil war that claimed 60,000 lives.

PEOPLE

Indo-European Tajikistan is a Persian-speaking outpost in predominantly Turkic Central Asia. The Tajiks are a widely spread people – fewer than half the world's Tajiks live in Tajikistan, and they claim as their cultural centres Bukhara and Samarkand, both in present-day Uzbekistan. The southern region of Badakhshan was annexed by Kabul in the 18th century and there are now more Tajiks in Afghanistan than Tajikistan, while half a million more Tajiks were displaced during the civil war. Uzbeks comprise 25 per cent of the population. Throughout much of Tajikistan, clan ties run deeper than notions of ethnicity.

MARKETPLACE

Independence and then civil war proved economically disastrous for Tajikistan, and the annual national budget remains less than that of a major Hollywood movie. Over 80 per cent of Pamiris earn less than US$200 per month. Almost one million Tajiks work abroad, mostly in Russia; remittances from them comprise an important element of the economy.

TRADEMARKS
- Roof of the World
- Marco Polo sheep
- Civil war
- The Great Game (the 19th century rivalry between Russia and Britain in the region)
- The Pamirs

NATURAL BEAUTY

The Fan Mountains in the west of the country are studded with dozens of gorgeous turquoise lakes. The western Pamirs offer remote valleys between rugged peaks, whereas the eastern Pamirs are made up of rolling, high-altitude valleys broken by deep blue lakes such as Kara Kul. The Wakhan Valley is an ethereally beautiful valley shared with Afghanistan and bordered by the snowcapped giants of the Hindu Kush.

MYTHS & LEGENDS

The ghost of Alexander the Great haunts Central Asia, and nowhere is his presence felt more than in Tajikistan. Central Asians know Alexander as 'Iskander' and he is celebrated in place names across the region, including beautiful Iskander-Kul in the Fan Mountains. He's thought to have founded Alexandria Eschate (Farthest Alexandria) near the modern city of Khojand and to have married the Sogdian princess Roxana after defeating her father in the mountains northwest of Dushanbe.

SHEEP GRAZE UNDER THE SNOWY PEAKS OF THE PAMIRS

CULTURE

Tajikistan is proud of its Persian heritage, honouring such illustrious Persian poets as Rudaki, Firdausi and Omar Khayam – all of whom are also claimed by Iran. The average Tajikistan family is large, often with seven or eight children. Men wear stripy coloured cloaks and *tupi* (skullcaps); women wear colourful dresses over striped trousers. About 80 per cent of Tajikistan's people are Sunni Muslim, though Pamiris follow the Ismaili sect of Islam. Radical Islam took root in the 1990s but lost its foothold after the removal of Al-Qaeda and the Taliban in neighbouring Afghanistan.

RANDOM FACTS

- Sogdian, the language of the Silk Road, is still spoken in remote valleys in the Pamirs and beyond.
- The Pamiri Ismailis of eastern Tajikistan venerate the Swiss-born Aga Khan as a living god.
- Koh-I Samani is the highest mountain in the former Soviet Union, at 7495 metres.

CUISINE

All the Central Asian standards such as *shashlyk* (mutton kebabs), *plov* (pilaf of rice and vegetables), *laghman* (noodle stew) and *non* (bread) are present. *Kurtob* is a Tajik dish layered with bread, yoghurt, onion and coriander and eaten with your hands out of a communal bowl. *Chakka* is curd mixed with herbs. Russian, Turkish and even Ecuadorian cuisine is available in the capital Dushanbe.

ECOTOURISM

Two excellent ecotourism projects in the Pamirs are providing income and a sustainable direction for tourism, and have revolutionised independent travel in the Gorno-Badakhshan region. The French NGO Acted (http://phiproject.free.fr) runs a homestay programme in the far-eastern Murgab region, including yurt stays in the neighboring Gumbezkul Valley. The Aga Khan's Mountain Societies Development Support Programme (MSDSP) runs a fledgling tourism programme in the western Pamir, based in Khorog, and also has a network of homestays – see www.pamirs.org.

TOP FESTIVAL

Navrus, on 21 March, is the year's biggest bash. Visitors are likely to see song and dance performances and maybe even some *buzkashi* (a polo-like game played with a headless goat or calf carcass) out at Hissar fort west of Dushanbe. This is the one time such traditional foods as *sumalak* (ground wheat sprouts cooked with oil, flour and sugar) are prepared. During the Navrus dinner seven items all beginning with the sound 'sh' are laid out on the table, including *shir* (milk), *shakar* (sugar) and *sharob* (wine).

ESSENTIAL EXPERIENCES

- **Travelling the Pamir Highway from Khorog to Osh, one of the world's great road trips**

- **Exploring Silk Road forts along the Tajik side of the Wakhan Corridor**

- **Bedding down in a Kyrgyz yurt on the Pamir plateau**

- **Diving in hand-first into a bowl of *kurtob* (layered bread, yoghurt, onion and coriander in a creamy sauce) in leafy Dushanbe**

- **Hiking out to a string of outrageously turquoise lakes in the Fan Mountains, a trekkers' paradise**

△ A SEVERE LOOK IN A SEVERE LANDSCAPE – THE AKSU VALLEY

MAP REF 15

BEST TIME TO VISIT MARCH TO APRIL, SEPTEMBER TO NOVEMBER (VALLEYS), JULY TO SEPTEMBER (PAMIR)

△ OVERHEAD OPULENCE: COLOURFUL DECORATIVE ART ADORNS A CEILING

PHOTOGRAPHER STEPHANE HERBERT / CORBIS

THE HEAD ACCOUNTANT OF A COTTON FACTORY IN REGAR DISPLAYS THE MERCHANDISE

AN ETHNIC KYRGYZ FAMILY INSIDE THEIR YURT IN THE PAMIR MOUNTAINS

KYRGYZSTAN

KYRGYZSTAN IS CENTRAL ASIA'S MOST WELCOMING REPUBLIC, A LAND OF MOUNTAIN VALLEYS, HERDSPEOPLE AND YURTS.

CAPITAL CITY BISHKEK   POPULATION 5.2 MILLION   AREA 198,500 SQ KM   OFFICIAL LANGUAGES KYRGYZ, RUSSIAN

A HERD OF YAKS BROWSES THE TREELESS EXPANSE OF THE TIAN SHAN MOUNTAINS

LANDSCAPE

Kyrgyzstan is an overwhelmingly mountainous country, dominated by the jagged peaks of the Tian Shan, bordering China's Xinjiang province, and the Pamir Alay, bordering Tajikistan to the south. Mountain spurs hem in the Fergana Valley, shared with Uzbekistan, and the huge alpine lake of Issyk-Kul. Up in the central highlands the landscape consists of rolling *jailoo* (alpine pastures) and high-altitude lakes that are dotted with nomads' yurts in summer.

HISTORY IN A NUTSHELL

The earliest inhabitants of the region were Turkic nomads, including Scythians and Turks, waves of whom moved across Asia displacing other nomadic peoples en route. The Kyrgyz people of today trace their roots back to the Yenisei Valley of Siberia; their ancestors began migrating south in the 10th century under the influence of Mongol incursions. The Karakhanid empire ruled in the region between the 10th and 12th centuries, and had its capitals in Kyrgyzstan. In 1862 the area became part of the Russian tsarist empire, controlled from a string of forts centred on Bishkek. Rebellions in 1916 and the 1930s were a result of clumsy Soviet collectivisation, but Kyrgyzstan did not become independent until 1991.

PEOPLE

About two-thirds of the people of Kyrgyzstan are Kyrgyz. The remainder are Uzbeks (14 per cent) and Russians (11 per cent), with minorities of Dungans (Muslim Chinese), Koreans and Germans, many of whom were deported here during World War II.

MARKETPLACE

The Kyrgyz economy was left out on a limb after the collapse of the Soviet Union. Despite the most liberal privatisation programme in Central Asia, the economy is still shaky at best, reliant on livestock raising, gold-mining, hydroelectricity and tourism. Unemployment is somewhere between 20 and 30 per cent.

TRADEMARKS

- Yurts
- Felt rugs
- Horses
- Alpine valleys
- *Kymys* (fermented mare's milk)
- Silly hats

NATURAL BEAUTY

The Arashan Valley above Karakol offers classic alpine scenery, with lush meadows, rushing streams and snowy peaks that could have been lifted straight out of the Canadian Rockies. Just an hour's drive from the capital Bishkek, the Ala-Archa Canyon provides wonderful trekking, summertime skiing and glacier climbing. Lake Issyk-Kul offers golden beaches within sight of a range of snowy peaks. In contrast, Song-Köl is a high-altitude lake frequented by migratory birds and Kyrgyz herders.

WILD THINGS

The Tian Shan is believed to preserve the world's second-largest snow leopard population. Marco Polo sheep and ibex are also present in the mountains, as are marmots, wolves and brown bears. The walls of the Fergana Valley have some lovely pistachio and walnut forests, while the border with Kazakhstan is one of the world's tulip hot-spots.

RANDOM FACTS

- The city of Bishkek is named after the wooden plunger used to churn fermented mare's milk.
- The Kyrgyz people are outnumbered almost three to one by their livestock.
- The Manas epic is 20 times longer than the Odyssey.
- It takes about three hours to erect a Kyrgyz yurt.

THE SKELETON OF A YURT GOES UP AT TASH RABAT

CULTURE

Present-day Kyrgyz culture is still closely tied to its nomadic past. Yurts, which are constructed by piling felt onto a frame of wood and reeds, are the preferred accommodation in the summer pastures. Sheep, the main livestock, provide the raw material for *shyrdak* (felt carpets), the perfect portable handicraft for a nomadic nation. The Kyrgyz people's traditional reliance on the horse finds expression in summer games including *kok boru* (a polo-like game played with a headless goat carcass, called *buzkashi* in other countries), long-distance horse races and horseback wrestling.

MYTHS & LEGENDS

The Manas is an ancient epic poem (described as the 'Iliad of the Steppe') that tells of the formation of the Kyrgyz people through the exploits of their warrior-hero Manas. White-bearded bards known as *manaschi* still perform fragments of the poem – a complete recitation of it takes over 24 hours to finish.

IN ART

Central Asia's most famous writer of modern times is the Kyrgyz novelist Chinghiz Aitmatov. His novels *Jamilla* and *The Day Lasts Longer than a Century* offer revealing insights into Soviet-era Kyrgyzstan. One film worth looking out for is Aktan Abdykalykov's 1998 *Besh Kumpyr,* about a young boy adopted by five old ladies. Part of American Robert Rosenberg's novel *This is Not Civilization* describes the life of a Peace Corps worker who is stationed in a remote Kyrgyz village.

ECOTOURISM

Kyrgyzstan has Central Asia's most impressive homestays and ecotourism projects. These projects were established to provide an alternative and sustainable income to communities that were left out in the cold following the fall of the Soviet Union. Community Based Tourism (CBT: www.cbtkyrgyzstan.kg) has a network of homestays across the country, through which travellers can rent horses, guides and vehicles at very modest rates. Yurts provide an environmentally sensitive form of alpine accommodation and homestays help put tourist money directly into the pockets of dozens of local families.

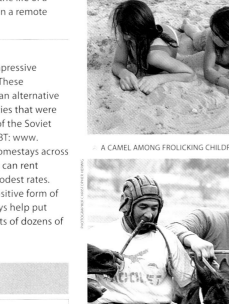

A CAMEL AMONG FROLICKING CHILDREN AT LAKE ISSYK-KUL, BISHKEK

THE OUSTED PRESIDENT AKAEV, DEPICTED IN BLACK METAL

PHOTOGRAPHER CHRISTOPHER HERWIG

ESSENTIAL EXPERIENCES

- Releasing your inner nomad on a horse trek in the mountains ringing Lake Issyk-Kul

- Getting your passport stamped at the Torugart or Irkeshtam Passes, Central Asia's remotest border posts

- Drinking *kymys* (fermented mare's milk) and listening to a *komuz* (Kyrgyz lute) in a homestay yurt

- Listening to a bard reciting the Manas epic in the summer pastures of Kochkor

- Picturing the life of a Silk Road trader in the remote caravanserai of Tash Rabat

- Shopping for spices in the Osh bazaar in the Kyrgyz Fergana Valley

PHOTOGRAPHER YURIY LIBERMAN / CORBIS

CHANGING GUARDS OUTSIDE THE NATIONAL MUSEUM, BISHKEK

PHOTOGRAPHER CHRISTOPHER HERWIG

KAZAKHSTAN

BISHKEK · Tokmak — Issyk-Kul · Karakol

Talas ·

Ala-Archa Canyon

· Kyzyl Kul · Naryn

· Jalal-Abad

UZBEKISTAN

· Osh

· Kyzyl-Kiya CHINA

Kyrgyz Fergana Valley Sary-Tash

TAJIKISTAN

MAP REF J5

BEST TIME TO VISIT JUNE TO OCTOBER

WELCOMING ACCOMMODATION ON THE *JAILOO* (PASTURE) OF SARALA-SAZ ≫

A GENTLEMAN AND HIS GOSHAWK, NEAR BALIKCHI ≫

THE FAST AND FURIOUS GAME OF *KOK BORU*

KAZAKHSTAN

THIS EURASIAN GIANT, ONCE A LAND OF NOMADS AND HORSEPEOPLE, IS RECOVERING FROM THE FALLOUT OF THE SOVIET UNION WITH THE HELP OF SOME OF THE WORLD'S LARGEST OIL RESERVES.

CAPITAL CITY ASTANA   POPULATION 15.2 MILLION   AREA 2.7 MILLION SQ KM   OFFICIAL LANGUAGES KAZAKH, RUSSIAN

LANDSCAPE

Straddling Europe and Asia, Kazakhstan is continental in size. It stretches from sub-Siberia to the north to the Central Asian deserts of the south; from the Caspian Sea in the west, across to the Altay and Tian Shan mountain range bordering China. Stunning Mt Khan Tengri pegs the eastern border of Kazakhstan, Kyrgyzstan and China. In between is the steppe, which is as flat as a pancake for hundreds of miles.

HISTORY IN A NUTSHELL

A procession of eastern nomadic empires – from Sakas to Mongols – have swept through Kazakhstan for millennia. After Genghis (Jenghiz) Khan, Kazakhstan became part of the Turkic Chagatai khanate. The 16th century saw the steppes divided between three Kazakh hordes, who ruled a huge empire from horseback. The last 300 years were dominated by Russians, first tsarist then Soviet, who used the republic as a testing ground for weapons and a dumping ground for exiles. Kazakhstan gained a reluctant independence in 1991.

PEOPLE

Descendents of nomadic horsepeople, Kazakhs are closely related to their neighbours, the Kyrgyz. A hundred years of Russification and Sovietisation has created a modern lifestyle, however, with European-style dress and a dependence on the Russian anguage. Kazakhstan has a declining population. The far south is largely Kazakh; the north is mainly Russian.

MARKETPLACE

Kazakhstan is home to some of the largest oil finds in recent years, and has become a pivotal piece in the new global struggle to secure oil reserves. Though it's not exactly an Asian tiger, President Nazarbaev sees his country as a 'Central Asian snow leopard', despite the fact that corruption is endemic and only a small percentage of the population has benefited financially from the oil. Kazakhstan was the breadbasket of the Soviet Union and remains a huge wheat producer.

TRADEMARKS

○ Steppes
○ Horse sausage
○ 'Yeeees, I like…', Ali G's mate Borat Sagdiyev, Almaty's famous fictional resident
○ Nuclear-testing sites and cosmodromes
○ Rusting fishing boats stranded by the dying Aral Sea

NATURAL BEAUTY

The southeast, with its striking alpine valleys, wildflowers and glacial lakes, is the most beautiful corner of the country. The glorious Zailiysky Alatau range is less than an hour's drive from downtown Almaty. Another pristine hiking hotspot is the Altay Mountains, near the Russian and Mongolian border in the far northeast.

RANDOM FACTS

○ Kazakhstan is the ninth-largest country in the world.
○ The Tenghiz and Kashagan fields in the west of the country are home to some of the largest proven oil reserves on earth.
○ The country's capital is Astana, which means… er… 'capital' in Kazakh.

ECOTOURISM

Though they are still in their infancy, half a dozen ecotourism projects have taken root in southeast Kazakhstan, including at Lepsinsk, the Aksu-Zhabaghly Nature Reserve and Kurgalzhino Nature Reserve outside Astana. Homestays, horse riding and even flamingo spotting are available – see www.ecotourism.kz.

SURPRISES

○ Kazakhstan shifted its capital 1000 miles north from Almaty to Astana in 1997.
○ The only nomads you'll find in Kazakhstan these days are stuffed and mounted in a dozen dusty Soviet-era museums.
○ Almaty means 'Father of Apples' and is thought to be the genetic home of the wild apple.

CUISINE

Ropey kebabs, *nan* bread, oily fried rice and greasy dumplings are the standards here. Enjoy. The national dish is *beshbarmak* – meat, fat and offal stewed in a pot for hours and served on squares of pasta. *Kazy* is one of several popular kinds of horsemeat sausage, and is generally washed down with a shot of vodka and a grimace. Kazakhs let their nomadic roots show with their love of *qymyz* (fermented mare's milk) and *shubat* (fermented camel's milk).

ESSENTIAL EXPERIENCES

○ **Reading Dostoevsky's *The House of the Dead* at Semey, his place of exile for five years**

○ **Trundling across the empty steppe for days to a nowheresville town like Aralsk, Atyrau or Aktau**

○ **Staring at fleets of Mafiosi-looking Mercedes in booming Almaty or Astana**

○ **Making the pilgrimage to the Timurid-era Kozha Akhmed Yasaui Mausoleum in Turkistan, Kazakhstan's most impressive piece of Central Asian architecture**

○ **Trekking to the lovely green Köl-Say lakes, southeast of Almaty**

MAP REF   I3

BEST TIME TO VISIT APRIL TO NOVEMBER

PLOTTING THEIR NEXT MOVE IN FRONT OF ZENKOV CATHEDRAL, ALMATY

DISUSED EQUIPMENT AT THE TIAN SHAN ASTRONOMICAL OBSERVATORY

YOUNG WOMEN AT A WELCOMING CEREMONY, ASTANA

THE MIDDLE EAST

HERE IN THE CRADLE OF CIVILISATION, THE REMNANTS OF THE GREATEST EMPIRES OF THE ANCIENT WORLD YIELD TO THE LYRICAL CALL TO PRAYER FROM A BLUE-TILED MOSQUE. TOGETHER THEY MARK THE PASSING OF TIME, AS IF LIFE HAS CHANGED LITTLE IN CENTURIES, EVEN AS EVERYTHING SEEMS TO CHANGE FROM ONE DAY TO THE NEXT.

The Middle East stretches from the Central Asian steppes of eastern Iran to the Mediterranean, where Israel, Lebanon and Syria lie somewhat uncomfortably by the water's edge. The region is dominated by its deserts; the Empty Quarter (Rub al-Khali or Abode of Silence) is one of the largest in the world and is shared by most of the countries of the Arabian Peninsula – Saudi Arabia, Yemen, Oman and United Arab Emirates (UAE). Mountains provide a geographical counterpoint to the arid plains and seas of sand, most notably Mt Damavand in Iran, the highlands of Yemen, southwestern Saudi Arabia and snowcapped Lebanon. The story of the Middle East is also the story of its rivers, with the Tigris, Euphrates and Jordan flowing reassuringly through history even as great civilisations and tumultuous events have come and gone.

But it is the confluence of cultures and great religions that at once unifies and divides the region. The three great monotheistic faiths – Judaism, Christianity and Islam – all arose from Middle Eastern soil, and they continue to shape the region's present and its future. Every country in the Middle East (with the notable exception of Jewish Israel) is predominantly Muslim, but many countries have small but significant Christian minorities. Within the Muslim communities of the region, the schism between Sunnis and Shiites belies the apparent religious homogeneity. Shiites form either the largest groups or significant minorities in Iran, Iraq, Lebanon and Bahrain.

Further layers of identity exist in the form of ethnic groups. Arabs predominate, but Kurds span the borders of many countries and Iran is overwhelmingly Persian. The Jews – once numerous across the Middle East – are now confined to Israel.

An arid climate and barren soil have forced the peoples of the region to congregate in zones of agricultural fertility. The great cities of Babylon, Nineveh, Persepolis and Petra emerged from these productive regions; home to the Babylonians, Assyrians, Persians and Nabataeans, they were the cradles of civilisation, and their names still resonate with biblical power. Cities of great, if lesser, antiquity, such as Baghdad, Damascus, Mecca and Jerusalem, have since taken up the mantle of historical and spiritual significance.

In modern times, it could almost be said that oil is the new religion. It has transformed once-impoverished, deeply traditional outposts in the desert or the Gulf into economic powerhouses whose financial wellbeing sends ripples across the globe in the form of oil prices. But within the region, oil's geographical specificity has fostered massive inequalities and an unprecedented transfer of migrant workers from poor countries to rich. In oil-rich UAE, annual GDP per capita is an enviable US$43,400. Oil-poor Yemenis get by on US$900.

Everywhere in the Middle East, however, the future belongs to the young, whether rich or poor – almost 40 per cent of wealthy Saudis and struggling Syrians alike are younger than 15 years old.

TEXT: ANTHONY HAM

IRAN

IRAN IS ONE OF THE MOST MISUNDERSTOOD COUNTRIES ON EARTH, AND ONE OF THE MOST HOSPITABLE, SURPRISING AND REWARDING ANYWHERE.

CAPITAL CITY TEHRAN   POPULATION 68.7 MILLION   AREA 1.6 MILLION SQ KM   OFFICIAL LANGUAGE FARSI

LANDSCAPE

Like so many other aspects of Iran, the country's geography is unexpected. There are two great deserts, the Dasht-e Kavir and Dasht-e Lut. But there are also three dominant mountain ranges: the volcanic Sabalan and Talesh ranges in the northwest; the vast Zagros in the central west; and the Alborz, which skirts the Caspian Sea and is home to most of Iran's impressive ski fields. Temperatures vary wildly and on the same day it could be –5°C in Tabriz and 35°C in Bandar Abbas. Iran is not known for its wildlife and that which is notable, such as the Asiatic cheetah, is often endangered.

HISTORY IN A NUTSHELL

Persian history was long dominated by the rise and fall of empires. Cyrus the Great's Achaemenid Empire was first among them, starting in the 6th century BC and building fantastic cities such as Persepolis, before the Macedonian upstart Alexander the Great put an end to it in 331 BC. The Sassanians extended the empire to Egypt before its sudden demise, caused by the arrival of Islam in 637. During the next millennium Genghis Khan and Timur (Tamerlane) severed many heads, the Safavids oversaw a

flowering of Persian arts, and the Qajars squandered them. Reza Shah ended that in 1925 and renamed the country Iran, and his son became the last *shah* (king of kings). He was overthrown in the 1979 revolution that brought Ayatollah Khomeini and other hardline Islamic clerics to power.

PEOPLE

About 58 per cent of Iranians can be classified as Persians, descendants of the Aryans who first settled in Iran in around 2000 BC. The Persians are complemented by Azerbaijanis (25 per cent) as well as small populations of Lors and Kurds – all of whom live in the mountainous northwest of the country – and by equally small groups of Turkmen, Arabs and Baluchi people. Farsi is spoken by almost everyone, but each ethnic group also has its own language or dialect. The most unifying aspect of the people is religion: officially 89 per cent are Shia Muslims, the rest being Sunni Muslims, Zoroastrians, Baha'is, Christians and Jews.

MARKETPLACE

Iran is more developed than many people think. Oil and its export drives the economy and, while few

Iranians are employed in the industry, everyone benefits through subsidised fuel prices (petrol costs US$0.10 per litre). With fuel so cheap, Iranians use more than twice as much as Western Europeans. Most of the population is under 30 and unemployment is a big issue.

TRADEMARKS

o Oil
o Black chadors
o Carpets
o Ayatollahs
o Fiery protests with flaming US flags
o Art-house films

NATURAL BEAUTY

It seems as if there's a mountain at the end of every Iranian street. Whether it's looking up the avenues of Tehran to the snow-covered peaks of the Alborz range, staring out to the Zagros peaks from Imam Square in Esfahan, or climbing up to one of the shattered remains of the Castles of the Assassins, Iran is much more of a visual feast than you expect. In their silent, solitary way, Iran's deserts are just as enchanting.

THE INKY CHADORS OF THREE WOMEN DISTILL THEM INTO SILHOUETTES

^ REMEMBRANCE OF THINGS PAST: THE RUINS OF PERSEPOLIS, THE ANCIENT CAPITAL OF PERSIA

^ A MULLAH MAKES A DIGNIFIED FIGURE AT THE ENTRANCE TO THE MULLAH SCHOOL OF ESFAHAN

^ THE DOME OF THE ARG-E KARIM KHANI, SHIRAZ, APPEARS LIT FROM WITHIN

AN ORNATE MASK WORN OVER A CHADOR

THE SWEEPING LINES OF TEH AZADI TOWER DRAW THE EYE TO ITS BLUNT PINNACLE, TEHRAN

A PASTORAL IDYLL

URBAN SCENE

Early-20th-century traveller Robert Byron probably summed up Esfahan best when he ranked it 'among those rarer places, like Athens or Rome, which are the common refreshment of humanity'. The city embodies the artistic harmony from the Safavid era and has been wowing visitors since the early 1600s. At its centre is vast Imam Square, the world's second-largest (after Tiananmen Square), embellished with the majestic Imam and Sheikh Lotfollah mosques, and the Ali Qapu Palace. Equally enchanting is the Zayendeh River and its romantic stone-arch bridges.

CULTURE

Everyone who visits Iran will encounter *ta'arof*, a system of formalised politeness. It can be confusing: a shopkeeper will refuse to take your money, or an offer of food will be turned down several times before finally being accepted. It's designed to give the person making the offer the chance to save face if they actually cannot provide a meal or afford their

purchase. A good rule is to refuse any offer three times but, if the person continues to insist, do accept. Shopkeepers will naturally expect to be paid, so keep offering.

POETIC HEROES

Iran's great poets have been dead more than 500 years, but their influence remains enormous. Almost everyone can quote at least a few verses of Ferdosi, Hafez, Omar Khayyam and Sa'di, and you can often hear long recitals at their respective mausoleums, which are also big domestic tourist attractions. But the idea of poets being heroes? These poets are credited with protecting the Persian language and culture during times of occupation, for which Iranians are eternally grateful.

CUISINE

The Persian philosophy of food has been evolving since Achaemenid times, when physicians decided a good diet involved a balance of 'hot' and 'cold' foods. Hot foods, such as the ubiquitous red meat kebabs, are always served with cold foods, usually yoghurt, cheese, radishes and fresh green herbs. So if you

order two very cold foods together – say, fish and *dugh* (a yoghurt drink) – the waiter will think you're completely mental.

FUTURE DIRECTIONS

With all this nuclear nonsense and sabre rattling going on, the future direction of Iran is anyone's guess, really. But it can be safely assumed that the ruling clerics won't easily relinquish power. Until they do, Iran's 'democracy' will continue to represent a dubious freedom, at best.

ESSENTIAL EXPERIENCES

○ **Meeting someone, and then finding yourself sitting on a Persian rug in their home, drinking tea, eating dates and talking politics an hour later**

○ **Watching the sun set on Esfahan's magnificent Imam Square as you smoke orange-flavoured tobacco through a *qalyan* (water pipe)**

○ **Listening to impromptu poetry recitals in the garden of Hafez's tomb in Shiraz**

○ **Soaking it all up from the hill behind the sublime Persepolis**

○ **Discovering abandoned props on the stage of history like Kuh-e Khajeh, where you'll find the archaeological remnants of an unbaked mud village from the Parthian era**

○ **Exploring the lanes and teahouses in the delightful stepped village of Masuleh**

PHOTOGRAPHER MAJID GETTY

PHOTOGRAPHER JANE SWEENEY LONELY PLANET IMAGES

⌃ THE STERN FACES OF FEMALE POLICE OFFICERS DURING THEIR GRADUATION

⌃ BLOOD-RED TENDRILS OF WOOL DRYING

FROM THE TRAVELLER

The locals like to take advantage of the cool shade within the inner arcades of the Khaju Bridge, over the Zayendeh River in Esfahan. This old bridge is a place of pleasant relaxation during the heat of the day, and becomes a mystical space filled with Persian songs in the evening: its acoustics are outstanding. I used to sit here every evening listening to the mysterious songs and hand-clapping of locals, and often dropped by during the day to enjoy its relaxed atmosphere.

MARIAN GOLIS   CZECH REPUBLIC

AZERBAIJAN

TURKEY   • Tabriz

TURKMENISTAN

Masuleh•

Gombad-e Kāvus •

☼ TEHRAN

Mashhad •

• Hamadān

IRAQ

AFGHANISTAN

Esfahan • Kuh-e Khajeh

• Yazd

KUWAIT

Shiraz • Persepolis   • Kermān

• Bushehr

• Bam   • Zāhedān

• Bandar-e Abbās

PAKISTAN

SAUDI ARABIA

MAP REF // F7

BEST TIME TO VISIT MARCH TO MAY, SEPTEMBER TO NOVEMBER

A BUSTLING CROWD AROUND THE LUMINOUS HAZRAT-E MASUMEH SHRINE IN QOM

PHOTOGRAPHER MARCUS ROSE / PANOS

A MEETING OF MINDS IN A SYNAGOGUE, TEHRAN

WOMEN WATCHING A SOLAR ECLIPSE IN IMAM SQUARE, ESFAHAN

TEXT ANTHONY HAM

IRAQ

IRAQ MAY HAVE BECOME A BYWORD FOR CONFLICT BUT IT'S ALSO A LAND OF SOARING LANDSCAPES, RESONATING WITH THE GREAT CIVILISATIONS OF HISTORY – WHICH HAVE LEFT BEHIND MANY ANCIENT SITES.

CAPITAL CITY BAGHDAD   POPULATION 26.7 MILLION   AREA 437,070 SQ KM   OFFICIAL LANGUAGES ARABIC, KURDISH

⌃ THE HAPPY OCCASION: A BAGHDAD WEDDING

LANDSCAPE

Iraq is as geographically diverse as its people, dropping steeply from the towering mountains of the northeast down to the western deserts, then through the fertile central plains and all the way to the swamps of the Shatt al-Arab waterway, which empties into the Gulf. Flowing through the country, and dominating Iraqi history, are the Tigris and Euphrates rivers.

HISTORY IN A NUTSHELL

Iraq's early history is like a map of the great civilisations of antiquity – the Sumerians, Babylonians, Assyrians and Persians all ruled large parts of the world from ancient Mesopotamia. From AD 750, the Abbasid caliphate ruled the lands of Islam from their capital in Baghdad, until the Mongols laid waste to the Abbasids and their city in the 13th century. The Ottomans ruled Iraq for centuries, followed briefly by the British before Iraq became independent in 1932. Saddam Hussein seized power in 1979, whereafter he fought wars against his neighbours (such as Iran in the '80s) and his own people (the Kurds) before invading Kuwait and attracting the ire of the US and its allies. After a decade of crippling sanctions, US-led forces invaded Iraq in March 2003. Saddam was quickly defeated, but building a peaceful Iraq is proving infinitely more difficult.

PEOPLE

Three-quarters of the population is Arab, followed by a patchwork of Kurds (15 per cent), Persians (three per cent), Turkomans (two per cent), Yezidis, Assyrians and Chaldeans. Iraqis are predominantly Muslim, but these are divided, often bitterly, between Shiites (around 60 per cent) and Sunnis (around 35 per cent). There are, however, small but historically significant communities of Christians (Chaldeans, Assyrians, Syrian and Roman Catholics, Orthodox Armenians and Jacobites). A dwindling number of Sabaeans, or Mandeans, also remain in Iraq – their religion honours John the Baptist.

MARKETPLACE

Despite abundant oil beneath Iraq's soil, Iraq's economy is a mess, blighted by destroyed infrastructure and the effects of war and sanctions. Annual GDP per capita stands at US$3400, although nationwide figures mean little in a country where there remains a great disparity in peace and security between the regions.

TRADEMARKS

- Cradle of civilisation
- Saddam Hussein the Bogeyman
- Long-suffering people
- Extant ruins from Babylon and Sumeria
- Holy Shiite cities

RANDOM FACTS

- Iraq has a very youth-oriented population, with the average age of locals being 19.7.
- Prior to the US-led invasion, almost all of Iraq's export revenues came from oil.
- The USA now receives more than half of Iraq's exports.
- The average life expectancy at birth for an Iraqi is 58.8 years.

THE MARSH ARABS

For thousands of years, the Marsh Arabs – a Shiite Muslim people – inhabited the swampy, reed-filled marshes of southern Iraq. They lived a self-contained life, cultivating rice, raising cattle and weaving palm products in villages accessible only by water. Perhaps because the Marsh Arabs have always had a reputation for resisting rulers who encroached on their life, Saddam Hussein drained the marshes,

RANKS OF WORSHIPPERS AT THE KADHIMAIN MOSQUE, BAGHDAD

WATER WORLD: MARSH ARABS COLLECTING REEDS

forcing many into exile and placing this unique way of life under threat.

IN ART

○ *The Marsh Arabs*, by Wilfred Thesiger, is a window on the lost world of Marsh Arab life in the 1950s.

○ *The Shi'is of Iraq*, by Yitzhak Nakash, tells you everything you needed to know about Iraq's majority community and the shapers of its future.

○ Two excellent accounts of the 2003 US invasion of Iraq and its aftermath are Asne Seierstad's *A Hundred and One Days: A Baghdad Journal*, and *Salam Pax: The Baghdad Blog*.

○ *Kilometre Zero*, directed by Hiner Saleem, generated much critical acclaim at the 2005 Cannes Film Festival.

○ Kazem al-Sahir is the biggest-selling singer in the world and his 2004 CD *Bare footed* is outstanding.

MYTHS & LEGENDS

When Haroun ar-Rashid (he of Arabian Nights fame) became Abbasid caliph in AD 786, Baghdad had existed for just 24 years. By the time he died in 809, Baghdad was the world's most celebrated city. The caliph transformed Baghdad from a provincial outpost into a city of expansive pleasure gardens, palaces, libraries and distinguished seats of learning where medicine, literature and sciences flourished. His patronage of the arts and translation of texts from across the world ensured the survival of many works of classical literature. Hard as it is now to believe, Baghdad was the richest, most beautiful city in the world.

IMPORT

↗ Invading armies
↗ Security contractors
↗ Foreign correspondents unable to leave their hotels
↗ Once-exiled Iraqi politicians and businesspeople
↗ Foreign insurgents

EXPORT

↖ Shia Islam
↖ Regional instability
↖ More bad news stories than any other country
↖ Writing (invented by the Sumerians)
↖ Humankind – the Garden of Eden is believed to have been in Iraq

FUTURE DIRECTIONS

It is a brave analyst who dares predict Iraq's future. Euphoria among Iraqis over Saddam's demise has given way to fears that the country may plummet into civil war. There are reasons for hope – an elected Iraqi government is now in place and Iraqi security forces are slowly taking over from foreign troops – but Iraqis dream of a future free from foreign intervention and a future as free from the repression of Saddam as from the daily uncertainties and deprivations of the US-led occupation.

⌃ SETTLEMENTS LIKE RAFTS ON THE MARSHES NEAR NASIRIYA

PHOTOGRAPHER GIACOMO PIROZZI // PANOS

PHOTOGRAPHER HIEN LAM DUC // PANOS

ESSENTIAL EXPERIENCES

○ **Finding the Baghdad of legend on the banks of the Tigris River**

○ **Marvelling at the ingenuity of the ancients at the 3rd-century BC Arch of Ctesiphon**

○ **Treading carefully through the ruins of Babylon, the showpiece of ancient Mesopotamia**

○ **Exploring the stunning architecture and polyglot heritage of Mosul**

○ **Admiring the scenic setting of high-altitude Amadiya**

○ **Wondering whatever happened to the Assyrian Empire at the formerly powerful walled city of Nineveh**

⌃ THE DISTINCTIVE SPIRALLING MINARET OF THE MALWIYA MOSQUE

```
TURKEY          ● Zakho
        ● Sinjar  ● Mosul
SYRIA   Ash Sharqat ●   ● Kirkuk
              ● Tekrit
              ● Samarra        IRAN
        ● Rutba    ⊙ BAGHDAD
JORDAN      Kerbala ● ● Babylon
              Najaf ●
                    Nasiriyya ●
                          Basra ●
SAUDI
ARABIA
              KUWAIT
```

MAP REF // C7

BEST TIME TO VISIT MARCH TO MAY, SEPTEMBER TO NOVEMBER

PHOTOGRAPHER MARCO DI LAURO // GETTY

⌃ IRAQIS KICKING UP THEIR HEELS AT AN AMUSEMENT PARK

PAST AND PRESENT COLLIDE IN RURAL IRAQ

PRIMARY SCHOOL STUDENTS RALLY BEHIND THE IRAQI FLAG

TEXT JENNY WALKER

LANDSCAPE

Much of Kuwait's 185 kilometre by 208 kilometre landmass comprises a gravel plain with little or no water. Rains encourage a brief blush of vegetation each spring before the extreme summer arrives to take its revenge. Kuwait's redeeming feature is a long coast of sandy bays, dunes and marshes, with nine offshore islands.

HISTORY IN A NUTSHELL

Attracted to the confluence of two great rivers, Stone Age man settled on the northern shores of Kuwait Bay from 4500 BC. The Bronze Age people of Dilmun followed suit on Failaka Island, which the Greeks turned into an important trading post from the 3rd to 1st centuries BC. Kuwait City grew out of Bedouin encampments on the mainland, swelling with summer nomads. By 1760 the city's permanent inhabitants, including the current ruling family Al-Sabah, had built up an impressive seafaring trade. The Kuwaitis repulsed many foreign incursions, including an attack on the Red Fort by the Saudis. Under the rule of Mubarak the Great (r 1896–1915), the British were enlisted to keep piracy and the Turks at bay. With the discovery of oil, Kuwait was transformed into a modern state, and declared independence in 1961. In 1990, Saddam Hussein invaded after accusing Kuwait of stealing Iraqi oil

KUWAIT

COUCHED IN ONE OF THE MOST CONTESTED CORNERS OF THE WORLD, THE CITY-STATE OF KUWAIT HAS REINVENTED ITSELF AS A DYNAMIC COUNTRY IN THE 21ST CENTURY.

CAPITAL CITY KUWAIT CITY   POPULATION 2.4 MILLION   AREA 17,820 SQ KM   OFFICIAL LANGUAGE ARABIC

MOVING OUT OF A 'MILITARY EXCLUSION ZONE', NORTH OF KUWAIT CITY

from an oilfield that straddled the border. In a bombing campaign named Desert Storm, Allied forces drove the Iraqis out, but not before many pipelines had been torched. Despite the regeneration of Kuwait since the invasion, the ongoing hostilities in Iraq are menacing this otherwise vibrant city-state.

PEOPLE

Kuwait's population is comprised of 37 per cent Kuwaitis, many of Bedouin ancestry, and 63 per cent expatriates. Despite one or two inland communities, Kuwait is best described as a coastal city-state. Most Kuwaitis are Sunni Muslims but there is a substantial Shiite minority – a source of concern given tensions across the border.

MARKETPLACE

Despite the cost of rebuilding after the invasion, Kuwait has a robust economy thanks to its ownership of 10 per cent of the world's oil reserves. Banking, overseas investment and the largest cargo fleet in the world also contribute to the country's thriving condition.

TRADEMARKS

- Kuwait Towers
- Frequent bullying by neighbours
- Oil installations
- Market, ancient and modern
- Infinite beaches

SURPRISES

- In Kuwait, water is more valuable and expensive than oil.
- The Oil Display Centre in Al-Ahmadi is interesting even for those without a PhD in geology.
- Modern Kuwait City displays few visible wounds of its battering in the 1990s invasion.

URBAN SCENE

Kuwait City is the heart and soul of the country. It is the moneybags, port and harbour, traditional shelter for nomadic herdspeople, purveyor of luxury goods and upholstered sofas, the Kew garden of plastic flowers and the Acapulco of nonalcoholic cocktails. If it isn't happening in Kuwait City, then it must be oil extraction.

RANDOM FACTS

- The oil slick that resulted from Iraqi sabotage of Kuwait's Sea Island Terminal measured 64 kilometres by 160 kilometres.
- Kuwait is an enormous, densely packed city, measuring 25 kilometres by 12 kilometres.
- The public chewing of gum is banned during Ramadan.

CULTURE

There are few visible relics in Kuwait City but that's not to say there is no history. The spirit of the past lives on in rituals such as the *diwaniya* (gathering), where men take up position in tents outside each

other's houses and sip sweet tea – much in the manner of their Bedouin forefathers, escaping the heat of the summer plains.

ENVIRONMENTAL REGENERATION

The oil spillages from 65 million barrels of oil, which covered 50 square kilometres of desert, appeared to be one wound of the Iraqi invasion that would never heal. With the help of the Japanese, however, the oil has been turned into soil good enough for blooms of hope.

ESSENTIAL EXPERIENCES

- Marvelling at a 'city restored' from the iconic Kuwait Towers
- Making exciting ethnographic connections at Tareq Rajab Museum
- Planting a smacker on a black-spotted sweetlips in the Scientific Centre aquarium
- Dining in style on the *Al-Hashemi II*, the world's largest wooden boat
- Pausing for a sobering reminder of war at the Al-Qurain Martyrs' Museum
- Wading into the sunrise on one of Kuwait's fine beaches

MAP REF · D7

BEST TIME TO VISIT OCTOBER TO APRIL

STUCK IN TRAFFIC – WITH TIME TO TAKE IN ELECTION PUBLICITY – SALMIYA

COME FLY WITH ME: CHILDREN TAKE TO THE SKY WITH KITES, KUWAIT CITY

SAUDI ARABIA

SAUDI ARABIA, ONE OF TRAVEL'S LAST FRONTIERS, AMPLY REWARDS THOSE WHO FIND THEIR WAY PAST THE FORMIDABLE BARRIERS TO ENTRY WITH CORAL CITIES BY THE SEA, STUNNING MOUNTAINS AND RUINS TO RIVAL THE BEST IN THE MIDDLE EAST.

CAPITAL CITY RIYADH   POPULATION 27 MILLION   AREA 1.9 MILLION SQ KM   OFFICIAL LANGUAGE ARABIC

LANDSCAPE

Saudi Arabia, which is roughly comparable to the size of Western Europe, is dominated by the Nafud Desert in the north and the Empty Quarter (Rub al-Khali or Abode of Silence) in the south. The flat salt plains of the Gulf coastline are a world away from the Red Sea coastline in the west. The latter is overlooked by precipitous mountains which soar up to Jebel Soudah in the southwestern Asir Highlands, a northeastern outpost of Africa's Great Rift Valley.

HISTORY IN A NUTSHELL

The Nabataeans, a people of Bedouin origin, dominated the frankincense caravan trade 2000 years ago in northern Arabia, resulting in their spectacular cities of Petra (in Jordan) and Madain Saleh. The Prophet Mohammed was born in Mecca in AD 570 and by the time he died in AD 632 he had overseen the birth of Islam. Mecca and Medina became the two holiest cities of Islam and were ruled over by the Umayyads, Abbasids and the Ottomans. In the 18th century, a pact between Mohammed ibn Abd al-Wahhab and the royal Al-Saud family laid the foundations of modern Saudi Arabia in a marriage of conservative Islam and Al-Saud political power. The

discovery of oil in the 20th century grafted fabulous wealth onto what is still a traditional Bedouin society.

PEOPLE

Indigenous Saudis are overwhelmingly Arabs, although around 5.5 million inhabitants (more than 20 per cent of the population) are non-Saudis whose presence in the kingdom depends on temporary work contracts. Islam is the state religion and, officially, all Saudis are Muslim.

MARKETPLACE

Saudi Arabia is the world's largest oil producer, with 25 per cent of known reserves and annual export revenues in excess of US$70 billion. However, one quarter of the Saudi workforce is unemployed and one of the fastest population growth rates in the world has seen GDP per-capita income fall to US$12,800, less than half what it was in the 1980s; in neighbouring UAE, the figure is US$43,400, while the average Yemeni takes home just US$900.

TRADEMARKS

○ Home of Islam
○ Lawrence of Arabia
○ Astonishing oil wealth
○ Uneasy coexistence of tradition and modernity
○ Women in all-encompassing *abeyya*
○ Camels and endless seas of sand

WILD THINGS

The Arabian oryx, which is believed to have spawned the unicorn myth, is Saudi Arabia's most iconic animal but for most of the past century it has stood at the brink of extinction, and it even disappeared from the wild altogether in the early 1970s. Fortunately, a captive breeding programme has proven so successful that 149 oryx have been released into the Rub al-Khali since 1995 and up to 500 oryx are now believed to survive in the wild.

RANDOM FACTS

○ Al-Hasa oasis, near al-Hofuf, is the largest oasis in the world, with two million palm trees.
○ The number of seats in government held by women is zero.
○ The proportion of Saudi territory covered by desert is 95 per cent.
○ Oil accounts for 90 per cent of Saudi export revenues.

A MICROCOSMOS AT JIDDAH

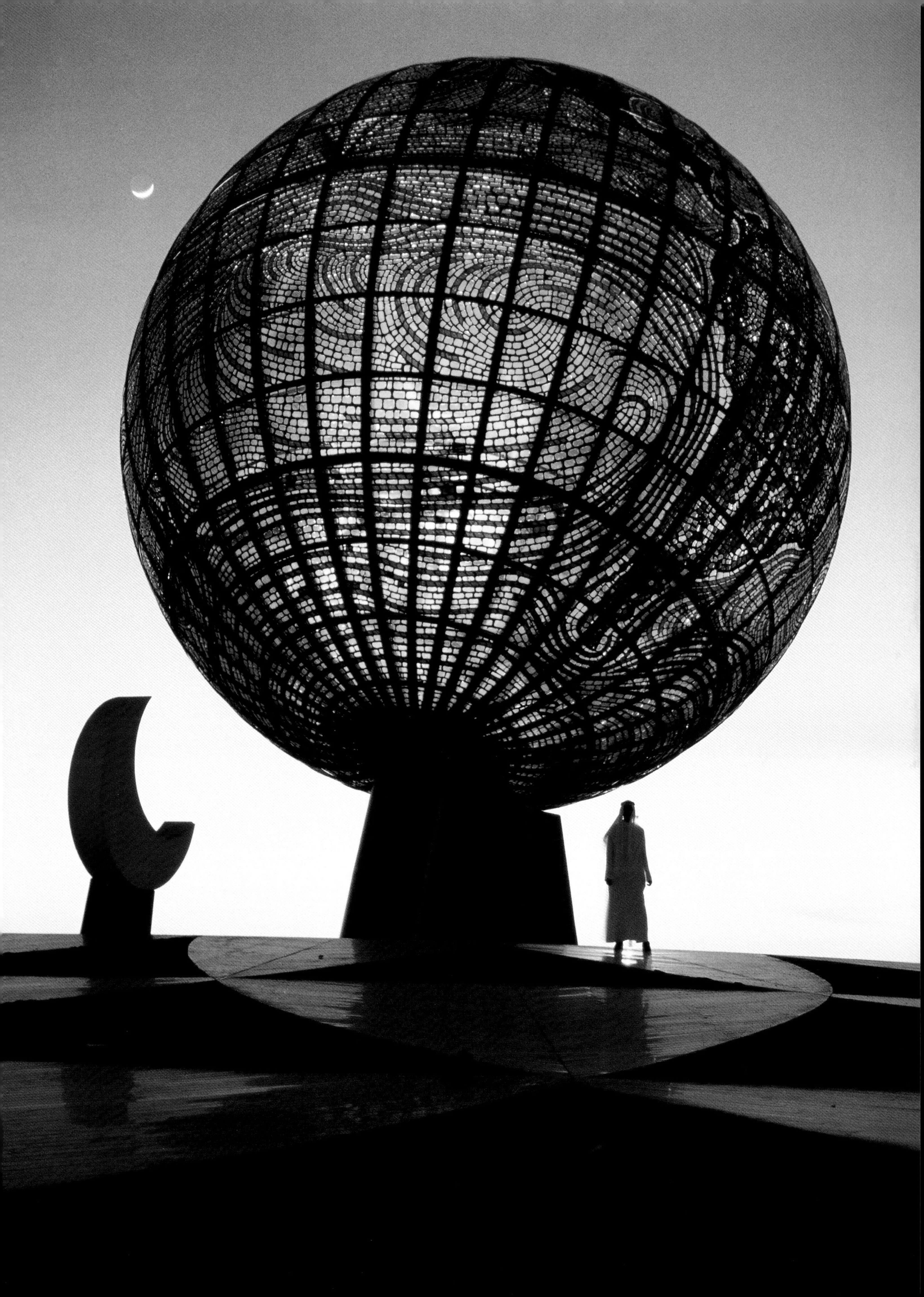

⌃ A HIGH POINT: A PILGRIM GIRL PRAYS ON JEBEL AL-NOOR, THE 'MOUNT OF LIGHT', SIX KILOMETRES FROM MECCA

PHOTOGRAPHER ANDREW TESTA PANOS

⌃ A MONUMENT TO THE COAST, RED SEA

⌃ THE MASSIVE KINGDOM TOWER ALMOST BLENDS INTO THE SKY, RIYADH

PHOTOGRAPHER ABID KATIB / GETTY

PHOTOGRAPHER KAZUYOSHI NOMACHI / CORBIS

GLEAMING SURFACES INSIDE THE MOSQUE OF THE PROPHET, MEDINA

PHOTOGRAPHER JEREMY HORNER / PANOS

THE PALM-TREE PLUMAGE OF THE OASIS OF NAJRAN

PHOTOGRAPHER TOR EIGELAND / CORBIS

THE MOTHER OF ALL MILK MOUSTACHES

NATURAL BEAUTY

Saudi Arabia's variety of landscapes can be a breathtaking surprise. The Empty Quarter is home to some of the most lonely but magnificent desert terrain in the world, with vast sand seas daily fashioned to perfection by the wind. In the north, particularly around Madain Saleh, the orange desert sands offer up fantastic stone monoliths. In the country's southwest, layered horizons of rocky peaks plunge down to the Red Sea coastline where, just offshore, coral reefs promise some of the best diving and snorkelling in the world.

IMPORT

↗ Big American cars
↗ 5.5 million foreign workers
↗ 3.5 million Muslim pilgrims every year
↗ Almost 100 per cent of the country's food
↗ Explorers like Wilfred Thesiger, Bertram Thomas and Sir Richard Burton

EXPORT

↖ Islam
↖ Osama bin Laden and 15 of the 19 September 11 hijackers
↖ The oil and natural gas that keeps the world running
↖ Saudi princes spending big in Europe
↖ A lurid genre of sensational royal family exposés

ON PAPER

○ *Arabian Sands*, by Wilfred Thesiger, is a classic in the canon of Arabian exploration.
○ *Cities of Salt*, by Abdelrahman Munif, is an evocative novel that traces the impact of oil on traditional Saudi society.
○ *Seven Pillars of Wisdom*, by TE Lawrence, gave birth to the Lawrence of Arabia myth and is a wonderful read.
○ *Voices of Change*, by Abu Bakr Bagader (ed), contains short stories by Saudi Arabian women.

THE BEDOUIN

Saudi Arabia's nomadic Bedouin people form the bedrock of Saudi society and their *ardha* (sword dance) is the national dance of Saudi Arabia. The Bedouin of the Najd (north of Riyadh) have always considered themselves the true Arabs, with their ancestral roots in Bedouin nobility. Those of the Hejaz are generally more cosmopolitan after 14 centuries of continual interaction and intermarriage with pilgrims. Despite the oil-fuelled rush to the cities, up to three million Bedouin still claim to live a nomadic existence.

URBAN SCENE

Riyadh has one foot planted firmly in the past; the other is pressed down hard on the accelerator as the city rushes headlong into the future. In the heart of old Riyadh, the Masmak Fortress is mud-brick and has stood at the heart of Saudi Arabian life for centuries, while elsewhere the extensive mud ruins of Dir'aiyah mark the spiritual heartland of the ruling Al-Saud family. At the same time, the Riyadh skyline is dominated by the sci-fi apparitions of the Kingdom and al-Faisaliah Towers, as young Saudi men race through the streets in the latest American cars. It's an at times unsettling, at times intoxicating mix.

SURPRISES

○ The adult female literacy rate is almost 71 per cent.
○ Osama bin Laden's Saudi citizenship was revoked in 1994.
○ Around 60 per cent of the Saudi population is under 15 years old.
○ Saudi Arabia's external debt is US$34.55 billion.

FUTURE DIRECTIONS

Modern Saudi Arabia finds itself at odds with both itself and the outside world, all the while struggling to balance its traditional past with its oil-rich present. The result is a profound uncertainty over the kingdom's future and a power struggle between conservative and liberal forces within the Saudi royal family. Saudi Arabia has enough oil reserves to last for 70 years, meaning that the prize is as great for whoever wins as the consequences are significant for the rest of us.

PHOTOGRAPHER REZA / GETTY

ESSENTIAL EXPERIENCES

- **Exploring the extraordinary rock-hewn tombs of the ancient Nabataean city of Madain Saleh**

- **Meandering through the souqs and coral-built houses in the Red Sea port of Jeddah**

- **Riding the cable car down the cliffs to the hanging village of Habalah**

- **Following in the footsteps of Wilfred Thesiger by venturing deep into the Empty Quarter (Rub al-Khali)**

- **Exploring the Yemeni-style palace and multistorey mud-brick fortress houses of Najran**

- **Experiencing Saudi Arabia in microcosm in Riyadh, where old and new collide at breakneck speed**

- **Diving the coral reefs off the Red Sea coast**

MAP REF   D8

BEST TIME TO VISIT JANUARY TO FEBRUARY

⌃ A CAMEL GIVES ITS OWNER A BIG WET ONE

AN AUSTERE ALCOVE AT THE NAJRAN FORT

SCULPTURES OF ANTIQUE ARABIC LAMPS ARE ILLUMINATED IN JIDDAH

BAHRAIN

A FORMER CENTRE OF THE PEARLING INDUSTRY AND NOW A HUB FOR MODERN ENTERTAINMENTS, BAHRAIN HAS ONE OF THE EASIEST-GOING LIFESTYLES IN THE GULF.

CAPITAL CITY **MANAMA**   POPULATION 698,590   AREA 665 SQ KM   OFFICIAL LANGUAGE **ARABIC**

LANDSCAPE

Bahrain consists of an archipelago of 33 mostly flat, gravel islands, including the disputed Hawar Islands and spits of sand appearing above low tide. The country is fearfully hot and humid in the summer (May to September) but pleasant during the rest of the year.

HISTORY IN A NUTSHELL

Settlement on Bahrain Island dates from 10,000 BC but the period of greatest archaeological interest revolves around the Dilmun civilisation (3200–330 BC). This organised copper-trading society was highly religious, as the Temple of Barbar, tombs and burial mounds dotted around Bahrain Island indicate. Dilmun was absorbed by the empire of Babylon, and the Greeks settled in the area for a while. Much of Bahrain's subsequent history remains indistinct until the 16th century. A thriving pearl industry attracted the Portuguese, who built a classic fort, Qal'at al-Bahrain, to protect their interest only to be ousted in 1602 by the Persians. The current ruling family, the Al-Khalifa, arrived in the mid-18th century; anxious to keep piracy and the Turks at bay, they struck a treaty with the United Kingdom, remaining under British protection until independence in 1971. After the collapse of the pearl market in the 1930s, Bahrain was rescued from economic depression by the discovery of oil. As the forerunner of the black-gold phenomenon, Bahrain set the standard for modernisation under the leadership of the Al-Khalifa family. When the oil began to run out, however, civil unrest followed, with demands for greater democracy. The government relented in part and today Bahrain has a constitutional democracy and is enjoying a period of economic success.

PEOPLE

Bahrain's population (half of which is under 25) is concentrated in one-third of one island, a fact likely to change as the urban sprawl is pushed southwards. Most Bahrainis are Arab, though many are partially of Persian descent. The majority are Shiite Muslim, but the Al-Khalifa family leads a sizable minority of Sunnis.

TRADEMARKS

○ Natural pearls
○ Formula 1
○ Nodding donkeys
○ Ancient burial mounds
○ Tatrees (traditional embroidery)

MARKETPLACE

Thanks to early steps to diversify the economy, Bahrain is now an important offshore banking centre and focus of international investment. Alongside oil, gas and heavy industry, tourism, given a boost by the success of the Grand Prix, is generating a tidy revenue.

IMPORT

○ Expatriate workers
○ Tolerant attitudes to foreigners
○ Michael Jackson
○ Saudi Arabian holidaymakers
○ Food – there's little agricultural land

EXPORT

○ Oil, as the first country in the Gulf to strike black gold
○ Wild pearls
○ Ceremonial gowns with tatrees
○ People – Bahrain has long been a transit hub

WILD THINGS

Nourished by sweet water springs, Bahrain's oyster beds deliver pearls that display a highly prized distinctive hue and depth of lustre. Bahrain may not have much in the way of wild things to speak of, but since the collapse of commercial diving, it is floating on pearls.

RANDOM FACTS

○ There are 85,000 burial mounds in Bahrain, occupying five per cent of the country's landmass
○ Opened in 2004, the Grand Prix Stadium took 7000 people and 3.5 million hours of labour to build
○ King Fahd Causeway, linking Bahrain to Saudi Arabia, has 12,430 metres of viaducts
○ At its peak, the pearl trade employed 2500 dhows

MYTHS & LEGENDS

For many centuries people have speculated on the precise geographical location of paradise on earth. Although the landscape of the present day doesn't much resemble the fabled garden, Bahrain is indicated to be the original Garden of Eden in the *Epic of Gilgamesh*, the world's oldest poetic saga, as well as in the Old Testament itself. Whether it is true or not, it's a myth that has certainly tickled the fancy of Bahrain's Tourist Board.

ESSENTIAL EXPERIENCES

○ **Bargaining for rags and riches around Bab al-Bahrain**

○ **Catching the breeze in Muharraq Island's wind-towers**

○ **Sniffing the excitement – and the high-octane – at the Formula 1 Grand Prix**

○ **Delving into history to find pearls in shallow waters**

○ **Watching pigeons wheel above the humps and bumps of the Royal Tombs**

MAP REF   E8

BEST TIME TO VISIT **OCTOBER TO APRIL**

THE TENDER TRAP: A MAN MAKING FISHING NETS ON SITRA ISLAND

PHOTOGRAPHER TIM GRAHAM / ALAMY

PHOTOGRAPHER MICHAEL JENNER / ALAMY

A YOUNG GIRL SPARKLES IN TRADITIONAL FINERY

CONDUCTING THE BUSINESS OF LIFE IN A *MANAMA* SHOP

TEXT JENNY WALKER

LANDSCAPE

About 160 kilometres long and 80 kilometres wide, and surrounded on three sides by water, much of Qatar's landmass is comprised of flat gravel plains. Through a phenomenon called geological uplift, the bedrock of the country has risen by two metres in 400 years while the water table has sunk correspondingly. As a result, there is little natural vegetation. Spectacular sand dunes ring the inlet at Khor al-Adaid on the Saudi border. Between May and September temperatures are extreme, with 90 per cent humidity and sandstorms. The winter months are pleasant, with chill evenings and occasional rainy days.

HISTORY IN A NUTSHELL

The peninsula has been inhabited from 4000 BC, but other than a mention by Herodotus and Ptolemy, there is little documentation of Qatar's early history. Qatar played an important role in the spread of Islam by transporting sea-faring jihad warriors. In the 16th century, the Portuguese were expelled by the Turks, who remained there for the following four centuries. The dynamic Al-Thani family, the present-day rulers of Qatar, arrived in the mid-18th century and laid the foundations of the modern capital, Doha. Under British protection, the Al-Thanis ousted the Turks. Qatar finally proclaimed independence in 1971.

QATAR

THINK OF QATAR AND ONE CAN'T HELP BUT PICTURE THE SOPHISTICATED, SPORTS-CONSCIOUS CAPITAL CITY, DOHA, WHICH ASPIRES TO BE THE GULF'S NEXT FASHIONABLE DESTINATION.

CAPITAL CITY **DOHA**   POPULATION **885,360**   AREA **11,430 SQ KM**   OFFICIAL LANGUAGE **ARABIC**

OLD-FASHIONED HORSEPOWER VERSUS THE PELOTON IN THE TOUR DE QATAR

The discovery of oil in the 1930s changed the fortunes of the country, turning it from an impoverished backwater to one of the richest per-capita countries in the world. Under the guidance of Sheikh Khalifa, it gained one of the world's most all-encompassing welfare states. Sheikh Hamad unceremoniously replaced his father in 1995 and propelled the country into the 21st century.

PEOPLE
Qatar's small indigenous population is of Najdi (central Arabian) ancestry, followers of the austere Wahhabi sect of Islam. Almost 50 per cent of Qatar's population lives in the capital, where locals are generally outnumbered by expatriate workers.

MARKETPLACE
Qatar has one of the fastest-growing economies in the world thanks to its ownership of almost six per cent of the world's natural gas reserves.

TRADEMARKS
- High-profile sporting events
- Camel racing
- Falconry
- A sea of sand
- The clack of prayer beads

URBAN SCENE
Ice-skating in midsummer heat, shopping for peregrine falcons, watching football in a coffee shop, paddling in the shallows, an evening of jazz, rugby or line-dancing: these are some of the many and varied pleasures of Doha.

RANDOM FACTS
- The 33-piece 'dhikr' necklet of Islamic prayer beads, each representing a name or attribute of Allah, are traditionally used by men but strung by women.
- About 2000 falcons are trained for sport or hunting each year.
- When Al-Jazeera Independent Satellite TV Channel went online, it received a staggering 611 million emails in the first year, making it one of the 50 most-visited websites in the world.

MYTHS & LEGENDS
The ancient art of falconry is a favourite pastime in Qatar. Falconry dates back to the 7th century BC when, according to tradition, the violent king of Persia was captivated by the sight of a falcon catching a bird on the wing. He netted the falcon to learn more of its grace and beauty and his study of the bird's nature transformed him into a calm and wise ruler.

FUTURE DIRECTIONS
Modern Qatar, with its increasingly vocal contribution to Gulf politics, economy and culture, is proving itself a regional force to be reckoned with. By hosting international sporting events and investing in luxury modern resorts and malls, Doha may yet come to rival the booming cities of neighbouring Gulf states.

SURPRISES
- Alcohol is not illegal.
- Women are free to drive and work.
- Although most of Qatar is desert, it has only a small section of sand dunes.
- 'We wish you a merry Christmas' is a popular mobile ring-tone.

ESSENTIAL EXPERIENCES

- **Jogging with the latest iPod along Doha's corniche (coastal road)**
- **Parading a strong backhand on the tennis courts of Doha's luxurious resorts**
- **Spending a day at the races at the camel track in Al-Shahhainiya**
- **Lazing under the stars by the inland sea of Khor al-Adaid**
- **Camping by the shallow waters and fascinating rock formations at Bir Zekreet**

MAP REF // E8

BEST TIME TO VISIT **OCTOBER TO MARCH**

A MONUMENT TO PERFUME (OR 'I DREAM OF JEANNIE') IN DOHA

WOMEN ABSORBED IN THE NEWS WHILE SELLING CARPETS

LARA DUNSTON & TERRY CARTER

UNITED ARAB EMIRATES

THE UAE OFFERS THE BEST OF BOTH WORLDS: AN EXOTIC EAST ROOTED IN BEDOUIN CULTURE, A TOLERANT ISLAM AND THE SUBLIME ARABIAN SANDS, COMBINED WITH THE BEST OF WESTERN MODERNITY.

CAPITAL CITY ABU DHABI   POPULATION 4.3 MILLION   AREA 88,880 SQ KM   OFFICIAL LANGUAGE ARABIC

ANCIENT *DHOWS* FRAME MODERN BUILDINGS AT DUBAI CREEK

LANDSCAPE

Comprised of barren coastal plains, rolling sand dunes, flat arid desert and dramatic mountains, the UAE has a climate that's harsh for much of the year, and in summer (June to August) the temperature can reach 48°C with 95 per cent humidity. The ocean offers little relief, being only around 10°C cooler. Despite this heat, there's a surprising amount of fauna and flora here and it's a haven for migratory birds.

HISTORY IN A NUTSHELL

Archaeological evidence exists of humans living here as far back as 8000 BC and of cultivation of date palms from around 2500 BC. Islam and Arabic arrived with the Umayyads in the 7th century. European nations took advantage of the UAE's strategic position on the trade route to India, until the British East India Company, which established trading links in 1616, took control. In 1892 the British reinforced their power through 'exclusive agreements' with the sheikhs, and the region became the Trucial Coast. After tough times early in the 20th century, oil began to flow in Abu Dhabi in 1962 and in Dubai from 1969. In 1968 the British attempted to create a state encompassing the Trucial States, Bahrain and Qatar. Despite setbacks, the leader of Abu Dhabi, Sheikh Zayed bin

Sultan al-Nayan persisted and the federation of the United Arab Emirates (UAE) was born on 2 December 1971, with Sheikh Zayed as president.

PEOPLE

The bulk of people live in the rich emirates of Abu Dhabi and Dubai, with everyone else in the poorer emirates: Sharjah, Ajman, Ras al-Khaimah, Fujairah, and Umm al-Qaiwain. Officially, Emiratis comprise 20 per cent of the population but many estimate it's closer to 10 per cent. This makes it a thoroughly multicultural country, with expatriates from all over the world. The downside, of course, is that Emiratis are diminishing in number and losing their culture. While Arabic is the official language, English is widely spoken, and you can hear everything from Urdu to Tagalog in the streets.

MARKETPLACE

Currently experiencing a period of sustained growth, the UAE's GDP grew by over seven per cent in 2004 (well above the world average) and its GDP per capita was around US$20,400. While it's assumed the bulk of revenue comes from oil, non-oil industries now comprise 72 per cent of GDP. In terms of diversification, Dubai is a leading light, with

phenomenal success in tourism, financial services, media and shipping.

TRADEMARKS

» Sheikh Zayed, father of the country
» The ubiquitous camel
» Bedouin hospitality
» Oil wealth
» Majestic falcons
» Red desert sands
» Elegant veiled women
» Burj al-Arab, Dubai's iconic, 321-metre-high sail-shaped hotel

ECOTOURISM

The UAE might appear more interested in theme parks than national parks, but the Dubai Desert Conservation Reserve (DDCR) encompasses nearly five per cent of the entire Dubai emirate. In 1997, a 27-square-kilometre area was allocated to create an eco-desert resort in the spirit of an African safari lodge, and al-Maha Desert Resort & Spa opened in 1999. To reintroduce native fauna, native flora was replanted in the reserve, and descendants of a herd of Arabian oryx sent to Arizona in the 1960s were returned, along with several other species, to great success.

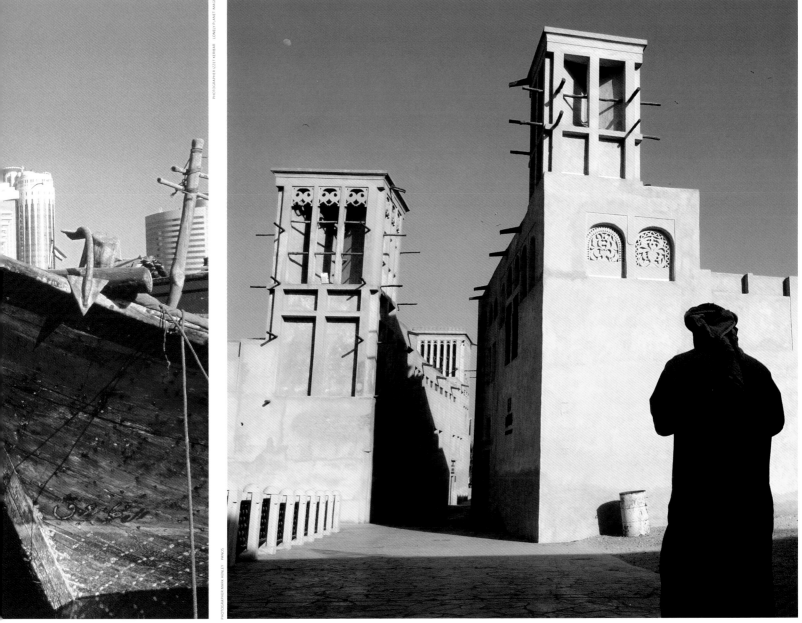

PHOTOGRAPHER IZZET KERIBAR LONELY PLANET IMAGES

PHOTOGRAPHER MARK HENLEY PANOS

THE AIR CONDITIONING OF OLD: WIND TOWERS IN THE RESTORED BASTAKIA QUARTER, BUR DUBAI

URBAN SCENE

The UAE's two largest cities are multicultural and cosmopolitan, yet couldn't be further apart in feel. Abu Dhabi is the New York to Dubai's LA. Abu Dhabi may be the oil-rich national capital but it's the country's cultural and intellectual heart, with glamorous Dubai being the centre of business. While Abu Dhabi clings to its traditions, in Dubai an alternative arts scene and DJ culture are flourishing, and a young Emirati fashion scene is growing.

CULTURE

The Arab culture, Bedouin heritage and Islamic religion permeate everyday life, making Emiratis the region's most social, hospitable and tolerant people. They adapt well to change, their way of business is based on risk-taking, and they're generally adventurous (watch them drive!), but their dress is modest and customs conservative. Visitors shouldn't take advantage of this. Dress respectfully, don't photograph women, and don't eat in public during the day in Ramadan – you'll increase your chances of meeting locals and leave all the richer.

SURPRISES

○ The country can go for a couple of years without significant rain.

○ However, in 2005 it actually snowed!

TOP FESTIVAL

The Dubai Shopping Festival started as a way to promote retail trade and today sees hordes of shopping-mad tourists fill Dubai's hotels, malls and restaurants in January and February. The great weather, festival events, nightly fireworks and huge discounts are key attractions. But the best fun is the

kitsch Global Village, with daily cultural performances mixed with a little (you guessed it!) shopping. Flush with success, Dubai started Summer Surprises (July and August) – the shopping is the same, the surprise is doing it in 45°C temperatures!

RANDOM FACTS

○ The UAE is one of the world's fastest growing countries.

○ Its citizens are entitled to free housing, health care and education.

○ The country has the world's fifth largest oil reserves.

○ Women comprise over 50 per cent of the university student population but only 30 per cent of the workforce.

○ There are about four million mobile phone subscriptions – nearly one for every person.

○ The country had 40 million date palms at last count.

○ Young Emirati women eat hot chilli sauce with everything and are known to carry it in their Gucci handbags!

FUTURE DIRECTIONS

The UAE's main focus is continued rapid growth and securing its post-oil economy; however, the dependence on a foreign workforce to perform the majority of work (particularly in the private sector, where UAE nationals are virtually nonexistent) is of concern. While Emirati traditions currently remain strong, the shrinking number of Emiratis means that keeping its culture alive could be the UAE's biggest challenge yet.

△ ALWAYS CONNECTED IN DUBAI

PHOTOGRAPHER TARIK ALAMY

PHOTOGRAPHER MARK HENLEY PANOS

△ ALL THAT GLITTERS IN THE GOLD SOUQ, DUBAI

PHOTOGRAPHER HUGH SITTON PHOTOGRAPHY ALAMY

○ THE BURJ AL ARAB HOTEL READY FOR TAKE-OFF, DUBAI

ESSENTIAL EXPERIENCES

● **Shopping the souqs for gold, spices, carpets and Burj Al-Arab paperweights**

○ **Taking a 50 fil (US$0.15) *abra* (boat) ride across bustling Dubai Creek**

○ **Dipping into the crystal-clear waters of the Arabian Sea**

○ **Having some henna done or smoking some *sheesha* (water pipe)**

○ **Heading to Al-Ain's dusty camel souq, then strolling through the cool shady date-palm oases**

○ **Driving the east coast from Dibba's fishing village of Fujairah for the Friday bullfights**

OMAN
Ras al-Khaimah
Umm al-Qaiwain
Sharjah
Dubai Fujairah
QATAR Sharjah Desert Park

ABU DHABI

Ruwais
Al-Ain

OMAN

SAUDI ARABIA

MAP REF :: F9

BEST TIME TO VISIT **NOVEMBER TO MARCH**

PHOTOGRAPHER MARK HENLEY PANOS

PHOTOGRAPHER LANA SLEZIC PANOS

A NETWORK OF CRANES AT THE CONSTRUCTION SITE OF THE BURJ DUBAI TOWER LOOM OVER THE AL-MUROOJ COMPLEX

A DIFFERENT SORT OF CAMEL RIDE AT A CAMEL MARKET

TEXT JENNY WALKER

OMAN

RESPECTFUL OF ITS RICH NATURAL AND CULTURAL HERITAGE, OMAN IS A MODERN ARAB COUNTRY WITH TRADITIONAL VALUES.

CAPITAL CITY **MUSCAT**   POPULATION **3.1 MILLION**   AREA **212,460 SQ KM**   OFFICIAL LANGUAGE **ARABIC**

AL-JALALI FORT COMMANDS A FORMIDABLE DEFENSIVE POSITION, MUSCAT

LANDSCAPE

Oman forms the eastern part of the Arabian Peninsula, an area of arid deserts and desolate mountains. It comprises gravel plains, sand dunes, a portion of the Empty Quarter (Rub al-Khali) and 2000 kilometres of coastline. Abundant springs create pockets of vegetation in the wadis and oases, supportive of a rich flora and fauna. In the winter, hailstones pelt the northern mountains, while in summer, temperatures on the plains soar to extremes. Dhofar, the southern region of Oman, has its own microclimate, with light rain and fog in summer that turn the desert green.

HISTORY IN A NUTSHELL

Oman's ancient existence was due to the lucrative frankincense trade. This precious commodity, produced from the aromatic sap of *Boswellia sacra*, a tree that grows best on the hillsides of Dhofar, was traded across the Indian Ocean from as early as 5000 BC. Islam was embraced in the 7th century AD. The Bani Nabhan dynasty ruled from 1154 to 1624, a period characterised by frequent wars and tussles with the Portuguese. However, by 1650 Oman began to enjoy peace and prosperity, marked by cultural achievement and spectacular fort-building. This resulted, by the 19th century, in a sizable empire that included parts of the African coast. Oman's colonial interests diminished in the 20th century, however, and a rift developed between coastal Oman, ruled by the sultan, and the interior, ruled by religious leaders. Sultan Said, with British assistance, reunified the country through the Jebel Wars of the 1950s but his isolationist policies turned Oman into a backwater. In a dramatic palace coup in July 1970, Said's son, Qaboos, took the throne. Since then, Sultan Qaboos has helped Oman blossom into a modern nation in what is aptly described as the 'Renaissance'.

PEOPLE

Oman's population is predominantly Arab, with 80 per cent belonging to the austere Ibadi sect of Islam. The country's colonial past has led to intermarriage with Swahili-speaking East Africans and Baluchi-speaking Iranians. The population also includes distinct ethnic groups, like the mountain-dwelling Jebbalis of Dhofar and the Bedouins of the Empty Quarter.

MARKETPLACE

In comparison with its neighbours, Oman has limited oil reserves. Since 1970, therefore, efforts to diversify the country's economy have been encouraged, with agriculture along the Batinah coast and port projects in Sohar and Salalah. Investing in human resources is seen as the key to self-sufficiency, and to this end all Omanis are given free education. 'Omanisation' (replacing expatriate staff with home-grown labour) is actively practised.

TRADEMARKS

- Frankincense trees
- Nesting turtles
- Off-road exploration
- Camel-rearing in the sand dunes
- 1000 forts and castles
- Pristine 2000-kilometre coastline

NATURAL BEAUTY

Curvaceous sand dunes throw long shadows at sunset, and the mountains are spliced with slivers of green plantation. Terraces and orchards wrap around the flanks of rust-red hillsides, while phosphorescent waters are spangled with stars by night and patrolled by squid, cuttlefish and rays by day.

WILD THINGS

Oman is home to some of the region's most endangered species. The Arabian leopard is protected in the wilderness of Jebel Samhan; the oryx was

A CASUAL AFTERNOON ON THE MUSANDAM PENINSULA

successfully reintroduced to the Jiddat al-Harasis in the 1980s; Ras al-Jinz is a nesting site of international importance for the green turtle.

URBAN SCENE

With a backbone of mountains and a belly of attractive beaches, plus fashionable hotels and souqs for coffee-sipping, Muscat is one of Arabia's understated delights. Main towns, like Nizwa and Sur, celebrate continuity with the past; Salalah, the semi-tropical summertime capital of the south, has leafy shoulders in an English county and rhythmic hips in Zanzibar.

MYTHS & LEGENDS

Any Omani sailor worth his salt will tell you that Sinbad of Arabian Nights fame was of Omani origin. The adventures of Sinbad are still played out in myth and reality: in 1980, the British explorer Tim Severin and an Omani crew set sail in the *Sohar*, a *dhow* made from palm trees and without a single nail, on an eight-month journey to Canton in China, earning this traditional sailing vessel legendary status.

CUISINE

Forget coffee-shop *shwarmas* and camel kebabs: Omani cuisine is all about home-cooking. A visitor to an Omani household is usually entertained with a fruit-paring extravaganza by the host, featuring pomegranates from Jebel Akhdar. With any luck, it will be followed by *shuwa*, melt-in-the-mouth mutton marinated in syrups, wrapped in banana leaves and baked in the hot earth of the summer desert. The meal may conclude with dates, cardamom coffee and that all-important Omani sweetmeat made from sugar and rose-water: halvah.

FUTURE DIRECTIONS

Oman is anxious to embrace the best parts of the modern world through industrialisation and a continually improving infrastructure of education, health care and roads. Nevertheless, the country nevertheless remains mindful of its cultural and religious values: indeed, this is one nation in the region that has refused to sell its soul to commercial interests. With progressive measures in place to protect its pristine environment, it's likely that this little-visited country will become an icon of sustainable tourism in the future.

△ AN INVITING, CRYSTALLINE POOL IN WADI SHAB

△ VICTORY OVER NATURE: A BEDOUIN CHILD WITH A CAUGHT SHARK

ESSENTIAL EXPERIENCES

○ **Bargaining with gusto for mosque clocks in Mutrah Souq**

○ **Wading tentatively through pools of toads in emerald Wadi Shab and Wadi Tiwi**

○ **Shedding a tear for turtles returning to the sea at Ras al-Jinz**

○ **Tottering nervously on the rim of Oman's grand canyon, on top of Jebel Shams**

○ **Surveying date plantations from the crenellations of Nakhal Fort or Jibrin Castle**

○ **Evoking the spirit of the past by bruising the stem of a frankincense tree in Dhofar**

MAP REF // F9

BEST TIME TO VISIT SEPTEMBER TO APRIL

△ DELICATE HENNA HAND DESIGNS ARE THE FINAL ACCESSORY

DISTURBING A DUNE METICULOUSLY SCULPTED BY THE WIND

A SHADELESS WALK THROUGH TOWN

A VIEW ACROSS THE CRENELLATIONS OF THE ANCIENT DESERT FORT AT NAKHAL

YEMEN

IF A LAND OF MOVING DESERTS, SPECTACULARLY SITED MOUNTAIN VILLAGES AND ANCIENT AND ENIGMATIC RUINS APPEALS, YEMEN SHOULD NOT BE MISSED. IT'S A COUNTRY KNOWN FOR THE WELCOME AND WIT OF ITS PEOPLE.

CAPITAL CITY SAN'A   POPULATION 21.5 MILLION   AREA 527,970 SQ KM   OFFICIAL LANGUAGE ARABIC

HIGH JINKS AT MAHRAM BILQIS, THE TEMPLE OF THE SABAEAN MOON GOD ILUMQUH

LANDSCAPE

Measuring about the size of France, Yemen can be divided roughly into three main areas: hot and humid (along the coastal strip), high and mountainous (in the central highlands) and hot and dry (in the Empty Quarter to the east). Like Yemen's habitats, its wildlife is also diverse, although if you want to see it, it pays to be patient!

HISTORY IN A NUTSHELL

It was the ancient Sabaeans who first placed the region firmly on the historical map. Dominating the lucrative trade in frankincense, their empire grew to dominate almost all of modern-day Yemen. Over the centuries, successive invading powers looked covetously towards Yemen for expansion. Seated at a strategic crossroads between Africa and Asia, it was a target too tempting to resist. Ancient Egyptians, Abyssinians and Persians all passed through its portals. In the 15th century, European powers also vied for control of the Red Sea Coast, but it was the Ottomans, and in the 20th century the British, who made the greatest inroads. After the occupiers had been outed, a dispute over succession broke out, leading to an eight-year war and dividing the country in two: the south pursued a Soviet-style socialism, and the north remained more conservative. Reunification took place in 1990, but after the elections of 1993 (when the north's General People's Congress dominated, causing increasing resentment in the south), relations began to sour again. In 1994 the south attempted to secede, leading to a six-month civil war. Though Yemen is unified again and peaceful, tensions between the different political parties, ideologies and tribal factions continue to simmer.

PEOPLE

Yemen's ethnic make-up is dictated by its geography. Along the coastal region, the population is more closely linked to the African mainland. In the central region, the lighter skin of the Semitic Arabs is apparent, while Bedouin tribespeople inhabit the desert regions to the east. Yemen boasts one of the world's highest population growth rates (between three and four per cent annually), and is a very young country (almost half its population is under 15 years old). Islam is the country's state religion and most Muslims are Sunnis.

MARKETPLACE

Yemen is still a firmly rural society, with 73 per cent of its population living in the countryside. Agricultural products account for at least 20 per cent of GDP, though the scarcity of water is an ever-pressing problem. Oil is Yemen's economic mainstay, making up around 70 per cent of the government's revenue. Other industries with reported potential include mineral mining and tourism.

TRADEMARKS

- The legendary land of the Queen of Sheba
- Truculent tribespeople
- Frankincense
- Hostage-snatching
- *Jambiya* – the beautiful carved dagger carried by every Yemeni man
- Intricate silver jewellery
- Picturesque painted *dhows* bobbing on the Red Sea
- *Qat* – the mildly narcotic leaf and a national obsession

NATURAL BEAUTY

Yemen's spectacular mountain villages and forts are famous. As Yemen has endured a war every seven years on average, many rural homes are perched precariously on the highest hilltops. The celebrated and beautiful rock palace at Dar al-Hajar sits on a rocky spire.

PHOTOGRAPHER DANIELE PELLEGRINI / GETTY

PHOTOGRAPHER CHRIS STOWERS / PANOS

URBAN SCENE

In 1984 Old San'a was declared a Unesco World Heritage Site in its entirety. The town is so perfectly preserved that it's said you can walk a square kilometre in any direction without encountering a single new building. The old city is particularly famous for its tower houses. Reaching up to eight storeys, they have been called the 'world's first skyscrapers'. San'a boasts no less than 14,000 of them.

WILD THINGS

Lying over 500 kilometres south of Yemen, the island of Suqutra has developed in almost total isolation from the rest of the country, resulting in remarkable flora and fauna. Activities include turtle, dolphin and bird watching and outstanding diving.

CULTURE

Yemeni hospitality is legendary; it's thought to have originated in the ancient and sacrosanct Bedouin creed that no traveller in need of rest or food should be turned away. Such a code of conduct ensures the survival of all in a difficult desert environment with scant resources.

↗ THE AL-GHOWAIZI FORT ON ITS HIGH PERCH, AL-MUKALLA

↗ THE CRUEL CURVE OF THE TRADITIONAL *JAMBIYA* (DAGGER)

RANDOM FACTS

○ The Yemenis are known throughout the Arab world for their fine sense of humour.

○ Twenty per cent of Yemeni text messages contain poems, jokes or political or philosophical aphorisms.

○ The urine of the Arabian one-humped camel is used by the Yemeni Bedu as a cure for many ailments, from liver complaints to dandruff.

○ In past times, the date palm was named *omm al-faqir*, meaning 'mother of the poor': its nutritional qualities could sustain the poor in times of hardship.

MYTHS & LEGENDS

Yemen is the legendary home of the Queen of Sheba. According to the Bible, she paid King Solomon a memorable visit with gorgeous gifts and a ridiculous retinue. He in turn won over the queen with his wisdom and she bore him a child. To this day, Yemeni girls are named Bilqis (her Arabic name) in her honour.

ARCHITECTURE

Yemen's rich and varied architecture depends on three things: available building materials (like stone, reeds or mud), climate (tropical or highland) and historical influences (such as African, Ottoman or Asian). Water has also been important. Some of the country's oldest structures are extraordinary feats of civil engineering, such as the great dam at Ma'rib.

ESSENTIAL EXPERIENCES

○ **Milling about with merchants and market-goers in the old souq of San'a – one of the largest and best-preserved in the whole of the Arab world**

○ **Strolling around Shaharah, one of Yemen's most spectacular mountain villages, with its beautiful bridge and stunning mountain scenery**

○ **Marvelling at Shibam, the 'Manhattan of the desert', with its ancient skyscrapers set in a dramatic desert setting**

○ **Puzzling over the ancient and enigmatic dam and temples at Ma'rib, called the 'Cradle of Civilisation' in southern Arabia**

○ **Goggling at the weird and wonderful flora and fauna of the island of Suqutra**

○ **Feasting on fresh fish cooked in a traditional clay oven**

MAP REF // D10

BEST TIME TO VISIT OCTOBER TO MID-MARCH

↗ A PALETTE OF SPICES FOR SALE, TAÏZZ

THE OTHER-WORLDLY DRAGON'S BLOOD TREE ON SUQUTRA

VEILED WOMEN IN CONICAL HATS WORK THE FIELDS IN HADRAMAUT

MUD-BRICK METROPOLIS: THE CITY OF SHIBAM IS KNOWN AS THE 'MANHATTAN OF THE DESERT' FOR ITS 14,000 ANCIENT SKYSCRAPERS

TEXT LARA DUNSTON & TERRY CARTER

SYRIA

FOR WHAT IS DEEMED A 'ROGUE' STATE, SYRIA IS AN AMAZINGLY FRIENDLY COUNTRY TO VISIT, AND ITS CRUSADER CASTLES, ROMAN RUINS, REFINED CUISINE AND ANCIENT CITIES CHARM OUTSIDERS.

CAPITAL **DAMASCUS** POPULATION **18.9 MILLION** AREA **185,180 SQ KM** OFFICIAL LANGUAGE **ARABIC**

DEFYING DIZZINESS: A WHIRLING DERVISH PERFORMS IN DAMASCUS

LANDSCAPE

Syria's narrow stretch of coast is backed by formidable mountains and carved up by deep ravines, which drop dramatically off into fertile farmland and an arid stony desert that's home to rich archaeological ruins, such as Palmyra. The Anti-Lebanon mountain range divides Syria from Lebanon.

HISTORY IN A NUTSHELL

Home to the world's oldest civilisations (dating back to 6600 BC), like many Middle Eastern nations Syria has experienced a succession of invasions and occupations – by the Egyptians, Babylonians, Alexander the Great, the Crusaders, Sassanids, Persians, Umayyads, Abbasids, Ayyubids, Mamluks, Mongols, Ottoman Turks, British, French and Israelis. Under 400 years of Turkish rule, Damascus and Aleppo became great trading cities on the pilgrimage route to Mecca. In the 19th century Syrian intellectuals started an Arab reawakening, encouraged during World War I by British colonel TE Lawrence (aka Lawrence of Arabia). Emir Faisal was made king until the French, who had the mandate over Syria and Lebanon, forced him into exile. The pan-Arab Baath party took control in 1963, although it wasn't until the 1967 Six-Day War (launched and won by Israel when Syria lost the Golan Heights) that Hafez al-Assad seized power. He ruled with an iron fist until his death in 2000. His son, Bashir al-Assad, promptly took over.

PEOPLE

Syria is mainly a Muslim Arab country, with 90 per cent of the population encompassing Sunni, Shiah, Alawite, Druze and Ismaili Muslims. The other 10 per cent are largely Armenians and Eastern Orthodox Christians. Syrian Muslims may be conservative but they are tolerant, open and hospitable. While Arabic is the official language, Syrians are well educated, and the average person on the street might speak English, Persian or even Russian!

MARKETPLACE

Situated for thousands of years along strategic east–west trade routes, Syria has based its socialist economy on energy, agriculture and manufacturing. Major exports include crude oil, fruit, vegetables, cereals, spices, raw cotton and clothes. Most large enterprises are nationalised, while small businesses are privately owned. Syria has been slow to join the global economy – and US economic sanctions against the country haven't helped. Almost 60 per cent of the population is under the age of 20 and unemployment is around 25 per cent.

TRADEMARKS

- Labyrinthine souqs
- Hand-crafted old Iran of good wood and hammer
- Rose-water-saturated sweets
- The Great Saladin, champion of the Arabs and archenemy of the invading Crusaders
- Roman ruins and a Roman centre
- Queen Zenobia at Palmyra
- Café storytellers

MYTHS & LEGENDS

The ruined basilica of Qala'at Samaan, north of Aleppo, takes its name from a peculiar individual named Simeon. Born in AD 392, Simeon was a shepherd's son who opted for a monastic life, retreating to a cave where he lived under a regime of self-imposed severity. His pious nature attracted visitors who came to seek his blessing. Somewhat resentful of these pilgrims, Simeon erected a three-metre-high pillar upon which he took up residence, so that people couldn't touch him. The legend goes that as his intolerance of people grew so did his pillars, the last of which was 18 metres high. His

A PORTFOLIO OF POSTCARDS AT THE PALMYRA RUINS

increasingly eccentric behaviour drew the faithful from as far as Europe, and St Simeon would preach daily from his perch. By the time of his death in 459, Simeon had spent close to 40 years aloft and an enormous church was built around the famous pillar.

CULTURE

Arab and Bedouin culture and the Islamic religion permeate everyday life in Syria. Ramadan is an opportunity for Syrian Muslims to renew their relationship with God. From dawn until dusk, they abstain from eating, drinking, smoking and sex. Lambs and goats are often tethered in the street during *Eid al-Adha*, the Feast of Sacrifice at the end of *haj* (the annual pilgrimage to Mecca), as the *Eid* culminates in a ritual slaughter. Islam's influence is also evident in the elegant calligraphy of sacred Quranic inscriptions and the splendid architecture of the Umayyad Mosque. Heroic tales from Arab history are told with intricate artistry in miniature paintings.

CUISINE

Syrian food is a delight, and is similar to Lebanese cuisine. A restaurant dinner can start late (not before 9pm) and finish even later. The affair begins with plenty of *mezze* (small starters and dips), followed by meat dishes such as kebabs, and sweet desserts featuring honey, syrup and rose-water. Street food staples include *felafel* (mashed chickpeas shaped into a ball and fried) and *shwarma*.

MUSIC

Syria's music is rooted in Bedouin traditions and Arab popular music. The Bedouin have simple but mesmerising musical traditions; however, the music you hear on the street has little to do with these. Popular music is a synthesis of indigenous Arab styles, harmony and instruments, centred on a star performer backed by anything from a small quartet to a full-blown orchestra, and often featuring the local *oud* (Middle Eastern lute). Contemporary Arab dance music marries traditional music with trip-hop, lounge, acid jazz, and drum'n'bass, and has taken the Middle East and Europe by storm.

ESSENTIAL EXPERIENCES

○ **Soaking up the sublime at Umayyad Mosque, Damascus**

○ **Wandering around the ancient Roman ruins of Palmyra in winter**

○ **Shopping for antiques on a Street Called Straight, Damascus**

○ **Discovering one of the Roman theatres in the heart of Bosra's black basalt fortress**

○ **Listening to the *hakawati* (professional storyteller) at An-Nafura coffee shop, Damascus**

○ **Exploring the eerie ghost towns of the Dead Cities**

○ **Visiting Qala'at Samaan to wonder how St Simeon could spend nearly 40 years perched on a pillar**

○ **Lining up for delicious *foul* (a tasty, semi-mushed fava bean soup) at Haj Abdo al-Fawwal's on Salat al-Hatab, Aleppo**

PHOTOGRAPHER IMAGESTATE // ALAMY

≫ A VENDOR WITH AN ELABORATE DEVICE FOR SERVING COLD DRINKS

TURKEY   Ain Diwar ●

        Hassake ●

    ● Aleppo   *Lake al-Assad*
    ● Idlib   ● Raqqa
  ● Lattakia

  ● Hama   Deir ●
Tartus ●   ez-Zur
    ● Homs
          ● Palmyra
LEBANON

  ✪ DAMASCUS   At-Tanf

                    IRAQ
ISRAEL
and the   ● Suweida
PALESTINIAN   JORDAN
TERRITORIES ● Bosra

PHOTOGRAPHER CHRISTINA DAMEYER // LONELY PLANET IMAGES

MAP REF // B6

BEST TIME TO VISIT **MARCH TO MAY (SPRING)**

≫ BRASS SERVING TRAY IN THE AZEM PALACE OF DAMASCUS

FLOODLIT WATER WHEELS NEAR THE ORONTES RIVER

FROM THE TRAVELLER

Most hotels in Hama offer daytrips, many in classic cars like this 1952 Pontiac. The day before, I rode in another vintage car with plush seats and air-con – but for this ride to Palmyra we were sweating on vinyl with only desert air to soothe us. After a while we gestured for a break. The gleaming car paused against the expanse of desert was an irresistible shot.

NANCY CHUANG   USA

A SOCIABLE AFTERNOON WITH THE *SHEESHA*

TEXT FRANCES LINZEE GORDON

LEBANON

THOUGH IT'S ONE OF THE SMALLEST COUNTRIES IN THE WORLD, LEBANON PACKS A PUNCH: HEAPS OF HISTORY AND CULTURE, BEAUTIFUL BEACHES AND BUCOLIC VALLEYS, AND A REPUTATION – ALBEIT MARRED BY THE RECENT WAR – AS BOTH THE PARTY CENTRE OF THE MIDDLE EAST AND ITS CULINARY CAPITAL.

CAPITAL CITY **BEIRUT**   POPULATION **3.9 MILLION**   AREA **10,400 SQ KM**   OFFICIAL LANGUAGE **ARABIC**

SURROUNDED BY RUINS, A STATUE IN MARTYR'S SQUARE SEEMS TO APPEAL FOR HELP

LANDSCAPE

Four main geographical areas run almost parallel to one another from north to south in Lebanon: the coastal plain in the west; the Mt Lebanon Range (home to Lebanon's famous cedar forests and its highest mountain, Qornet as-Sawda at 3090 metres); the wine-growing Bekaa Valley; and the Anti-Lebanon Range in the east, which marks the border with Syria. Lebanon has a Mediterranean climate: hot and dry in the summer and cool and rainy in the winter.

HISTORY IN A NUTSHELL

Until the break-up of the Ottoman Empire after World War I, Lebanon formed part of the region known as Syria and shared that country's history. Between the wars, it fell under a French mandate. The country's strategic location and relatively stable, West-leaning government made it a major trade and banking centre as well as an international playground, earning it the title 'Paris of the Orient'. However, after independence in 1946, the Muslim population became more and more frustrated, increasingly resenting their lack of power and participation in government (combined with the inflammatory influx of large numbers of displaced and restive Palestinians). In 1975 civil war broke out between a Muslim, leftist coalition and the Christian right-wing militias. In between intervention by Syria and two occupations by Israel in 1978 and 1982 (in an attempt to eradicate the Palestine Liberation Organisation), the civil war blazed at huge cost to the country and its people. In August 1992 parliamentary elections were held for the first time in 20 years, but fighting with Israel continued. In May 2000 the Israelis finally withdrew from Lebanon, and in 2005 the 29-year Syrian military presence also finally came to an end. The new spirit of optimism and growth proved short-lived, however. In July 2006 the kidnapping of two Israeli soldiers by Hezbollah militants triggered a 34-day conflict between the two countries that left over 1000 Lebanese dead and much of southern Lebanon in ruins. Following the deployment of a UN peacekeeping force, the long-suffering – but ever-optimistic – Lebanese find themselves rebuilding their beloved country once again.

PEOPLE

Lebanon is one of the most densely populated countries of the Middle East and nearly 90 per cent of its population lives in urban areas. Around 400,000 Palestinian refugees live in the country – accounting for nine per cent of the total population. An estimated 59.7 per cent of Lebanon's population is Muslim; 39 per cent is Christian.

MARKETPLACE

The civil war of 1975–91 devastated Lebanon's infrastructure and cut national economic output by half. After the war, Lebanon worked hard to rebuild itself and mend its finances, but at the cost of incurring a huge debt. Despite the introduction of economic austerity measures, the national debt at the beginning of the 21st century stood at US$32 billion (over 150 per cent of GDP) and unemployment was at a massive 24 per cent. The outbreak of war between Hezbollah and Israel in July 2006 didn't help matters and much of Lebanon's carefully constructed infrastructure (including motorways, bridges and airports) was reduced to ruins. Tourism, an important economic activity, was also hit hard. Lebanon faces yet more years of hard work and economic hardship to recover from this latest bitter blow.

TRADEMARKS

- Spectacular Roman sights
- Lebanon's cedar forests – said to date to Biblical times
- Delicious mezze – Lebanese food is famous

DANCE GROUP AL-NOUJOUM KICK-STARTS FESTIVITIES AT A WEDDING IN THE CHOUF MOUNTAINS

REBUILDING LIVELIHOODS ON A BEIRUT BEACH, THE BOMBED-OUT HOLIDAY INN HOTEL IN THE BACKGROUND

NATURAL BEAUTY

Small in size it may be, but Lebanon is well formed,
with fine beaches, snowclad mountains and
picturesque ports to romantic Crusader castles,
vine-swathed valleys and ruins set spectacularly
by the sea.

URBAN SCENE

Out of the ashes and scars of the civil war, Beirut
began to rise phoenix-like in an exciting rebirth. The
rejuvenation of the Central District was one of the
most ambitious urban redevelopment projects ever
undertaken. The capital had become famous for its
hippest-of-hip bars and nightclubs and vibrant
restaurant scene. The war with Israel in 2006 brought
a halt to all that, but you can bet your last Lebanese
lira that it won't be long before Beirut is back in
business again, offering all of its former hedonistic
pleasures and pursuits.

WILD THINGS

Though years of war and uncontrolled hunting have
taken its toll, Lebanon's wildlife is slowly returning.
Wolves, wild boars, gazelles and ibexes are very
occasionally seen. More impressive is the birdlife:
Lebanon is an important migratory staging ground
and off the coast alone no less than 135 species have
been recorded. In April, migrating storks can be seen
in the Bekaa Valley.

CULTURE

After years of sectarian conflict in Lebanon, it's best
not to ask about someone's religion immediately, or
about their whereabouts, role or experiences in the
civil war. Almost everyone in the country lost a friend
or family member in war. Excessive drinking and all
drugs are taboo, and appearance and status is of
supreme importance. In Lebanon, looking smart will
get you everywhere.

ARCHITECTURE

Keen to contribute to the rebuilding of his beloved
city, Beiruti architect Bernard Khoury is more than
making his mark, as well as making a name for
himself around the world. One of his daring designs
is the famous BO18, a building that more closely
resembles a bomb shelter than a nightclub and
features a sliding roof and seats that fold away into
tables on which patrons can dance. Khoury's other
designs (including some boldly avant-garde
restaurants) have won him international fame and
acclaim. His latest work-in-progress is the restoration
of the Beirut City Centre Building.

TOP FESTIVAL

Largest of Lebanon's many arts festivals and the
oldest and most prestigious in the Middle East is the
Baalbek International Festival, which first took place
in 1955. The festival is held among the spectacular
Roman ruins of Baalbek, and takes place annually
during July and August. Featuring music (including
opera, jazz, pop and world music), poetry, dance and
theatre, it has evolved into a major international
cultural event attracting an audience of some
40,000 people.

ESSENTIAL EXPERIENCES

○ **Sizing up Sun City at Baalbek – the region's
  top Roman site and one of the world's
  most wonderful**

○ **Touring Tyre and tripping though 5000
  years of history**

○ **Living it up in Beirut with its glitzy beach
  clubs, fine dining and hard partying**

○ **Measuring up the Mamluk architecture and
  medieval markets of Tripoli**

○ **Being in Byblos – with its Crusader castle,
  impressive Roman ruins, picturesque port
  and sumptuous souqs**

SYRIA

Al-Mina ● Tripoli
Chekka ● (Trablous) ● Hermel
Batroun ●
Byblos (Jbail) ●
● Jounieh
BEIRUT ✪
Zahlé ●
Aanjar ●
Sidon ●
(Saida) ● Jezzine
SYRIA
Tyre ●
(Sour)
ISRAEL & THE
PALESTINIAN
TERRITORIES

MAP REF // B6

BEST TIME TO VISIT MARCH TO MAY,
SEPTEMBER TO OCTOBER

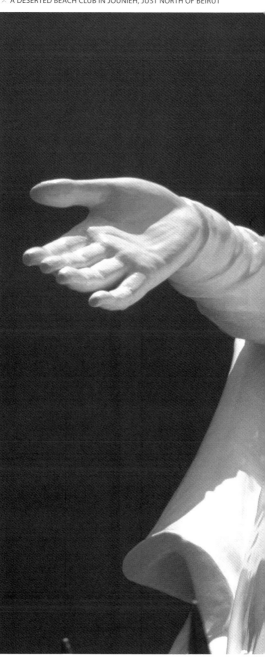

↗ A DESERTED BEACH CLUB IN JOUNIEH, JUST NORTH OF BEIRUT

PHOTOGRAPHER COREY WISE   LONELY PLANET IMAGES

PHOTOGRAPHER CHRISTINE SPENGLER   CORBIS

↗ A BRIDE EXHIBITS UNDIMINISHED NATIONAL PRIDE IN BEIRUT

A SMALL CHAPEL AMID THE ICE-BLUE LANDSCAPE OF THE CENTRAL MOUNTAIN RANGE

AN OPULENT BATHROOM INSIDE THE PALACE OF BEITEDDINE

DWARFED BY OUR LADY OF LEBANON, A MASSIVE BRONZE STATUE IN HARISSA

TEXT BRADLEY MAYHEW

JORDAN

A HAVEN OF PEACE IN A TOUGH NEIGHBOURHOOD, JORDAN IS A HIGHLIGHT OF THE MIDDLE EAST AND SO MUCH MORE THAN JUST AMAZING PETRA.

CAPITAL CITY **AMMAN** POPULATION **5.9 MILLION** AREA **91,970 SQ KM** OFFICIAL LANGUAGE **ARABIC**

THE SIMPLE YET STRIKING TOMB OF NABI YOSHA, SALT

LANDSCAPE

Tiny Jordan can be divided into three regions; the low-lying and fertile Jordan Valley, home to the Dead Sea and part of the Africa's Great Rift Valley; the central plateau, home to the main historical centres and cut by dozens of beautiful wadis (dry river valleys); and the Eastern Desert, an empty quarter that makes up 80 per cent of the country's land mass.

HISTORY IN A NUTSHELL

A young state with a long history, Jordan has been traversed by an endless series of invaders, mostly en route to somewhere else. They left behind a string of impressive remains, such as biblical cities, Roman amphitheatres, Byzantine mosaics, Arab palaces, Crusader castles and Ottoman mosques. Home-grown superstars the Nabataeans cornered the spice market 2000 years ago to fund the rise of Petra, the region's most fantastic ancient city, carved out of rock. Recent history has been inextricably linked to the neighbouring Arab–Israeli conflict.

PEOPLE

Over 98 per cent of Jordanians are Arabs. Of these, the most famous are the Bedouin, guardians of the conservative heart of Jordanian culture. Around 60 per cent of Jordan's population are Palestinian, most of whom arrived as refugees from the West Bank. A small community of Christians live in the mosaic town of Madaba.

MARKETPLACE

Jordan was hit hard economically by the first Gulf War (1990) and the recent US invasion of Iraq, both of which cut off its main export market and its supply of cheap oil. The country is repositioning itself as a regional service centre and a business-friendly springboard for the reconstruction of Iraq.

TRADEMARKS

○ Rose-red Petra
○ *Keffiyeh* (red-and-white checked headdress)
○ *Nargileh* (water pipe)
○ Roman ruins
○ Late King Hussein and Queen Noor
○ Bedouin people
○ Lawrence of Arabia

NATURAL BEAUTY

Nowhere is the desert more beautiful than at Wadi Rum, where red sand dunes compete for your attention with natural rock bridges and towering sandstone bluffs that just ache to be climbed. Hidden from view are Jordan's wadis – narrow watercourses lined with palm trees and waterfalls, miraculous threads of green that are the true oases in the desert. The sunset views of the Dead Sea and the Promised Land (Israel) from Mt Nebo will stir your soul, as they did Moses'.

CULTURE

The roots of Jordanian notions of hospitality, honour and respect for elders lie deep in the desert, though Jordan is increasingly an urban society. Clan and tribal affiliations are all-important to the Bedouin, though only a minority live a nomadic life these days. Islam dominates the rhythms of daily Jordanian life.

CUISINE

Jordanian food encompasses all of the Middle East's greatest hits, including hummus, *shwarma*, *shish tawooq* (chicken kebabs), *kofta* (meatballs) and a million different types of incorrigibly sweet pastries, drenched in rose syrup and washed down by a refreshing mint tea or cardamom-flavoured coffee. The local Bedouin speciality is *mensaf,* a succulent roast lamb dish served on a bed of rice and pine nuts.

THE EXPRESSIVE EYES OF A BEDOUIN WOMAN ARE ENHANCED BY KOHL

ECOTOURISM

The Royal Society for the Conservation of Nature (www.rscn.org.jo) runs a series of excellent ecotourism adventures in Jordan's nature reserves. The highlights are splashing up Wadi Mujib canyon and hiking the sandstone bluffs at Dana, which also has a great eco-lodge and local handicraft initiative. Profits from these activities fund the management of the reserves.

MYTHS & LEGENDS

Jordan provides the physical backdrop to some classic biblical stories, most of which feature Charlton Heston, if we remember correctly. It was in Jordan that Moses first set eyes on the Promised Land; where John the Baptist was beheaded by Herod at Salome's bequest; and where Lot's wife turned to salt after turning to watch the destruction of Sodom and Gomorrah.

RANDOM FACTS

○ Jesus is believed to have been baptised by John at Jordan's Wadi al-Kharrar (Bethany-Across-the-Jordan).

○ The ruins of Sodom and Gomorrah, the original Sin Cities, lie in shame at the southeast corner of the Dead Sea.

○ The Dead Sea is the lowest point on earth, at 408 metres below sea level, but it's less commonly known that it has shrunk by 30 per cent in the last 50 years.

○ Bedouin women tattoo their faces to protect against the 'evil eye'.

FUTURE DIRECTIONS

Jordan continues to tread a precarious tightrope. On the one hand it's forging ahead as a modern, cosmopolitan and technologically advanced Arab state, led by a young, modernising king. However, outside Amman, the nation's reality is one of Islamicised cities, politicised Palestinian refugees and the deeply conservative Bedouin people. Surrounded by the political maelstroms of Israel, Palestine and Iraq, and not far from the hot spots of Saudi Arabia and Syria, Jordan's future may well depend on the events that unfold outside its borders and beyond its control.

FROM THE TRAVELLER

There was no respite from the sun, even as we took a break from driving through the hot and dusty desert of Wadi Rum. I spied our guide Zedane squatting against a large rock, who looked surprised when he noticed my camera pointing in his direction, instead of the other way at the scenery around us.

PAUL GUGLIEMINO // AUSTRALIA

ESSENTIAL EXPERIENCES

○ **Giving the thumbs up after watching chariot races at the Roman ruins of Jerash**

○ **Dining out on *mezze*, *paella* and pizza in sophisticated Amman**

○ **Exploring the hidden tombs, trails and canyons of Petra**

○ **Following in the sandy footprints of Lawrence of Arabia at Wadi Rum**

○ **Diving into the big blue off the coast of Aqaba**

○ **Reading a newspaper while floating in the Dead Sea, just because you can**

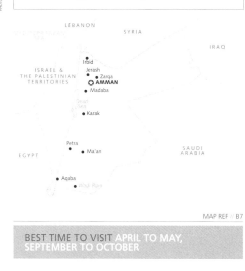

LEBANON
SYRIA
IRAQ
ISRAEL & THE PALESTINIAN TERRITORIES
● Irbid
● Jerash ● Zarqa
✪ AMMAN
● Madaba
Dead Sea
● Karak
EGYPT
● Petra
● Ma'an
SAUDI ARABIA
● Aqaba
● Wadi Rum

MAP REF // B7

BEST TIME TO VISIT **APRIL TO MAY, SEPTEMBER TO OCTOBER**

↗ AN ANCIENT MOSAIC MAP OF THE HOLY LAND IN MADABA

↗ THREE GIRLS STRIKE A PRETTY POSE AT AMMAN'S ROMAN THEATRE

BATHERS APPLYING FULL-BODY MUD MASKS AT THE DEAD SEA

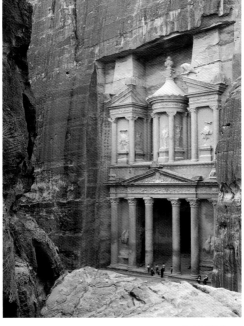

THE FACADE OF THE TREASURY (AL-KHAZNEH), PETRA

CROP CIRCLES IN WADI RUM: CROPS ARE GROWN ON CIRCULAR IRRIGATED PATCHES OF LAND IN THIS BARREN LANDSCAPE

PALESTINE

PALESTINE'S RUGGED HILLS, ANCIENT OLIVE GROVES AND CITIES RICH IN HISTORY ARE COMPLEMENTED BY A LIVELY CAFÉ SCENE IN RAMALLAH AND MILES OF MEDITERRANEAN BEACH.

CAPITAL CITY RAMALLAH (DE FACTO) POPULATION 3.9 MILLION AREA 6000 SQ KM OFFICIAL LANGUAGE ARABIC

LANDSCAPE

The future state of Palestine consists of two non-contiguous territories separated by Israel: the hilly, 5640-square-kilometre West Bank of the Jordan River; and the flat, 360-square-kilometre Gaza Strip along the Mediterranean. The Palestinians claim East Jerusalem, annexed by Israel in 1967, as their official capital.

HISTORY IN A NUTSHELL

Muslim rule and Arab civilisation arrived in the Holy Land in the 7th century. Filastin (Palestine) fell to the Crusaders in 1099 but was reconquered by Saladin a century later. Four hundred years of Ottoman Turkish rule were brought to an end by the British during World War I. Palestinian Arab opposition to Jewish immigration hastened the end of Great Britain's League of Nations Mandate (1918–48). In 1947 the United Nations General Assembly voted to partition Mandatory Palestine into two states, one Arab and one Jewish. In the ensuing war, Jordan took the West Bank, Egypt claimed the Gaza Strip and some 750,000 Palestinian Arabs became refugees. Israel captured the West Bank, Gaza and East Jerusalem in 1967. The *Intifada* that rose against Israeli rule lasted from 1987 to 1991. The Oslo Peace Process established in the early '90s collapsed into violence in 2000.

PEOPLE

Virtually all the people living in the West Bank and Gaza Strip (except for 240,000 Jewish settlers) are Arabs; 94 per cent are Sunni Muslims and the remaining minority are generally Christians. Many residents of Palestine are refugees who fled what is now Israel during the 1948 Arab–Israeli war.

MARKETPLACE

Palestinian–Israeli trade and tourism flourished in the 1990s but the violence that began in 2000 has devastated the Palestinian economy. Per-capita GDP is estimated to be US$1100 in the West Bank and US$600 in Gaza. More than one-third of Palestinians are unemployed and hundreds of thousands, especially in Gaza, are dependent on the UN for their basic needs.

TRADEMARKS

- Felafel
- Elaborately embroidered women's dresses
- Black-and-white checked *keffiyeh* (men's cloth headdresses)
- Yassir Arafat
- Intifada
- Israeli army roadblocks

NATURAL BEAUTY

A range of rocky hills that extend from the north to the south forms the backbone of the West Bank. On their eastern side, seasonal wadis slice through the arid landscape on their way to the Jordan River and the Dead Sea, the lowest place on earth.

THE WALL

In recent years, a new element has been added to the West Bank landscape. In order to prevent infiltration by suicide bombers – and, say Palestinians, to annex Palestinian land – Israel is constructing an electronic 'security barrier', also known as the 'separation wall' because some segments consist of eight-metre-high concrete slabs.

RANDOM FACTS

- Jericho is believed to be the world's oldest continuously inhabited city.
- Palestine's only beer, Taybeh, is brewed near Ramallah.
- The Samaritans have lived on Mt Gerizim near Nablus for over two millennia.
- Palestine has one of the world's fastest rates of population growth.

CUISINE

The cheapest way to get a quick, filling meal in Palestine is to head for one of the many eateries specialising in felafel (fried balls of ground chickpeas) and hummus (a thick chickpea paste), which often comes with *fuul* (steaming fava bean paste). One of the most delicious Palestinian desserts is *knafeh*, a scrumptious Nablus speciality made from cheese, thin strands of shredded wheat (often coloured a lurid orange) and sugary syrup.

FUTURE DIRECTIONS

They may differ about everything else, but there's one thing that the Palestinian, Israeli, Egyptian and Jordanian governments have always agreed on: regional tourism benefits everyone. As we go to press the situation in Palestine looks grim, but if political stability and security can be established Palestine has huge potential as a tourist destination.

ESSENTIAL EXPERIENCES

- **Strolling among carpets of West Bank wildflowers in early spring**
- **Marvelling at the 7th-century golden Dome of the Rock on Jerusalem's al-Haram ash-Sharif – Temple Mount**
- **Ducking your head as you enter Bethlehem's Church of the Nativity through its tiny door**
- **Feasting on *pomelo* (bomli), a huge citrus fruit grown locally around Jericho**
- **Exploring Wadi Qelt, a deep desert canyon with a monastery built into the cliff face**

MAP REF // B7

BEST TIME TO VISIT YEAR-ROUND

THREE DEMURE GIRLS AT FRIDAY PRAYERS IN THE AL-RIMAL DISTRICT

PHOTOGRAPHER AHIKAM SERI / PANOS

PHOTOGRAPHER AHIKAM SERI / PANOS

A GLIMPSE OF PARADISE ON THE ISRAELI SEPARATION WALL BY BRITISH GRAFFITI ARTIST BANKSY

SHEEP ARE SLAUGHTERED IN BURNING PITS DURING A SAMARITAN PASSOVER CEREMONY ON MT GERIZIM

ISRAEL

A VIBRANT, CULTURALLY DIVERSE DEMOCRACY, ISRAEL HAS BREATHTAKING LANDSCAPES FROM BIBLICAL TIMES, A DYNAMIC HIGH-TECH ECONOMY, SUPERB BEACHES AND A HIGHLY SPIRITED NIGHTLIFE SCENE.

CAPITAL CITY **JERUSALEM**   POPULATION **7 MILLION**   AREA **20,330 SQ KM**   OFFICIAL LANGUAGES **HEBREW, ARABIC**

WRAPPED UP IN ISRAEL: WORSHIPPERS WITH THE ISRAELI FLAG AT THE WESTERN (WAILING) WALL

LANDSCAPE

Israel's diverse geography ranges from snowy peaks in the far north to windblown sand dunes in the southern Negev Desert. The rocky hills of the Galilee, which are cloaked in wildflowers in winter and early spring, are bounded to the east by the Jordan Valley, where you'll find the freshwater Sea of Galilee (213 metres below sea level) and the mineral-rich Dead Sea (413 metres below sea level), the lowest point on earth. Hilly Jerusalem (800 metres above sea level) has chilly winters but delightfully warm, dry summers. Tel Aviv, its great secular rival on the country's 197-kilometre Mediterranean coast, is often sunny enough in winter to get a tan, but is hot and humid in summer.

HISTORY IN A NUTSHELL

Israel has had various names over the millennia. Called Canaan at the time of Abraham, in later biblical times it became known as the Land of Israel. A century after Jesus, in the wake of a failed Jewish revolt, the Roman province of Judaea (a candidate for liberation in Monty Python's *Life of Brian*) was renamed Syria Palaestina after the Philistines. Muslim rule began in the 7th century but was interrupted by the Crusaders, who established the Latin Kingdom of Jerusalem. Four centuries under the Ottoman Turks were brought to an end by the British during World War I, after which Palestine was ruled by Great Britain under a League of Nations mandate. The number of Jews in Palestine increased in the 1880s following pogroms in tsarist Russia, and in the 1920s and '30s. In 1947 the General Assembly of the United Nations partitioned Mandatory Palestine into two states, one Jewish and one Arab. Since then, Israel has fought six wars with its Arab neighbours and signed peace treaties with Egypt and Jordan. The Oslo Peace Process between Israel and the Palestinians imploded in 2000.

PEOPLE

Most of Israel's citizens are Jews; Sunni Muslim Arabs (including Bedouins) comprise 16.1 per cent of the population, and there are minority groups of Christian Arabs and Druze. About half of Jewish Israelis are Ashkenazim (those with European origins) and the other half are either Sephardim (descendents of Jews expelled from Spain and Portugal in the late 1400s) or Mizrahim (Jews from Asian and North African lands such as Morocco, Iraq, Yemen and Iran). Between 1990 and 2004, 916,000 immigrants arrived in Israel from the former Soviet Union and 53,000 came from Ethiopia.

MARKETPLACE

Israel started out in 1948 as an impoverished former colony that was overwhelmed by numbers of Jewish refugees and immigrants, many of whom had to spend years living in resettlement camps. Until 1973 the country's largely socialist economy grew by a remarkable 11 per cent every year. In the 1990s, the combined effect of economic liberalisation, a flourishing high-technology sector and the Oslo Peace Process resulted in the elevation of per-capita GDP to European levels. It has now reached US$24,600, and is currently growing at a rate of about five per cent a year.

TRADEMARKS

- *Kibbutzim*
- Raucous political debates, in the *Knesset* and everywhere else
- Brusque manners
- Heavily armed 19-year-old male and female conscripts on public buses
- Ultra-Orthodox Jews preparing for the Sabbath on Friday afternoon
- The lowest of low-rider jeans
- Security checks when you enter supermarkets, shopping malls and pubs

CITY HALL PATRIOTICALLY LIT DURING INDEPENDENCE DAY, TEL AVIV

A CONTEMPLATIVE MOMENT IN A BEDOUIN CAMP

- The highest temperature ever recorded in Asia, 54°C, was measured at Kibbutz Tirat Tzvi in 1942.
- Israel is the only country in the world that began the 21st century with more trees than it had at the beginning of the 20th century.
- In 1991 an El Al 747, with its seats removed, brought 1088 Ethiopian Jews (including two babies born en route) from Addis Ababa to Israel, setting a world record for the number of passengers carried by an airliner.
- Israel's first Olympic gold medal, in windsurfing, was won at the 2004 Athens Olympics.

NATURAL BEAUTY

The waters of the Dead Sea are so laden with salts and minerals that you can lie on your back with your hands and feet in the air while reading the newspaper. In nearby Ein Gedi spring, water cascades down a deep valley in the bone-dry desert, allowing a unique mix of flora and fauna to flourish. The Red Sea, at Israel's southern tip, has stunning coral reefs.

FROM THE TRAVELLER

It was 45°C on the day I visited the Dead Sea in Israel. Needless to say I was looking forward to a dip. It was horrible: like bathing in a hot bath after someone had tipped in a sack of salt. I put a finger to my lips and nearly burnt my tongue off. When I was back out on the shore I felt exactly like this sculpture. Still, what an experience!

HELEN ELLIS // AUSTRALIA

CLASSY COSTUMES FOR CLUBBING IN TEL AVIV

URBAN SCENE

Tel Aviv's bars and clubs are gaining increasing international attention thanks to their energy and no-holds-barred creativity. New watering holes ranging from classic French to ultra-hip open up every week.

WILD THINGS

Israel has over 500 resident and migrating bird species, making it one of the best places in the world for bird watching. In spring and autumn, millions of storks, cranes, cormorants, herons, pelicans and smaller species make their way from Eurasia to the warmer climes of Africa and back again. Bird enthusiasts view the scene in awe, as do enraged fishpond owners – the birds happily gulp down easy-to-catch snacks.

MODERN ARCHITECTURE

Jewish architects brought sleek, modernist Bauhaus architecture from Germany to Palestine in the 1930s. Adapted to local climatic conditions, the Israeli version features flat roofs, curved corners, deep balconies and strip windows whose horizontality is accentuated by vertical 'thermometer' windows that light the stairwell. Thanks to its Bauhaus heritage, Tel Aviv was declared a Unesco World Heritage Site in 2003.

TECHNOLOGICAL INNOVATION

Israel's technology sector is famously innovative: it has to be to compete with larger firms in bigger countries. Products developed here include drip irrigation, the first ingestible video camera (for noninvasive medical diagnosis), the Epilady electric hair remover, the Quicktionary pen-size scanner, ICQ instant messaging, the Pentium-4 microprocessor, MMX multimedia technology and keychain memory (disk-on-key).

ESSENTIAL EXPERIENCES

- Floating in the slimy, super-salty Dead Sea waters
- Spotting a flock of migrating storks
- Bobbing down the Jordan River on an inner-tube
- Placing a note to the Almighty in a crack in the Western Wall (you can also fax one in)
- Marvelling at the golden Dome of the Rock on Jerusalem's Temple Mount – al-Haram ash-Sharif
- Sipping a beer in a trendy Tel Aviv bar

MAP REF // B7

BEST TIME TO VISIT **YEAR-ROUND**

TAKE ME TO THE RIVER: WORSHIPPERS IN THE JORDAN

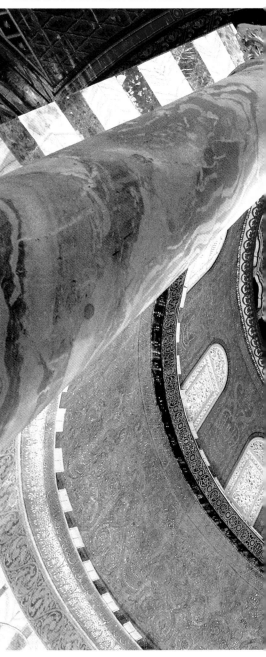

PHOTOGRAPHER MICHAEL COYNE . LONELY PLANET IMAGES

PHOTOGRAPHER PHILIPPE LISSAC . PANOS

A COPTIC EGYPTIAN MONK AT THE CHURCH OF THE HOLY SEPULCHRE, JERUSALEM

A DIZZYING LOOK UPWARDS INSIDE THE DOME OF THE ROCK, JERUSALEM

THEMES OF ASIA

TEXT ANDREW BURKE

FROM DESERT TO DELTA

⌃ THE SALT FLATS OF THE INHOSPITABLE DASHT-E KAVIR, IRAN   ⌃ FISHING BOATS WAIT TO BE RIGHTED BY THE RISING TIDE, QATAR   ⌃ A SCATTERING OF FEMALE STUDENTS ON THE BEACH IN DUBAI, UAE

It's summer in the Dasht-e Kavir, the more northern of the two deserts that lie across Iran like slowly dehydrating camels. Outside the temperature is toying with 50°C. The mix of sand and salt is as blinding in its whiteness as the desert is deafening in its total, unimaginable silence.

In the oasis town of Garmeh, lucky camels are taking refuge in whatever shade they can find. Outside its mud-brick walls dozens of varieties of date palm are thirstily lapping up the cool spring water that is Garmeh's reason for existing. Yet within this harsh, desolate environment a man named Maziar is living – really living – the sort of life most people will never even imagine.

Maziar is no mad dog, nor is he an Englishman. He, his wife, his parents and whichever visitors he has in his guesthouse are in rooms bedecked in bright Persian carpets around 10 metres underground, where the temperature is 25°C cooler. They play music, they sleep, they socialise – they live – until the sun slowly gives up its burning assault and is slowly and spectacularly interred beneath a sky full of colour. As the camels groan plaintively in the half-light around Garmeh, Maziar and his family watch from the flat roof of their home, which itself is made from the three ever-present elements of the oasis: sand, water and palms. Another cool evening has come. Dinner might be camel kebab, with dates for dessert. This is their life, lived to a rhythm fine-tuned over centuries by the greatest conductor of all, mother nature.

It's a story repeated all over the vast geographical mosaic that is Asia: people and place living in a sort of love-hate relationship. For many it's a matter of life and death; for many more the land is the main influence on their everyday existence. Sculpted over eons by a sea and sky that are both brutal and benevolent, the land often dictates what people wear, what sort of structure they call home, what they eat, what they drink, what they value, how they define poverty, what they call luxury, what they love, how fit they are and, for a mercifully decreasing number, how long they live.

About 1800 kilometres west of Garmeh, across the Zagros range which stretches angrily south like a giant crocodile's back, amid the blue waters of the Gulf and the sand and rocks and wadis of the northern Arabian Peninsula, Ahmed's relationship with the desert is similar. Ahmed is a Bedouin. He wears a long white tunic and *keffiyeh* (headdress), both reflecting some of the heat of the sun and allowing plenty of room for air to circulate underneath. He lives in a *beit ash-sha'ar*, a 'house of hair' made of black goat-hair that can be packed away and moved to whichever place the nomads next decide is worthy of grazing their herds.

For the Bedouin and others who have lived in the harsh conditions of the Middle East, the desert has been the architect of many of the pillars of their social code. Before the advent of sealed roads and air-conditioned Land Cruisers, crossing these empty, waterless places was an endeavour fraught with danger. Without the hospitality of others, journeys were quite likely to be fatal.

It's no surprise, then, that like the Arabs, the Iranians, Pakistanis and Afghans, the Bedouin are renowned for their hospitality. The Bedouin code revolves around the

FISHING BOATS IN TRANQUIL WATERS OFF THE PORT TOWN OF AL-MUKALLA, YEMEN ⌃

precept that no traveller may be turned away. Guests are welcomed with endless tea or coffee and the best food available. Beds are rolled out and, even if guests arrive as total strangers, they are treated like royalty. To be on the receiving end of this kind of selfless act is a heady experience, but giving is integral to desert-dwellers' survival: sooner or later they'll be in need of a similar act of generosity.

Imagine now that we're returning east and heading north, spinning across the world like a satellite. While Ahmed may not know it, below us in the Baluchistan Desert in Pakistan, on the wind-blown steppes of Turkmenistan and in the Gobi Desert in Mongolia are men and women living a similar life to him and his family, governed by a common master – the desert. That their lifestyles are so similar, irrespective of religion, language and distance, is a testament to the land's power.

For Passang in Nepal, life is very different. His home is in a village that tumbles several hundred metres down the side of a mountain, surrounded by modestly sized terraced fields, with other small homes dotted about the landscape. It's an implausibly beautiful place. The jagged peaks provide both a sense of protection and an immovable buffer against the outside world; in the shadow of this colossal mass of sheer-sided rock, it's easy to forget that there is any other world beyond it.

But for all the beauty that surrounds him, life for Passang and his family is just as harsh as Ahmed's. Almost their every act is a reaction to the mountains. With no road connecting the village to the world beyond the peaks and valleys, virtually all transport is on foot. Visiting a neighbour can involve a climb of several hundred

metres – villagers here are fit until they die. They are more or less self-sufficient in food, but their diet is dominated by potatoes, barley and vegetables, with the meat of sheep, cattle and yaks. Whether it's the human feet of porters or the four feet of the ubiquitous yak, the winding mountain paths (so beloved of Western trekkers) facilitate commerce in the Himalaya the way semitrailers and cargo ships do in the West. The yaks and porters traverse the steep-sided terrain carrying items such as soap, sugar, cigarettes, salt and cloth. Passang will bargain with the porter, perhaps offering him accommodation and a meal in return for a discount.

Even in war, the mountains are the dominant force here. Without helicopters, getting anywhere is a long, slow process that has for years played into the hands of the mobile Maoist rebels, who must love the natural protection afforded by the terrain as much as they dislike the privations they are forced to endure during a Himalayan winter.

The snow that falls on the Himalaya and on neighbouring Tibet during those winters, however, eventually enters Asia's major river systems, the most vital of all Asia's many geographical forms. The ice settled on the vast and sparsely populated Tibetan plateau melts into countless creeks and streams crisscrossing the land. Guided by gravity, these streams grow from dental floss–narrow rivulets into vast river deltas, via watercourses that sometimes crash and surge over the jaws of rapids and sometimes simply meander, sauntering across the continent like lazy, glistening serpents. These waters bring life to people, flora and fauna; their silt sustains fields of crops and the billions of fish that provide a major source of protein for many Asians. Their vitality is impossible to miss along the 3180-kilometre Indus, the 2948-kilometre Brahmaputra, the 4023-kilometre Mekong and the Yangzi, longest of all at more than 6000 kilometres. Collectively they are home to hundreds of millions of people, from fisherfolk in dugout canoes to city slickers paying thousands of dollars a month for a place with a view. It's not surprising that many of these major rivers have taken on a mythological element, and are respected, revered and feared in equal measure.

The life-and-death nature of living along these rivers is never more evident than during the monsoon season. As rains drench their way across the region, thousands of tributaries feed ever more water into the big rivers. If these are the arteries of Asia, then towards the end of the monsoon the continent's collective blood pressure rises dangerously high. In the Brahmaputra delta in Bangladesh it's not a question of *whether* the river will turn killer, but how many will die. It's a tragedy played out year after year in a part of the world known to the vast majority of humanity for this annual flood and nothing more. The lives and livelihoods being lost at the edge of the Bay of Bengal are presented to the rest of the world in ever-briefer television news reports. Yet still, after the waters drop, the bodies are recovered and the rescue boats have returned to port, Bangladeshis return to the Brahmaputra delta in search of the life the river can bring.

Between the sources of these rivers and the sea are wide tracts of farmland, thousands of towns and a good number of cities, both the frenetic – such as Shànghǎi, Dhaka, Karachi and Ho Chi Minh City – and the more laid-back – see Leh, Luang Prabang, Vientiane and Phnom Penh. There's jungle, too – some of the most awe-inspiring can be found along the Mekong in Laos.

In Laos, Kanchana lives near the town of Xieng Kok. It's a place of stunning beauty, on a bend in the Mekong just south of the border with China in what has become known as the Golden Triangle. The area is flanked by steep hills, blanketed in the sort of jungle that would make Tarzan feel right at home: huge old trees covered in lianas, with a canopy so thick that light only barely reaches the damp, steamy jungle floor. Here, in the half-light of the morning and late afternoon, Kanchana and her fellow villagers search for what are known generically as 'jungle products' – medicinal roots, mushrooms, barks, herbs and a mind-boggling array of frogs and toads. Change the names of the people, the bugs and the plants and you could be in any number of places in Borneo, Sumatra, Myanmar, the Philippines, Vietnam or Thailand. But even in this remote corner of Asia, population pressure (encouraging ever more slash-and-burn agriculture) and pure greed are having an impact.

There is, after all, 'gold' in them there hills – in the form of very large trees. The pillage of Asia's forests is well documented, but the damage continues. However, the situation is not all bad: along with the gold that logging brings to the very few, the environment is also coughing up other (though lesser) riches in a more sustainable form. Just a few hours downriver and inland from Huay Xai a group of locals and foreigners have tapped into the burgeoning demand for sustainable ways of experiencing nature at the Gibbon Experience. Here, up in the 25-metre-tall elders of the forest, visitors pay to stay in treehouses, zipping from one tree to another by flying fox and getting up close, if not personal, with the population of rare gibbons.

Sustainable tourism is a welcome addition to the huge variety of moneymaking possibilities in Asia, but it's the fossil fuels within the land which have most changed Asia's relationship with the planet. Their impact on the region has been enormous: from economic benefits in the oil-rich Gulf States to the practical consequences of cheap electricity in places like Singapore. (Its founding father, Lee Kuan Yew, calls air conditioning the greatest invention of the 20th century and credits it with an important role in the spectacular rise of the city-state.)

For desert-dwelling Ahmed, modernity brings a mobile phone and satellite television, which allow him to know better than any of his forebears when the next sandstorm will hit. For Passang it means Western trekkers in their brightly coloured Gore-Tex jackets pass through, happily paying small but significant amounts for tea and snacks. For Kanchana it brings new roads and heavy logging equipment to the jungle, and Chinese cargo boats down the sacred river in ever-increasing numbers. And for Maziar, globalisation takes his guesthouse to the world via the internet, while at the same time bringing downloads of African music and visitors from around the world to his disarming little oasis.

Fossil fuels and modern technology enable humans to master the elements much more than in the past. And while few Asians, or anyone else for that matter, would choose to reject the hospitals, transport, heating, air conditioning and everything else the modern world brings to their lives, the resulting homogenisation is an unfortunate side-effect. Modernity is, without doubt, a double-edged sword.

In the Iranian capital of Tehran, Mashid isn't complaining. Her car means she can escape the Big Brother–style gaze of the regime – not to mention the smog of a city that could be a monument to the cement mixer – and drive up into the Alborz Mountains. There, on the snow-covered slopes of Shemshak, she can ski, flirt and remove her headscarf safely away from the eyes of the morality police. In Iran, that's a liberty that only the mountains can bestow.

Mashid isn't alone in finding solace in the land – or, indeed, the sea. Asia is home to many a 'paradise', the sort of palm-lined, white-sand beaches that can be conjured up in almost everyone's imagination and idealised until the cows (or dolphins) come home. They're delightfully scenic parts of the world, like metaphorical valves whose sole purpose is to release pressure and replace it with that holy of holies, 'relaxation'. Their very names have, in several cases, become almost universally known: Bali, Samui, Phuket, Goa. For both the pilgrims to paradise and those who make their living from them, the land fulfils their dreams.

But perhaps it's Maziar's relationship with the exotic, seductive, beguiling but sometimes brutal figure of Asia that best sums up Asia's complex bond between people and place. There, in his oasis village, he has nothing, and he has everything.

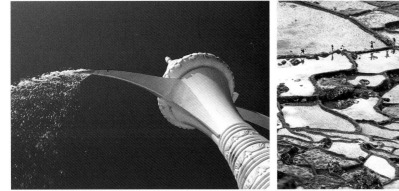

THE COFFEE-POT FOUNTAIN IN AL-ITTIHAD SQUARE, ABU DHABI, UAE   RICE PADDIES MIRROR THE SKY IN TANA TORAJA, INDONESIA   A CAMEL AND RIDER IN THE UNRELENTING DESERT LANDSCAPE

AMELIA THOMAS

LAND OF GODS

RELIGIOUS FINERY IN A PROCESSION IN PALESTINE

PILGRIMS WHIRL AROUND THE KAABA IN MECCA, SAUDI ARABIA

THE HEAD-ANOINTING OF THE JAIN SAGE GOMATESHVARA, INDIA

Wherever you find yourself in Asia, from the most remote and windswept mountaintop settlement to the frenetic, polished-steel megalopolises, you'll rarely be far from the sound of prayer. The falsetto strains of a *muezzin* emanate from a lofty marble minaret in Yemen; bells peal within a diminutive Filipino country church; drumbeats sound from a gaudy temple in the hustle and push of Bangkok; the low hum of a single, saffron-robed Tibetan monk drifts high in the foothills of the Himalaya. A whirlwind of creeds and colours, symbols and ceremonies, priests and patriarchs, rabbis, *granthis* and *sadhus*, makes this the most overtly religious, and, perhaps consequently, the most turbulent continent on earth.

Breaking down the world's religious population into a few basic percentages, it immediately becomes clear that once you set foot inside Asia, you've reached the land of the gods, the continent that has played by far the most prominent role in shaping all the major religions practised today. Christianity takes the largest chunk, with around 2.1 billion adherents accounting for some 33 per cent of the planet's population. And though the great modern bastions of Christianity don't lie within Asia, there are sizable Christian populations are scattered across Southeast Asia. The Philippines, with its population of almost 90 million, and the tiny, ravaged nation of East Timor, with just a million inhabitants, both have predominantly Christian populations – courtesy of 16th-century Spanish and Portuguese missionaries and spice traders. The religion's roots, of course, lie buried deep within Asian soil, beneath the verdant pastures and crystalline lakes of Galilee and the ancient stones of pretty, provincial and troubled Bethlehem.

The world's next largest religion is Islam, with 1.4 billion worshippers – a little over 20 per cent of the global population. Carried on trade winds towards East Asia between the 12th and 15th centuries by Arab and Indian merchants, Islam's modern-day stronghold is Indonesia, the largest Muslim-majority nation in the world, where it dominates the some 18,000 islands that comprise the vast archipelago. Pakistan and Bangladesh are the world's second- and third-largest Islam-dominated countries, as a result of the Partition of India in 1947, which caused millions of Muslims to flock west amid violence and chaos just as millions of Hindus migrated east. Islam's 6th-century Asian origins in what is today Saudi Arabia are concealed within two of the world's most revered, and paradoxically most restricted, pilgrimage cities: Mecca, in the southwest of the country, and Medina, further north.

The third of what some refer to as the 'Abrahamic religions' (though this label is hotly contested by many believers, who point to the myriad fundamental differences in doctrine and practice) is Judaism, which claims a comparatively tiny 0.23 per cent of the world's population. Minuscule, shrinking outposts of the faith still remain sprinkled across Asia, in Iran, India and the former Soviet republics of Kazakhstan, Tajikistan and Uzbekistan. The relatively new and fiercely ambitious state of Israel, founded in 1948, is home to around half of the world's 12 million Jews. In contrast to the youth of the Jewish state itself, the religion's lineage is the oldest of the grand monotheistic triumvirate, stretching back more than three millennia to the time of the biblical patriarch, Abraham, whom Jews believe was favoured by God as the founding father of their race.

The points from which these three far-ranging and frequently conflicting religions are said to have sprung form a compact, almost equilateral triangle at the very heart of the continent. This triangle is peppered with sites of immense significance, sometimes for a single one or pair of the faiths, and occasionally, tumultuously, for all three. The remains of the ancient Sumerian city of Ur stand at the bottom-right corner of the triangle. Once known as Ur of the Chaldees, it was part of ancient Mesopotamia, and is situated not far from the confluence of the great Tigris and Euphrates rivers. It was here, somewhere around 1900 BC, that Abraham is thought to have been born – the bridge from Judaism to Christianity and Islam, he appears not only in the Torah and Old Testament, but also in the Quran, as Ibrahim, a patriarch blessed by God who founded the Arab nation through his son Ismail.

Ur, or Tell al-Muqayyar as it's commonly known today, is relatively inaccessible to any but the hardiest travellers, situated as it is in southeastern Iraq, around 320 kilometres south of Baghdad. Since the US-led invasion of Iraq in 2003, Ur's ancient sites have been overseen by coalition forces and thus, in theory at least, are open to curious visitors. Nothing has been found in this bleak desert landscape to lead archaeologists directly back to the great patriarch himself. Still, tantalising hints of what the great city must have looked like during his lifetime are offered by the pottery-littered wastes surrounding the haunting Great Ziggurat. A stepped temple constructed in the 21st century BC to the moon god Nanna, the Great Ziggurat is – perhaps surprisingly – one of the world's best preserved such structures. It was from Ur that Abraham first wandered to Canaan, and then on towards the 'Promised Land' – one important divergence in the story has him making a crucial stop en route at the holiest and most fabled Islamic city of all: Mecca.

Mecca lies on the opposite side of the triangle, at its bottom-left corner. It was the birthplace of the prophet Mohammed, the great founder of Islam, who was born to a poor family of the Quraysh tribe in around AD 569. According to Islamic tradition, Mohammed didn't receive his first calling from God until he reached the age of about 40, after which he was forced to wait for another three years – amid much derision from his contemporaries, who largely worshipped Arabian tribal gods – before being contacted by God for a second time. Even before Mohammed's revelations, however, Mecca was already a great site of pilgrimage, due to the presence of the Kaaba, the holy shrine said to have been built by Ibrahim himself. Nowadays, the Kaaba remains the holiest site for Muslims across the globe: it's the direction to which the devout turn five times a day to recite the *salat* prayer, and the place to which each able-bodied Muslim is obliged to make the *haj* pilgrimage at least once during his or her lifetime, according to the *Arkan-al-Islam*, or Five Pillars of Islam.

The Kaaba itself, a small granite cube-shaped building swathed in embroidered silk, is engulfed by the massive Masjid al-Haram (the Sacred Mosque). Much expanded and ornamented since the inauguration of the Saudi regime in the early 20th century, the mosque is believed to be a representation of the house of God in heaven, and its mystical cornerstone, the Black Stone (perhaps an ancient fragment of a meteorite) is said to have been put in place by Mohammed himself.

Modern-day Mecca, in stark contrast to the tragic wastes of Ur, is a tourist destination *par excellence*, with world-class luxury hotels – some charging upwards of US$500 per night – lording it over simple hostels designed to accommodate the annual influx of more than three million pilgrims. Mecca remains out of bounds to non-Muslims, with roadblocks set up to weed out potential infiltrators. Only a handful of intrepid non-Muslims have ever managed to make it to the heart of this forbidden city; the irrepressible 19th-century British adventurer Sir Richard Burton was one. He famously entered in 1853, even being circumcised as part of his elaborate preparations to avoid detection.

The third point on the triangle, and a place with equally heavy modern restrictions on travel, is Bethlehem, situated in the conflict-ridden Palestinian Territories' West Bank. The New Testament city of Jesus' birth, Bethlehem today is a town of hardship and isolation. Imprisoned behind Israel's towering, controversial 'security wall', the Church of the Nativity, Manger Square and Star Street once saw up to a hundred tour buses per day arriving at the Grotto of the Nativity, reputedly the site of Christ's humble manger. Now, Bethlehem's quiet cobbled streets and shaded squares play host to only a trickle of Christian pilgrims and international visitors. Souvenir shops and restaurants remain locked; hotels, except for the few days around Easter and Christmas, have low occupancy rates. For visitors who do make it to Bethlehem, though, the Palestinian welcome remains warm, despite an unsteady present and uncertain future.

Just north of Bethlehem, however, is the city that encapsulates better than any other the boiling-point tensions simmering between the three great, related religions. In Jerusalem, the mystical, mythical and much disputed Temple Mount, or al-Haram al-Sharif, is the holiest place on earth for Jews, and the second-holiest for Muslims. It is, for Muslims, where Mohammed ascended to heaven; for Jews, it's the place where the First and Second Temples stood, and the site where redemption will take place when the Messiah arrives. Its al-Aqsa Mosque is the third-holiest in Islam, and was the direction towards which Muslims prayed before this was changed to Mecca. The Western or Wailing Wall below is one of the retaining walls that surrounded the Second Temple, and is the holiest site in Judaism. Just around the corner, the Via Dolorosa supposedly witnessed the last walk of Christ, and the Church of the Holy Sepulchre still contains the stone shelf on which his body lay after crucifixion. It may, at a glance, seem paradoxical that the three oft-conflicting religions all have such a small central point of significance, when to non-believers it seems they had the whole of the ancient Holy Land to choose from. Yet on the other hand, the extreme sacredness of Jerusalem, and its wrangled-over Old City in particular, also speaks clearly of the common ancestry and heritage of the faiths.

Journeying 5000 kilometres east across the vast Asian landscape, the traveller arrives in the territory of the two other mighty Asian religions, lodged firmly between the Middle Eastern wellsprings of piety and the Southeast Asian Muslim strongholds. This is the land that gave rise to the related creeds of Hinduism and Buddhism. The larger of the two, Hinduism, is also the more ancient; its central Sanskrit Veda hymns, which form the foundation stones of the faith, had their mystical origins here between 3000 and 1500 BC. Hinduism today has around a billion followers, around 13 per cent of the world's population. Its centre has never moved far from its origins in the huge, complex land of India. It's thought that the religion's evolution began in the nomadic Aryan tribes from the steppes of central Asia, who brought the Vedic tradition with them to India in about 1800 BC. Their beliefs and customs gradually intermingled with the animistic and shamanistic practices of aboriginal tribes, the nature spirit worship of the southern Dravidians, and the mother goddess cult of the sophisticated northwestern Indian Harappans. Out of this heady brew, Hinduism was born. Unlike Islam, Christianity and Judaism, Hinduism reveres no single deity or key historical figure; instead, it has a pantheon of colourful, fantastical gods – some scholars number them at around 300 million – all representing aspects of Brahman, the one eternal, infinite God. The flexibility about which god or gods the individual reveres, along with an emphasis on private

ANNAPURNA ONE THROUGH WIND-WHIPPED PRAYER FLAGS, NEPAL

BEFORE AND AFTER: A FAMILY GETS SHAVED AT A HINDU TEMPLE, INDIA

AL-AQSA MOSQUE AND DOME OF THE ROCK, JERUSALEM, ISRAEL

rather than congregational worship, means Hinduism has become one of the most personal, vivid and varying religions on earth.

Travellers to ancient Varanasi, on the banks of the holy river Ganges, experience Hinduism at its most ebullient during the spring festival of Holi. To be there is to be blinded by colour – perhaps literally, with the throwing of coloured *tika* powder – while being pulled headlong into the maelstrom of festivities that consume the city. (An alternative is to join the seething, worshipping millions at the Kumbh Mela, an enormous, frantic festival held every three years in one of four rotating Indian locations – the sites, according to Hindu legend, where four drops of *amrita*, the nectar of immortality, fell from the sky during an epic aerial battle between the gods and the demons.) Reputedly the oldest continually inhabited city in the world, Varanasi is also the location of a riverside temple-shrine to Lord Kashi Vishwanath, an incarnation of Lord Shiva, the preserver-god of the universe: thus, the city itself remains at the heart of all Hindu pilgrimage. Bathing at the city's *ghats* purges one of sins, and dying within the city walls can break the cycle of rebirth known as *samsara*.

North of Varanasi lies the place at which the world's fourth-largest religion was born, today encompassing nearly six per cent of the population, with devotees totalling at least 600 million worldwide. More accurately a philosophical system combining elements of faith than a religion, Buddhism had its beginnings with the enlightenment of the wealthy prince Siddhartha Gautama, later known as the Buddha, who was born in 563 BC to a chieftain family in Lumbini, in modern-day Nepal. From the initial teachings of the Buddha, cradled in Hinduism and based largely on the moderate 'Middle Way' and methods of achieving *nirvana*, Buddhism split into three main forms, which all spread widely across Asia. Southern or Theravada Buddhism, with its scriptures written in Pali, an ancient language close to Sanskrit, is the Buddhism of Thailand, Cambodia, Sri Lanka, Laos and Myanmar; Northern or Mahayana Buddhism is the most diverse of Buddhism's forms, and is today practised in Vietnam, Japan, South Korea and officially atheist China. Perhaps the most familiar form of Buddhism to the modern Westerner is Vajrayana or Tibetan Buddhism, which is headed by the Dalai Lama and practised in Northern India, Nepal and Mongolia.

Today, the exact spot in northern India where the Buddha achieved enlightenment beneath the Bodhi Tree is marked by a tree said to be its direct descendent, a *Ficus religiosa* or sacred fig, situated at the Mahabodhi Temple in Bodhgaya. Pilgrims flock to this place, the most important of the four holiest pilgrimage sites of Buddhism. It has resonance for Hindus too, since they believe the Buddha was the ninth incarnation of the Lord Shiva. Unlike many other of the world's pilgrimage destinations, Buddhist sacred places – rather like the religion itself – tend to be quiet and understated. Along with Bodhgaya, Lumbini retains a serene, small-town feel, save for a single main tourist bazaar. Pilgrims to the town can wander relatively undisturbed to the great Ashokan Pillar, erected just 300 years after the Buddha's birth by the great Buddhist emperor, Ashoka, to commemorate his own pilgrimage there. Of the four Buddhist pilgrimage destinations, incidentally, only Lumbini lies in Nepal: Kushinagar, where the Buddha died and was cremated, and Sarnath, the deer park where he gave his first teachings, are both located in northern India, the latter close to Varanasi.

On a journey to almost any destination in the massive continent of Asia, it's likely you will encounter a sacred place for at least one of the major world religions, which, despite the paths they later traced across the globe, remain distinctly Asian to the core. Their offshoots and variations are numerous; the points – geographical, theological and philosophical – at which they meet, mingle and diverge are many. Some Asian religions such as Sikhism, with its Punjabi stronghold and major pilgrimage site at the glorious Amritsar Golden Temple, remain relatively isolated and distinct – though the roots of the Sikh faith, too, are inextricably linked to those of its neighbouring creeds. Others, like the Chinese traditional religions that mix Taoism, Confucianism and Buddhism, defy categorisation. With the presence of religion so palpable throughout Asia, and with the great, soaring Himalaya containing the very closest points to heaven on the planet, it's likely that even the most staunchly atheist travellers will find themselves presented, either through local culture or simply through topography, with a vivid, compelling vision of god, gods or goddesses at least once during their visit.

TEXT CHINA WILLIAMS, ANDREW BENDER, AMY KARAFIN & JENNY WALKER

POP GOES ASIA

⌃ IRANIAN REBELS WITHOUT A CAUSE

⌃ JASON SCOTT LEE AS THE LEGENDARY BRUCE LEE

⌃ A FANBOY IN A MANGA COSTUME, JAPAN

Cast off that tweedy traditionalist thinking that Asia is all temples and ancient rituals. This land may be old but it's filled with teenagers who love bubble-gum pop music, luxury cars, high-tech gadgets and a good shoot-'em-up flick. These home-grown entertainments aren't merely imitations of Western exports – they're as intertwined with the regional psyches as the more lauded traditional arts.

Japan is the prime mover for Asian pop culture. J-pop, manga, *anime* and even karaoke have infiltrated commercial centres around the world. Hong Kong is another leader in producing cutting-edge entertainment; and while all of Asia loves to sing, India has enshrined the art form in the long-surviving Bollywood industry. The celebrities and songs may change over time, but fans' almost religious devotion to this unique form of escapism holds steadfast across generations.

Despite an exterior of traditionalism, the Middle East also supports a healthy popular culture scene, with Iranian club music migrating to European dance halls and satellite television beaming music videos and soap operas into homes. Although the perceived social liberties of the outside world are hot conversation topics in coffee houses and souqs, many instead choose the freedom exalted by their own cultures: the open road. In the Middle East, the automobile is the unifying excess.

ASIAN CINEMA CLASSICS

Let's begin with the silver screen, where Hollywood thinks it has won the race. Asian films are about more than duelling giant lizards – not to take anything away from

Godzilla (we dare you to try…). Northeast Asia, especially, has added as much to the global canon of film classics as any Western nation, and the global vernacular of pop-culture references became a lot cooler once Hong Kong got involved. Through movies, most notably, ours is a shrinking planet.

In every cinema circle, Japanese film-maker Akira Kurosawa (1910–98) is universally recognised as a master. Many of Kurosawa's acclaimed films, including *Rashōmon* (1950) and *Shichinin no Samurai* (The Seven Samurai, 1954), focus on the semi-historical wandering samurai in a lawless world. These films helped cement the samurai into the world's collective imagination and inspired other film-makers to explore frontier heroes and villains within their own cultures. Many of the American westerns, including *The Magnificent Seven* and *A Fistful of Dollars*, are direct homages to Kurosawa. Other masterpieces of Japanese film-making's golden age include Kon Ichikawa's *Biruma no Tategoto* (The Burmese Harp, 1956) and Yasujirō Ōzu's *Tōkyō Monogatari* (Tokyo Story, 1953).

Across the East China Sea, Hong Kong crowned another warrior class in film: the kung fu masters. Although a long line of kung fu stars preceded him, it was an American-born Chinese who made the genre an international success in the 1970s. Bruce Lee (1940–73) was lean and mean and had lightning-fast ass-kicking skills. He's credited for setting the standard for an entire generation of chop-socky kung fu films. In the 1990s, Tsui Hark's *Once Upon a Time in China* series resurrected on screen the genre of *wūxiá*, stories about chivalrous martial arts heroes, both men and

LARGER THAN LIFE: BOLLYWOOD FILMS SUCH AS *DEVDAS* INSPIRE AN ALMOST RELIGIOUS DEVOTION IN INDIA

women. These retooled Chinese folk tales used modern-day special effects to set the star, Jet Li, sailing through the air with fists raised and running across pursuers' heads as if crossing a stream strewn with rocks. Taiwanese director Ang Lee's film *Crouching Tiger, Hidden Dragon* (2000), starring Chow Yun-Fat and Michelle Yeoh, is a more recent incarnation of this genre. Today's Hong Kong film-maker to beat, however, is Stephen Chow, whose comedy *Kung Fu Hustle* (2004) was a break-out success. Zhāng Yìmóu's *Hero* (2002) and *House of Flying Daggers* (2004) were mainland China's answers to Hong Kong's dominance of action films. *Hero* sets itself apart from other *wǔxiá* films with its signature Chinese subplot about national unity.

In the 1980s Hong Kong added another dimension to action-hero cosmology with John Woo's 'gun-fu' movies, in which gunplay replaced the traditional exchange of punches and kicks. His blood-soaked epics – *A Better Tomorrow* (1986), *The Killer* (1989) and *Hard-Boiled* (1992) – captured the flamboyant fashions of the time with the ultimate unflappable leading man, Chow Yun-Fat. Woo has since gone on to direct Hollywood blockbusters such as *Mission: Impossible II* (2000).

More akin to Kurosawa's tales of blurred lines between good and evil are the films of Park Chan-Wook, South Korea's film-maker of the moment and director of the 'vengeance trilogy': *Sympathy for Mr Vengeance* (2002), *Oldboy* (2003) and *Lady Vengeance* (2005). They're grisly, personal stories that often recall Greek tragedies, complete with intractable suffering and well-meaning but doomed protagonists. In interviews, Park has said that his films aren't meant to endorse vengeance but rather to show its futility. Thailand's Pen-ek Ratanaruang has also earned a seat on international film circuits with his wry and visually stunning movies. *Last Life in the Universe* (2003) is a trilingual film (Thai, Japanese and English) that follows the friendship between two mismatched but lonely characters. It also contains the director's signature flourish, an absurdist shoot-out scene in which everyone in the room is killed.

The most historical genre of films in Asia can be credited to one of the continent's oldest nations: mainland China. The classics that have emerged from China's turbulent modern era capture that country's cultural upheaval and its richly visual tradition of storytelling. In Chén Kǎigē's *Yellow Earth* (1984), a young communist soldier is sent to a remote village in the north to collect rousing folk songs for propaganda. Instead, he converts a young peasant girl with the modernising communist message. Chén's follow-up masterpiece *Farewell My Concubine* (1993) follows the careers of two famous Peking Opera stars – one of whom, playing the concubine, finds it harder to move in and out of character than his male lead and friend. Beyond its classic story of unrequited love are the rumblings of the Cultural Revolution and the shifting alliances that an archaic art form such as opera must make to survive. Other visually epic films in the mainland-Chinese repertoire include Zhāng Yìmóu's films *Red Sorghum* (1987 – it was the break-out film for actress Gǒng Lì, the poster girl for Chinese cinema in the 1990s), *Raise the Red Lantern* (1991) and *Shanghai Triad* (1995).

BOLLYWOOD – A CLASS OF ITS OWN

The perfect counterbalance to the tragic drama of Chinese cinema is Bollywood. Everything about Bollywood is big and exuberant. The movies run up to three and a half hours long, not including intermission, and have six or seven (or 12) song-and-dance numbers with casts of hundreds. Costumes and palatial settings are as elaborate as the forces that keep the lover-protagonists apart. One film, or even one song, may be shot in several different countries, and distribution is worldwide. Actors are prolific. It's not unusual for the big names to shoot several films a year; veteran megastar Amitabh Bachchan once did 11. Bollywood bombshell and former Miss World Aishwarya Rai is almost as busy.

The roughly 1000 movies released each year play at city theatres and in tents across small-town India, where tickets cost 10 rupees (US$0.25) and may supplant the evening meal. About 3.6 billion tickets are sold annually – that beats Hollywood by a billion. Audiences come for 'masala movies', named for their mix of comedy (without irony), drama (happy ending guaranteed), action (sans violence) and romance (without kissing).

Off-screen it's another story: the industry is a masala of scandals. There's the usual superstar gossip of love affairs (here, a public kiss will do it) and bad behaviour. But it has the added spice of family intrigue: Bollywood actors all seem to be related. Big stars tend to have kids who become big stars, and they marry other big-shot children of other industry heavy-hitters – like royalty, or circus families.

The biz also has less noble connections to another kind of family: the Bombay underground, which has funded feature films for decades. Assassination attempts on producers and directors and the blackmailing of actors are not uncommon. Some movie-loving dons demand a say in casting and plot lines; directors of gangster films worry about mafiosos' reviews. Add to this the alleged tendency of dons to emulate their film counterparts and to name their children after movie heroes, and it all starts to sound like so many Bollywood movie high jinks.

But the films' influence on the real world is not limited to gangster circles. Bombay Hindi – a mix of broken Hindi, slang and words from other languages – was considered improper until it was popularised by films set in Bombay. Macho, street-smart heroes (especially those played by Amitabh Bachchan) speak Bombay Hindi, and now it's widely understood and accepted.

Likewise, fashion tastes across the country are shifting. *Salwaar kameez,* formerly worn only in the north, are now standard issue among girls in sari-wearing bastions like Tamil Nadu. *Kameez* hemlines rise and fall with the whims of Bollywood – or Kollywood or Tollywood, as the case may be. Southern India's Tamil- and Telugu-language film industries, once Bollywood's frumpy cousins, are now spiffing up, hiring Bombay's big-name celebs, and boosting output.

Those big names can make or break a film, but so can the music they lip-synch to: one good song is enough to secure ticket sales. The music, called *filmi* (the Hindi adjective for 'film'), plays in the streets across India, the good songs continuing long after their films have been forgotten. Kids act out the song-and-dance routines by the side of those roads: pint-sized versions of star-crossed lovers performing for an imaginary audience of billions.

DISNEY ON A RICE DIET

From *Pokémon* to *Sailor Moon* and *Akira*, anime (Japanese animation) encompasses all genres and demographics, with breathtakingly realistic visuals, exquisite attention to detail, complex and expressive characters and elaborate plots. Leading directors and voice actors have rock-star status, and characters become popular idols.

Hundreds of *anime* studios in Japan create everything from feature films and TV series to interstitials for video games. Many *anime* stories start as manga, the Japanese comic books whose roots go back to Japan's historic woodblock prints. Today, manga accounts for an astounding 40 per cent of all publication sales in Japan, and it's gaining popularity worldwide.

The artist credited with creating the signature *anime* style – characters with large oval eyes – was Osamu Tezuka (1928–89), considered the father of the genre. His first series was *Tetsuwan Atom* (Astro Boy, 1963), which followed the crime-fighting adventures of an android superhero outfitted with the usual comic book powers: jets in his arms and legs, lasers in his fingers and rear, an evil-intention-detecting heart and extraordinary strength and hearing. Another in Tezuka's catalogue is *Jungle Taitei* (Kimba the White Lion, 1965) – which appears to have strongly influenced Disney's 1994 hit, *The Lion King*.

Today's king of *anime* is Hayao Miyazaki, recognised for his highly imaginative and complex stories. His film *Mononoke-hime* (Princess Mononoke, 1997), about the historic transition between medieval and modern Japan, is a tale about a war between the forest spirits and the humans who want to exploit the land's resources. The movie broke the Japanese box-office record set by *ET*, but was later sunk by *Titanic*. His follow-up was *Sen to Chihiro no Kamikakushi* (Spirited Away, 2002), about a young girl who becomes imprisoned in a bathhouse for spirits and ogres; it won the Oscar for best animated film.

IT'S GOT A BEAT

Japan, the country that invented karaoke (in 1971), has also given the world its own uniquely spiced version of pop bands and crooners. The typical J-pop starlet is similar to her Western counterpart: teenage, female and cloyingly cute, with a shelf life, normally, of only a few moons. The stars who have graduated to icon status include Seiko Matsuda, who holds the title of most number one singles for a female artist, Chage & Asuka, and the groups Anzen Chitai and Hikaru Genji. These days, the J-Pop craze mixes solo artists and megagroups like the boy band SMAP and Morning Musume, a girl group that keeps things fresh by continually swapping out its dozen-or-so members.

K-Pop (Korean Pop) and Hong Kong's Canto-Pop aren't far behind the hit-record status of J-Pop. The 2006 Korean phenomenon is Rain, named one of the world's 100 most influential people of the year, who sells out concerts throughout Asia and is starring in a soap opera. In Canto-Pop, there is an entire constellation of twinkle-eyed, pretty stars, well known in Chinese-speaking communities worldwide: the thespian-crooner Andy Lau, Mr Nice Guy Jackie Cheung, ex-Běijīng waif Faye Wong, the immortal Sally Yip, and more recent arrivals like Sammi Cheung, Candy Lo, Grace Ip and bad boy Nicholas Tse.

CRUISING THE SAND STRIP

Songs and cinemas might entertain the masses further east, but the Middle East prefers expensive modern gadgets. In Syria it's not uncommon to see elderly men trotting down the road on a donkey laden with leafage; in Oman, boys loll by on camels trimmed with Bedouin regalia; in Yemen, women herd goats to the next piece of desert-fringed grazing land. What is more surprising to visitors to the Middle East, however, is that the road may be a double-lane highway, and the boy in all probability is whispering '*habibi*' (darling) into the receiver of a video-conferencing mobile phone. The women, under a variety of cloaks and *abeyya,* may well be wearing Wrangler and Nike. In the Gulf, the international computer and text messaging jargon has slipped seamlessly into the vernacular, with phrases like 'log on', 'download', and 'how RU' peppering the ritual *salaam* of traditional greeting. It's *haram* (forbidden) for women to be seen without the *hejab*; but almost more *haram* to be seen with the wrong handbag.

If there's one piece of pop culture that's common to the whole region, however, it must be *al-siera* – that is, not just 'car', but 'The Car'. The modern equivalent of the load-bearing camel has to be all things to all people. It has to transport caravans of goods, including woollen tents and television sets in Saudi Arabia, the fold-away barbecue in the United Arab Emirates, goods best not asked about in Iraq, and even the camel itself, deemed too precious these days to make its own journey in Oman.

While The Car has to travel goat-tracks in Iran on which most people wouldn't hazard a pair of boots, and run immaculate errands into the local mall for white-gloved ladies in Kuwait, it has a far more important function than mere transportation: it is expected to signal (even where the driver is not generally given to such habits) the exact size of the family fortune. It is therefore required to be four-wheel drive (whether backless, topless or bull-bars additional), preferably Toyota, and ultimately Land Cruiser. No other form of popular culture in the Middle East is quite as prominent, nor has any inspired quite as much love as the four-wheel drive: in Muscat there is a fine of five rials for driving a dirty one; in Doha the seats are trimmed with sheep pelts; in Manama the vehicles are lavished with prayer beads.

Seen as the safe family car in many other countries, in the Middle East the four-wheel drive *is* the family – the vehicle by which adolescent boys injudiciously prove themselves, the wheel behind which daughters show that Islamic women are fashionable too, the conveyor of the eight children of the neighbour's friend, the prize camel of the caravan.

TEXT | TONY WHEELER

FLASHING BACK TO THE
ASIAN HIPPY TRAIL

WINDOW SHOPPING IN SHÀNGHÃI, CHINA

SMILING DEITIES AT THE SHWEDAGON PAYA, YANGON, MYANMAR

ASCETIC LIFE IN THE RIZONG MONASTERY, LADAKH, INDIA

It was the era of the Magic Bus, the Hippy Trail, the Long and Winding Road – a time when half a dozen influences converged, the planets moved into a benevolent alignment and as a result, and perhaps just for a moment, things changed. Travel through Asia took off.

Some of those late '60s, early '70s influences on travel were boringly demographic, economic, historical and technological. The jet age was reaching maturity: jumbo jets took to the skies and the cost of travel plummeted. At the same time, the postwar baby boomers were coming of age – I should know, I was one of them – and setting off on their first big solo journeys.

There were a lot of boomers, so anything they did was bound to make an impact. They were also far better off than any previous generation, and were living through a remarkably long period without major conflicts. In the 26 years between the end of World War II and my departure, age 25, for Asia and beyond, the economic graph had shown a single upward-sloping line of increasing prosperity. (In contrast, the 21 years between the end of World War I and the start of World War II encompassed the Great Depression, an economic downturn of unprecedented severity.)

Not all the influences of the time were so mundane, though – there was also a magic in the air. Jack Kerouac's *On the Road* might have been published in 1951 but, along with the novels of Herman Hesse, it was one of the 'in-every-backpack' books of the '60s. The Beatles were in India and Indian fashions were in Notting Hill and Haight-Ashbury. Revolution was also in the air – Vietnam was as much a protest as a place. All these factors combined to bring Asia onto the boomers' collective radar

and kick off the era of Asian travel. It was a time when horizons widened. Europe might have seemed exotic to our parents, but the whole world was spread out before us, and if some of the places we encountered were delicious surprises, that was just the way exploration should be.

Maureen and I set off on our journey to the East in mid-1972, driving a beaten-up old car so cheap that if it collapsed we were prepared to park it by the roadside and walk away. It took us from London all the way to Kabul in Afghanistan. Looking back, that first 'big trip' was a succession of magic moments, still technicolour bright to this day.

Turkey was our first glimpse of Asia, the East, a different world. It seems appropriate that the leap from Europe to Asia – the crossing of the Bosporus – was on a ferry. It was also fitting that the first bridge connecting Istanbul's western and eastern halves was nearing completion just upstream from our ferry route. Things were about to change.

Fortunes have fluctuated in a number of places in the years since our first visit. At that time, Iran was a place pregnant with possibilities and yet roiling with internal conflicts and anger. It would soon tumble into the chaos and conflict that's yet to play itself out even today, and is threatening to drag in many other parts of the world. Afghanistan is an even sadder story, a place that alternately charmed and terrified us, but soon after tumbled into a maelstrom of horrific intensity.

Pakistan was then and is now a country where huge possibilities and potential added up to pitifully small end results. Back then our fellow travellers rushed through Pakistan, lured eastwards to the great attractions of India; now they simply avoid it. India was larger than life in 1972 and it's still larger than life today, although it's worth remembering that the number of visitors it attracts is still, in reality, very limited. For us, Nepal, and particularly Kathmandu, was the enchanted end of the rainbow, a place we fell in love with at first sight. Despite all its recent troubles it has been a long-term love affair of mine, and my fingers are crossed that the mountain kingdom will find a way out of its problems.

Nepal was the end of one rainbow, but it was also the starting point for another. From India we hopped across to Thailand, which was then a mysterious destination for the truly dedicated traveller or, alternatively, R&R patrons from the nearby Vietnam War. We hitchhiked through Malaysia and paused in Singapore, the steamy city-state which was about to morph into one of the world's great economic success stories. Indonesia was a place we barely knew or understood; at the time, when the country was moving out of the shadow of the tumultuous Soekarno years, that was probably true for much of the outside world. Bali charmed us instantly.

That first Asian exploration may have started out as a once-in-a-lifetime trip, but it has ended up as a rest-of-a-lifetime journey. A year later we published the first Lonely Planet guidebook, gleaned from our overland travel experience in Asia. The following year we took off on a 12-month exploration of Southeast Asia which allowed us to explore Indonesia in much greater depth, delve into Malaysia and Thailand and dip into Indochina (in 1974 Laos was still open, just). It also kicked off another long-term love affair, albeit a distinctly troubled one, with Burma, today's Myanmar. We even went to Portuguese Timor, a colony that would briefly become an independent nation before Indonesia swallowed it – only to cough it up, Jonah-like, as an independent nation a quarter of a century later.

The Southeast Asia trip led to the second Lonely Planet guidebook, the 'yellow bible'. I still get a huge kick out of its role as an introduction to the region for many travellers, young and old. In later editions it would expand to add other countries in the region; the final laggers – Vietnam, Laos and Cambodia – were included in the 1990s when they reopened to the outside world.

Those first trips in the 1970s laid the foundations for the following three decades of Asian wandering and, remarkably, there's still much more for me to do. On my first glimpse of China I didn't even set a toe inside the country. In 1977 China was still a closed shop: the lid of the Chairman's big red mystery box was firmly locked. The best you could do – and we did it – was to go up to the edge of Hong Kong's New Territories, stand on a hillside and gaze at the peasants working the fields across the border. Today the view would probably take in endless manufacturing plants churning out DVDs and laptop computers destined to stack shelves in the West.

Strictly organised and orchestrated group tours of China kicked off soon after Richard Nixon's ground-breaking 1972 visit, but it wasn't until the early 1980s that the first independent visitors began to sneak in. Their passports carried visas that were more likely to have been issued by mysterious backpacker tour offices in Hong Kong's Chungking Mansions than by any Chinese embassy. Those intrepid early explorers came back with tales of tough travel, touchy officials and bottomless bureaucracy.

Two decades later China has changed beyond belief. I travelled across southern China from the Vietnamese border to Shànghǎi in mid-2005, buying tickets in computerised bus stations and riding in modern air-conditioned buses down state-of-the-art superhighways. As we drove into every big city we'd pass a zone of car dealers where the latest luxmobiles from BMW and Mercedes were lined up for their new Chinese owners.

Japan also popped up repeatedly on my travel itineraries in the mid-1980s. In 1990, working on a new edition of our Japan guidebook, I managed to explore the western half of the country fairly thoroughly on a trip which included nights in everything from capsule hotels to love hotels, luxury *ryokans* to backpacker hostels, family *minshukus* to assembly-line business hotels. Nearby Korea didn't feature on my travel itineraries until the new century, but I've made up for lost time since, with repeat visits to South Korea and one memorable foray into North Korea – a country that still tops my list of the weirdest places I've ever visited.

In the 1990s the Middle East stamped its way into my passport, first with a visit to Jordan and Israel. On that trip I arrived in Israel by crossing the Allenby Bridge to the West Bank, and departed into the Egyptian Sinai. In subsequent years I've taken in the Gulf States. There have been repeat visits to Dubai, the only city in the world to rival the Chinese metropolises for pace and scale of change, and visits to other cities in the United Arab Emirates and other Arabian Peninsula countries, including the most interesting and perplexing of them all, Saudi Arabia. In 2006 I managed to four-wheel-drive my way around Oman, return to Afghanistan and even sneak into Iraq for a quick look around the northern region.

There's still all of Asian Russia and the former Soviet states of Central Asia to explore, as well as Mongolia – I'm going there in 2007 – and Taiwan, which has somehow slipped through my fingers thus far.

In three decades of Asian travel I've made regular repeat visits, for a whole host of reasons other than simply going back to update a guidebook. I've made a circuit of the region with photographer Richard I'Anson to follow the story of that most Asian of transport modes, the bicycle rickshaw. We documented that journey, covering 12 major Asian cities, in the book *Chasing Rickshaws*, which led a couple of years later to another Asian circuit. This time Richard and I traced the story of the most Asian of foods, rice. *Rice Trails* not only followed the path of rice from paddy field to mill to restaurant and home, but also recorded the story of the world's most important food, most beautiful crop and the myriad ceremonies and festivals associated with it.

I've been fortunate enough to have experienced the region as a whole host of different 'tourists'. My first visit was as a penniless backpacker: I've returned in a multitude of different disguises. Maureen and I have travelled through Asia with our young children and experienced how 'travel with children' can be an easy-going delight in places like Bali, an education in Japan or India and a challenge on walks through the Himalaya. As older and more affluent travellers, we've experienced the luxurious side of Asia, from stays in the Peninsula Hotel in Hong Kong to the Oriental in Bangkok. We've explored Asia as business travellers, too. Sometimes our book-publishing business has taken us to book fairs and publishing meetings through the regions, or to book-publishing plants in major printing centres like Singapore and Hong Kong. On other occasions we've participated and spoken at travel and tourism conferences and summits from Macau to Nagoya, Seoul to Hong Kong. In addition, Lonely Planet has endeavoured to put money and effort back into the Asian countries it has been so engaged with; we've been fortunate enough to see that effort pay off first-hand in aid projects all over the region.

In all this travel, and for all these different reasons, we've continued to be amazed by new discoveries in Asia. Of course there are wonders we've read about, seen in films and documentaries, and learnt to understand long before we actually encountered them. (Even so, the first sight of the Great Wall of China, the dark triangle of Mt Everest, the shimmering beauty of the Taj Mahal, the neon confusion of central Tokyo or the living beauty of a Thai coral reef all met and exceeded our

△ A LIVID PERFORMER AT A TIBETAN BUDDHIST FESTIVAL

▷ THE BIG SQUEEZE: AN OVERLOADED BUS IN BODH GAYA, INDIA

△ RICKSHAW OPERATORS TAKE A LOAD OFF, HONG KONG

CART DRIVERS HAVE A CONFABULATION IN A BIRGANJ STREET, NEPAL

expectations.) But Asia still regularly blows Maureen and I away with places that provoke the questions, 'Why didn't I know about this? Why haven't I seen this in a book, a film, a magazine?' Those were my first thoughts when I arrived at dawn in Myanmar's lost city of Pagan back in 1974; a few years ago Tsaparang, a virtually forgotten Buddhist city in far-west Tibet, gave me a repeat experience. Even in the last 12 months I've been privileged to stagger back, take a deep breath and say 'Wow' a number of times. Why didn't I know about the hill-top citadel of Arbil in the Kurdistan region of Iraq until I arrived there? How had the rock-cut Buddhist stupa of Takht-e Rustam in Afghanistan evaded my attention until I stood on the edge of a plateau and looked down at it?

Of course, I've only enjoyed so much of Asia by never becoming an expert on any of it. I have huge respect for our writers and researchers, who speak the language, have degrees on the history and know their corner of Asia intimately. I've been a dilettante, enjoying a taste here, a flavour there. On the other hand, I can say 'yes', 'no', 'please', 'thank you', 'a cold beer' and count to 10 in a host of different Asian languages and I've developed a taste for the cuisine of almost every Asian country I've visited. An Indonesian *nasi campur*, a Hainanese chicken rice, an Indian *thali*, a Japanese *bento* box – I wouldn't know which one to choose.

So that is my Asia, a region I've been wandering through for over 30 years without ever getting close to the end of that long and winding road. It's pushed me, it's tested me, it's left me hungry and exhausted, but it's also left me exhilarated and amazed. I still don't feel like I've scratched the surface of what Asia has to offer – this is a love affair that's going to last all the way to the end.

THE AUTHORS

CHINA WILLIAMS (COORDINATING AUTHOR)

Because of the name, China Williams was destined to meet and adore Asia. The fated rendezvous occurred with a teaching position in rural Thailand, where she developed a serious rice addiction and more freckles than skin. She has has written numerous Lonely Planet guidebooks to Thailand and other countries in Southeast Asia and currently lives in Montana, of all places, with her husband, Matt.

ANDREW BENDER

France was closed, so after college Andy moved to Japan instead. It was a life-changing experience, as Asian journeys so often are. Now based in Los Angeles and New York, he writes for publications including *Forbes* and *Travel + Leisure;* his Lonely Planet books include *Japan, Korea, Taiwan* and *Tokyo.*

JOE BINDLOSS

Joe Bindloss was born in Cyprus, grew up in England and has since lived and worked all over the place, though he currently calls London home. Joe has written for Lonely Planet all over Asia, from India and Nepal to Thailand and the Phillipines.

GREG BLOOM

Greg lives with his wife and baby daughter in Manila, where he splits his time between travel writing and editing reports for international organisations. Formerly the editor of the *Kyiv Post* in Ukraine, he writes frequently for Lonely Planet about the Philippines and countries of the former Soviet Union.

LINDSAY BROWN

Lindsay Brown, a travel writer and photographer, is a former conservation biologist and publishing manager of trekking guides at Lonely Planet. He has contributed to Lonely Planet's *India, South India, Pakistan & the Karakoram Highway,* and *Nepal* guidebooks.

ANDREW BURKE

Andrew Burke is a journalist and photographer who has worked and travelled in Asia for 15 years and lived there since 2001. Work and play have taken him to more than 20 Asian countries, though his specialities are Indochina and the Middle East. Andrew has written or contributed to 10 Lonely Planet books, including *Iran, Laos* and *China.*

TERRY CARTER & LARA DUNSTON

Australians Terry Carter and Lara Dunston made the Middle East their home after moving to the United Arab Emirates in 1998. Their first guidebook for Lonely Planet was *Syria & Lebanon,* followed by *Dubai.* A dozen books later, they still love writing about the atmospheric souqs, Oriental music, and delicious cuisine that make Damascus and Dubai two of their favourite cities.

PAUL CLAMMER

Paul has travelled widely in the Islamic world as a backpacker, tour leader and guidebook writer, from Casablanca to Kashgar. His great love is Afghanistan, which he's been visiting regularly since 2001, when he had dinner with two Taliban ministers a fortnight before the 9/11 attacks.

MARK ELLIOTT

British-born travel writer Mark Elliott has crisscrossed Asia for two decades. Amongst his many books, cult classic *Asia Overland* showed penniless backpackers how to traverse the continent on little more than a smile. Mark's fascination with Sri Lanka was particularly engaged by a 1987 Hill Country meditation retreat and by observing the momentous 2005 (non)election in Jaffna.

FRANCES LINZEE GORDON

First sparked by a school scholarship, Frances' fervour for travel continues unabated. She regularly visits the Middle East (for which she has a special passion) and contributes text and photos to a variety of publications. She recently completed a part-time MA in African and Asian Studies and Arabic in London.

JULIE GRUNDVIG

Julie Grundvig is a contributor to several Lonely Planet titles, including *Taiwan, China* and *Bluelist.* She holds an MA in classical Chinese and is associate editor for *Yishu: Journal of Contemporary Chinese Art.* She currently lives in Vancouver, BC, Canada.

ANTHONY HAM

In another life, Anthony represented asylum seekers from across the Middle East and completed a Master degree in Middle Eastern politics before setting off to write and photograph his way around the world. Anthony wrote Lonely Planet's *Saudi Arabia* book and coordinated *Middle East.*

AMY KARAFIN

Indian in several former lives, Amy Karafin headed straight to India after university in the US. Once there, she fortuitously discovered both meditation and its inverse, Bollywood. She has worked on two editions of Lonely Planet's *India* and is studying Hindi – primarily so that she can sing along to Bollywood movies.

MICHAEL KOHN

Michael Kohn's love of Asia was sealed on a manic overland bus journey across India at age 18. He later taught English in Osaka and edited a newspaper in Ulaanbaatar before hooking up with Lonely Planet in 2003. Along with Lonely Planet's *Tibet, Central Asia* and *Israel & the Palestinian Territories,* he is also the author of *Dateline Mongolia: An American Journalist in Nomad's Land.*

MARIKA MCADAM

Marika McAdam is a proud Melburnian who has based most of life's decisions on geography. Marika has a background in law and international relations and a future in neither. She is the sole author of *Bangladesh* and *Goa,* and contributor to the *Lonely Planet Guide to Experimental Travel.* Asia is in Marika's blood, and in her genes.

TOM MASTERS

Tom Masters lives and works in London but has a passion for diving and is a regular visitor to the Indian Ocean. When he's not enjoying the warm, clear waters of the tropics for Lonely Planet, Tom works as a documentary producer for British and American TV networks.

BRADLEY MAYHEW

Bradley has been travelling through Asia since graduating with a degree in Oriental Studies from Oxford University. Addicted to Central Asia and Tibet, he is the author of Lonely Planet guides to *Tibet, Central Asia, China, Nepal, Shanghai, Southwest China* and *Bhutan.* He has lectured on Central Asia to the Royal Geographical Society and is the author of the Odyssey Guide to Uzbekistan.

MAT OAKLEY

Mat was born in the English town of Watford, whose residents are united by a desire not to live in Watford anymore. After stints living and working as a journalist in Thailand, Laos, Australia and Fiji, he now lives in Singapore with his wife and two badly behaved Fijian cats.

TOM PARKINSON

Twelve years after reading *Into the Heart of Borneo* and four years after joining Lonely Planet, Tom finally made it east of his habitual European and African stomping grounds to explore the Malaysian jungles. For this book he revisited his time in the peculiar oil-soaked nugget-nation that is Brunei.

CHRIS PITTS

Chris studied Chinese literature in the US, China and Taiwan, before a chance meeting in a library elevator wound up letting him off in Paris *(parlez-vous chinois?).* He has written for Lonely Planet's *China* and *Shanghai,* though unfortunately he has yet to publish any of his classical Chinese poetry.

DEVIKA RAJAN

Devika left a senior position with the State Bank of India in 2004, responding to an urge to do something different. Since then, she has dabbled in travel writing and poetry, taken part in theatre workshops, and run a half marathon. She lives in Mumbai with her banker husband and her collection of books.

NICK RAY

A Londoner of sorts, Nick comes from Watford, the sort of town that makes you want to travel. Nick currently lives in Phnom Penh, Cambodia and has combed every corner of the Mekong region in his work as a guidebook author, tour manager and location scout for TV and film.

INDEX

ROBERT REID

A transplanted Okie now based in Brooklyn, Robert has updated many Lonely Planet guidebooks, including *Myanmar (Burma)* and *Southeast Asia*. In the golden '90s, Robert taught English and worked at *Vietnam News* in Ho Chi Minh City for a spell, before joining Lonely Planet's inner ranks as a Commissioning Editor and Publishing Manager for Shoestring guides.

SIMON RICHMOND

Simon Richmond's first visit to Malaysia was back in the early 1990s. At the time he was living and working in Tokyo. He's since travelled throughout the country from the sun-kissed beaches of Langkawi to the deepest jungles of Sarawak. He's the coordinating author of Lonely Planet's *Malaysia, Singapore & Brunei*.

DANIEL ROBINSON

Daniel Robinson grew up in California, Illinois and Israel and has a BA in Near Eastern studies from Princeton and an MA in modern Jewish history from Tel Aviv University. His recent writing on the Middle East includes reporting for the Associated Press and the 4th edition of Lonely Planet's *Tunisia* guide. He is based in Tel Aviv.

MARTIN ROBINSON

Martin Robinson has wrestled with *hangeul* (the Korean language) on Lonely Planet's last two editions of *Korea* and *Seoul*. He lived in South Korea for two years teaching English, working in a provincial governor's office and eating 50 types of *kimchi* (spicy vegetables). He's married and nowadays lives in New Zealand.

SARINA SINGH

Sarina Singh, a freelance journalist and former foreign correspondent, has worked on over 20 Lonely Planet titles including *Pakistan & the Karakoram Highway*. She has also written for international publications such as *National Geographic Traveler* and the *Sunday Times* and is the writer/director of *Beyond The Royal Veil*, a television documentary about Indian 'royalty'.

PAUL SMITZ

After numerous 'visits' to Hong Kong that involved little more than a stopover in the airport, Paul finally got the chance to take an extended tour of this dramatic cityscape. He seems to like Asia-Pacific exploration, having researched several destinations between Malaysian Borneo and New Zealand for Lonely Planet.

AMELIA THOMAS

Amelia is a journalist working in Israel and the Palestinian Territories. She recently covered Gaza and Upper Galilee for the Lonely Planet *Israel & the Palestinian Territories* guide, when conflict raged in both. She authored the upcoming Lonely Planet *132: Seize the Days*, and is currently writing a book on the last Palestinian zoo.

JUSTINE VAISUTIS

Justine's yen for the tropics has found her in many weird and wonderful places, but none quite so hot, sticky and fascinating as Indonesia. On her most recent foray there she clowned with orang-utans, got lost up river and dined on gargantuan prawns while researching Kalimantan for Lonely Planet's *Indonesia* guide.

JENNY WALKER

Jenny Walker's long association with the Middle East includes several titles for Lonely Planet and a thesis on the Arabic Orient (MPhil, Oxford University). She has recently completed a book on the off-road routes of Oman with her husband and has visited 88 countries in 25 years of independent travel.

TONY WHEELER

Tony travelled through Portuguese Timor, the colonial incarnation of East Timor, while researching the very first edition of Lonely Planet's *Southeast Asia on a Shoestring* more than 30 years ago. He returned to the country during the Indonesian occupation and revisited the independent nation to write the Lonely Planet *East Timor* guidebook.

WENDY YANAGIHARA

After a month-long sojourn in Vietnam, Wendy Yanagihara decided to spend a year in the metropolis formerly known as Saigon. She has travelled from the northern highlands to the Mekong lowlands, and has updated Lonely Planet's *Vietnam* and *Southeast Asia on a Shoestring*, powered by Vietnamese coffee.

PUBLISHER Roz Hopkins
COMMISSIONING EDITORS Ellie Cobb, Bridget Blair
EDITORIAL & PRODUCTION MANAGER Jenny Bilos
PROJECT MANAGER Adam McCrow
PUBLISHING PLANNING MANAGER Jo Vraca
IMAGE COORDINATOR Dana Topchian
IMAGE RESEARCH Pepi Bluck
DESIGN Mark Adams
LAYOUT DESIGNER Mik Ruff
DESIGN MANAGER Brendan Dempsey
CARTOGRAPHER Wayne Murphy
COORDINATING EDITOR Kate Whitfield
ASSISTING EDITORS Vanessa Battersby, Sarah Stewart, Melissa Faulkner, Kate Daly
MANAGING EDITORS Brigitte Ellemor, Barbara Delissen, Geoff Howard
PUBLISHING ADMINISTRATOR Fiona Siseman
PRE-PRESS PRODUCTION Ryan Evans
PRINT PRODUCTION MANAGER Graham Imeson

PUBLISHED BY
LONELY PLANET PUBLICATIONS PTY LTD
ABN 36 005 607 983
90 Maribyrnong St, Footscray,
Victoria, 3011, Australia
www.lonelyplanet.com

Printed through Colorcraft Ltd, Hong Kong
Printed in Malaysia

ISBN 978 1 741046 014

Text © Lonely Planet 2007
Photographs © Photographers as indicated 2007

PHOTOGRAPHS
Many of the images in this book are available for licensing from Lonely Planet Images.
www.lonelyplanetimages.com

LONELY PLANET OFFICES
AUSTRALIA
Locked Bag 1, Footscray, Victoria, 3011
Phone 03 8379 8000 Fax 03 8379 8111
Email talk2us@lonelyplanet.com.au

USA
150 Linden St, Oakland, CA 94607
Phone 510 893 8555 Toll free 800 275 8555
Fax 510 893 8572 Email info@lonelyplanet.com

UK
72-82 Rosebery Ave London EC1R 4RW
Phone 020 7841 9000 Fax 020 7841 9001
Email go@lonelyplanet.co.uk

PHOTO CREDITS
FRONT COVER Monks on a road north of Rangoon, Myanmar; Roland Neveu // On Asia. **INSIDE FRONT COVER** (from left) Nomad girl in western Tibet; Kazuyoshi Nomachi // Australian Picture Library. A pilgrim in the Mosque of the Prophet, Saudi Arabia; Kazuyoshi Nomachi // Australian Picture Library. **BACK COVER** (from left) Women working in paddy fields, Ben Tre Province, Vietnam; David Noton Photography // Alamy. Iranian women strolling down the Promenade; Rob Howard // Corbis. Muslim worshippers, Beijing; Richard Nowitz // Getty. Fishermen, Inle Lake, Myanmar; Gavin Hellier // Getty. **INSIDE BACK COVER** (left) Man in the Aksu Valley, Tajikistan; Christopher Herwig. (right and spine) Stairway at the Nakano Sun Plaza Hall, Tokyo, Japan; BSPI // Corbis. **p2** Woman sitting in rock garden, Japan; James Porter // Getty. **p4** (clockwise from left) Monk shaving his head; Bernard Napthine // Lonely Planet Images. Muslim worshippers, China; Richard Nowitz // Getty. Fishermen, Inle Lake, Myanmar, Gavin Hellier // Getty. Shwedagon Pagoda, Myanmar; Anders Blomqvist // Lonely Planet Images. Purim procession, Tel Aviv, Israel; John Arnold Images // Alamy. **p5** Taxi driver, Chowringee, India; Anthony Plummer // Lonely Planet Images. **p7** Black Hmong people in a field, Vietnam; Stu Smucker // Lonely Planet Images. **p8** (from left) The Great Wall of China; Alison Wright // Corbis. Street musicians in Jodhpur, India; Stewart Cohen // Getty. Man in front of a mosque, Mazar-e Sharif, Afghanistan; Stephane Victor // Lonely Planet Images. **p9** Fisherman casting a net, Yangshuo, China; Keren Su // Getty. **p11** Children singing the Japanese national anthem; Karen Kasmauski // Corbis. **p14** (from left) Kazuyoshi Nomachi // Australian Picture Library; Liu Liqun // Australian Picture Library; Medio Images // Alamy. **p15** (from left) J Marshall, Tribaleye Images // Alamy; Michael Gebicki // Lonely Planet Images; Bernard Napthine // Lonely Planet Images. **p15** (main image) A nomad girl in western Tibet wearing a home-made cosmetic; Kazuyoshi Nomachi // Australian Picture Library. **pp24–5** Women working in paddy fields, Ben Tre Province, Vietnam; David Noton Photography // Alamy. **pp72–3:** Calligraphy brushes for sale in a Seoul art shop, South Korea; John Elk III // Lonely Planet Images. **pp106–7** Indian man splashed with paints after Holy day at the Ranakpur Temple; Liz Thompson // Lonely Planet Images. **pp142–3** Men smiling, Turkmenistan; JTB Photo Communications Inc // Photolibrary. **pp164–5** Camel rider at Wadi Rum, Jordan, Sergio Pitamitz // Corbis.